Working with
Aspects of Language

Second Edition

MANSOOR ALYESHMERNI

University of Minnesota

PAUL TAUBR

Formerly Cleveland State University

Working with Aspects of Language

Second Edition

HARCOURT BRACE JOVANOVICH, INC.
New York / Chicago / San Francisco / Atlanta

Cover photograph by Norman Rothschild

ISBN: 0-15-503869-9

Library of Congress Catalog Card Number: 75-16673

Printed in the United States of America

Socrates: What do you say of him [the young boy who has just been guided to solve a problem in geometry], Meno? Were not all these answers given out of his own head?

Meno: Yes, they were all his own.

Socrates: And yet, as we were just now saying, he did not know [how to solve geometry problems]?

Meno: True.

Socrates: Then he who does not know still has true notions of that which he does not know?

Meno: He has.

Socrates: Without any one teaching him he will recover his knowledge for himself, *if he is only asked questions?*

From "The Meno," *The Dialogues of Plato*, Vol. I, 4th ed., trans. Benjamin Jowett (Oxford: Clarendon Press, 1953). Reprinted by permission of the Clarendon Press, Oxford. (Emphasis added.)

PREFACE

This workbook of exercises and readings accompanies the second edition of Dwight Bolinger's *Aspects of Language* (Harcourt Brace Jovanovich, 1975). Its purpose is not only to test the students' understanding of what they have read but to encourage them to make generalizations about language based on principles that they, as language users, know implicitly. Although the majority of the exercises deal with English, several exercises using other languages have been included to emphasize the universality of the linguistic processes discussed. Students will need a dictionary and, occasionally, a thesaurus; except for *Webster's Third International Dictionary,* which is the subject of several exercises in Chapter 16, no other reference books are required. An instructor's manual provides answers to the exercises and a bibliography of useful sources for each chapter.

Material for the exercises has been drawn from many of the standard sources in language study as well as from the individual works acknowledged. We have been especially influenced in content and format by two workbooks: John Algeo's *Problems in the Origins and Development of the English Language,* Second Edition (Harcourt Brace Jovanovich, 1972) and Harold V. King's *Guide and Workbook in the Structure of English* (Prentice-Hall, 1967). The chapters in this workbook were prepared as follows: Mansoor Alyeshmerni, Chapters 3, 4, 5, 6, 10, 12, 13, 15, and 17; Paul Taubr, Chapters 7, 8, 9, 11, 14, and 16. Both authors are responsible for Chapters 1 and 2.

We are indebted and grateful to many people for their assistance. Professor Bolinger reviewed each chapter and offered suggestions for many of the exercises. Professors Harold Allen and Daniel Bryan and the staff and students of the Communication Program at the University of Minnesota provided a great deal of assistance in the preparation of the original manuscript. Professors Iraj Bashiri, Jonathan Paradise, and George Koury advised us on the exercises involving Persian, Hebrew, and Arabic. At Harcourt Brace Jovanovich, we would like to thank William A. Pullin, who proposed that we prepare the original workbook and who has advised and assisted us with both editions; William Dyckes and Tina Norum, our editors, whose imagination and sensitivity to language have proved invaluable; and Marilyn Marcus, Taylor Gaither, Marian Griffith, Al Balodis, and Stephen Saxe, who provided creative solutions to the problems of designing and producing this book.

Finally, we wish to acknowledge the generous assistance and encouragement we received at every stage of the preparation of the manuscript from our wives, Mahryam Daniels Alyeshmerni and Marcia Vesely Taubr.

Mansoor Alyeshmerni
Paul Taubr

CONTENTS

4 SOUNDS AND WORDS

5 LEXICON

6 SYNTAX

12 VARIATION IN TIME: SOURCES OF VARIATION

13 VARIATION IN TIME: THE OUTCOME OF VARIATION

BORN TO SPEAK

Are children born to speak? Is speaking instinctive behavior, or is it a cultural achievement, like the ability to ride a bicycle? By what criteria can one judge whether an activity is instinctive or not? Is speech similar to such an undoubtedly instinctive activity as walking? Exercise 1 begins with a reading giving four criteria for distinguishing instinctive from acquired activity. Following the reading you are given some evidence that is commonly used to support the instinct hypothesis of language development. Exercise 2 presents a brief statement by Edward Sapir supporting an entirely different hypothesis, which you are to refute, defend, or qualify.

Among the evidence for the instinctiveness of language is the regularity in the stages in which children learn to speak. The third exercise gives you some experience with Roger Brown's scheme for classifying these stages.

EXERCISE 1: Is Language Instinctive or Acquired?

By what criteria does one judge whether an activity is instinctive or the result of a cultural achievement? Eric Lenneberg gives four criteria for distinguishing an obviously instinctive activity (walking) from an obviously cultural achievement (writing):

A. Is the activity essentially invariant within the species?

B. Is there a history of the development of the activity within the species?

C. Is there evidence for an inherited predisposition for the activity?

D. Does the activity have its own specific physical center in the brain and any other part of the body?

Lenneberg compares walking (bipedal gait) and writing in the selection below. As you read this, consider where language belongs. To what extent is it an inherited, instinctive activity, and to what extent is it culturally acquired?

The Four Criteria[1]

| *Bipedal Gait* | *Writing* |

CRITERION A

No intraspecies variations: The species has only one type of locomotion; it is universal to all men. (This is a special case of the more general point that inherited traits have poor correlations—if any—with social groupings: cf. black hair or protruding zygoma.[2]

Intraspecies variations correlated with social organizations: A number of very different successful writing systems have co-existed. The geographical distribution of writing systems follows cultural and social lines of demarcation.

CRITERION B

No history within species: We cannot trace the development of bipedal gait from a primitive to a complex stage throughout the history of human *cultures*. There are no geographical foci from which cultural diffusion of the trait seems to have emanated at earlier times. All human races have the same basic skeletal foot pattern. For significant variations in gait, we have to go back to fossil forms that represent a predecessor of modern man.

Only history within species: There are cultures where even the most primitive writing system is completely absent. We can follow the development of writing historically just as we can study the distribution of writing geographically. We can make good guesses as to the area of invention and development and trace the cultural diffusion over the surface of the globe and throughout the last few millenia of history. The emergence of writing is a relatively recent event.

CRITERION C

Evidence for inherited predisposition: Permanent and customary gait cannot be taught or learned by practice if the animal is not biologically constituted for this type of locomotion.

No evidence for inherited predisposition: Illiteracy in nonWestern societies is not ordinarily a sign of mental deficiency but of deficiency in training. The condition can be quickly corrected by appropriate practice.

---

[1] Eric Lenneberg, "The Capacity for Language Acquisition," in *The Structure of Language*, ed. Jerry A. Fodor and Jerrold J. Katz (Englewood Cliffs, N.J.: Prentice-Hall, 1964), pp. 583–84. This essay is a revised version of "Language, Evolution, and Purposive Behavior," in *Culture in History: Essays in Honor of Paul Radin*, ed. S. Diamond (New York: Columbia University Press, 1960), pp. 869–93. All citations are from the 1964 version of the essay. Reprinted by permission of Columbia University Press.

[2] Note, however, that although there are no significant intraspecies variations in gait, there are many distinctive but minor cultural differences. For example, Weston La Barre has observed differences between the Bengali, Punjabi, and South Chinese walk. See his "Paralinguistics, Kinesics, and Cultural Anthropology," in Thomas A. Sebeok et al., eds., *Approaches to Semiotics* (The Hague: Mouton & Co., 1964), p. 195.

CRITERION D

Presumption of specific organic correlates: In the case of gait, we do not have to *presume* organic correlates; we *know* them. However, behavioral traits that are regarded as the product of evolution (instincts) are also thought to be based on organic predispositions, in this case, on the grounds of circumstantial evidence and often in the absence of anatomical and physiological knowledge.

No assumption of specific organic correlates: We do, of course, assume a biological capacity for writing, but there is no evidence for innate predisposition for this activity. A child's contact with written documents or with pencil and paper does not ordinarily result in automatic acquisition of the trait. Nor do we suppose that the people in a society that has evolved no writing system to be genetically different from those of a writing society. It is axiomatic in anthropology that any normal infant can acquire all cultural traits of any society given the specific cultural upbringing.

✿   ✿   ✿

A series of statements supporting the instinctive base of language is given below. Each statement comes under the heading of one of the criteria discussed previously. In the space provided beside each statement, place the letter of the criterion to which it corresponds.

__A__ 1. Every human culture has a language.

_____ 2. An eight-year-old deaf child who had never had any training or any contact with other deaf children was admitted to a school for the deaf. Immediately upon his arrival he began to "talk" sign language with his contemporaries. "The existence of an innate impulse for symbolic communication can hardly be questioned" (Lenneberg, "The Capacity for Language Acquisition," p. 589).

_____ 3. "One still hears the foolish claim that a child born to German parents ought to be able to learn German more easily than some other language. Our experience discredits this. Ancestry makes no difference. A child learns whatever language it hears, one about as easily as another, and often two or more at the same time."[3]

_____ 4. The stages of [language] development are relatively clear-cut and are found in children everywhere in the world.[4]

_____ 5. Instinctive behavior develops according to patterns of organic maturation. Roger Brown distinguishes three stages of language development that follow the holophrastic stage (Bolinger, pp. 5–6 and p. 279).

_____ 6. "Learning a new language is always in some measure repeating an old experience. Variety may be enormous, but similarities abound" (Bolinger, p. 14).

_____ 7. In comparing the language development of identical and fraternal twins, one finds the following: the onset of speech and the speech development history of each

[3]Dwight Bolinger, *Aspects of Language*, 2nd. ed. (New York: Harcourt Brace Jovanovich, 1975), p. 2.
[4]Eric Lenneberg, *Biological Foundations of Language* (New York: John Wiley & Sons, 1967), p. 252–53.

child in a pair of identical twins is about the same. On the other hand, the onset of speech and the speech development history of each child in a pair of fraternal twins is often different (Lenneberg, *Biological Foundations of Language,* pp. 252–53).

_____ 8. There is no such thing as an incompletely developed natural language.

_____ 9. Within a country such as the United States, language habits vary according to region, social class, ethnic group, and many other factors, even when only speakers of English are considered.

_____10. Most of the modern European languages are descended from a common ancestor. Languages change slowly and steadily.

_____11. "Now it is felt that the organs of speech in their present form were shaped as much for sound production as for nourishment. The human tongue is far more agile than it needs to be for the purposes of eating" (Bolinger, p. 3).

_____12. Every language has a small group of distinct and discrete sound units that combine to form the words and sentences of the language.

_____13. We have no evidence that we can use to trace the spread of language at any particular place or time from a tribe having it to a tribe or tribes not having it.

_____14. As far back as we can reconstruct the languages of the world, there is no evidence that those spoken, say, four thousand years ago were different in nature from those spoken today.

_____15. "Language development, or its substitute, is relatively independent of the infant's babbling or his ability to hear. The congenitally deaf who will usually fail to develop an intelligible vocal communication system, who either do not babble or to whom babbling is of no avail . . . , will nevertheless learn the intricacies of language and learn to communicate efficiently through writing. Apparently, even under these reduced circumstances of stimulation the miracle of development of a feeling for grammer takes place" (Lenneberg, "Capacity for Language," p. 589).

_____16. There is no evidence, direct or indirect, that man was ever without a fully developed language.

_____17. Every language has words assembled according to set rules.

_____18. "If in the case of lower animals we assume without compunction that the communication trait is the result of an *innate predisposition elicited by environmental circumstances,* we have no reason to assume . . . that the language trait of man is purely acquired behavior . . ." (Lenneberg, "Capacity for Language," p. 600).

EXERCISE 2: The Nature of Language Acquisition

The following passage by Edward Sapir, an early twentieth-century linguist, presents the view that language is not based on inherited predispositions and capacities. Write a paragraph supporting, refuting, or qualifying the information in this passage.

The Nature of Language Acquisition[5]

Speech is so familiar a feature of daily life that we rarely pause to define it. It seems as natural to man as walking, and only less so than breathing. Yet it needs but a moment's reflection to convince us that this naturalness of speech is but an illusory feeling. The process of acquiring speech is, in sober fact, an utterly different sort of thing from the process of learning to walk. In the case of the latter function, culture, in other words, the traditional body of social usage, is not seriously brought into play. The child is individually equipped, by the complex set of factors that we term biological heredity, to make all the needed muscular and nervous adjustments that result in walking. Indeed, the very conformation of these muscles and of the appropriate parts of the nervous system may be said to be primarily adapted to the movements made in walking and in similar activities. In a very real sense the normal human being is predestined to walk, not because his elders will assist him to learn the art, but because his organism is prepared from birth, or even from the moment of conception, to take on all those expenditures of nervous energy and all those muscular adaptations that result in walking. To put it concisely, walking is an inherent, biological function of man.

Not so language. It is of course true that in a certain sense the individual is predestined to talk, but that is due entirely to the circumstance that he is born not merely in nature, but in the lap of a society that is certain, reasonably certain, to lead him to its traditions. Eliminate society and there is every reason to believe that he will learn to walk, if, indeed, he survives at all. But it is just as certain that he will never learn to talk, that is, to communicate ideas according to the traditional system of a particular society. Or, again, remove the new-born individual from the social environment into which he has come and transplant him to an utterly alien one. He will develop the art of walking in his new environment very much as he would have developed it in the old. But his speech will be completely at variance with the speech of his native environment. Walking, then, is a general human activity that varies only within circumscribed limits as we pass from individual to individual. Its variability is involuntary and purposeless. Speech is a human activity that varies without assignable limit as we pass from social group to social group, because it is a purely historical heritage of the group, the product of long-continued social usage. It varies as all creative effort varies—not as consciously, perhaps, but none the less as truly as do the religions, the beliefs, the customs, and the arts of different peoples. Walking is an organic, an instinctive, function (not, of course, itself an instinct); speech is a non-instinctive, acquired, "cultural" function.

---

[5]Edward Sapir, *Language* (New York: Harcourt Brace Jovanovich, 1921), pp. 3–4. Copyright, 1921, by Harcourt Brace Jovanovich, Inc.; renewed, 1949, by Jean V. Sapir. Reprinted by permission of Harcourt Brace Jovanovich, Inc. The selection has been retitled.

_____

_____

_____

_____

_____

_____

_____

_____

_____

_____

_____

_____

EXERCISE 3: Stages of Language Acquisition

Bolinger, following Roger Brown, recognizes four stages in the child's acquisition of language. The first is the *holophrastic* stage, when each utterance is a word that has just one meaning. During the second, or *joining*, stage "the child brings together two of his names for things or actions." There is also an increase in wordplay. In the third, or *connective*, stage he begins to join two or more words together with grammatical signs, such as articles, verb endings, and noun endings. The child begins to put sentences inside sentences in the fourth, or *recursive*, stage. Now he can make stylistic choices. Classify the sentences below as characteristic of one or another of these four stages.

1. _holo._ Awgone.
2. _____ Yellow block.
3. _____ What color?
4. _____ What he did at work today?
5. _____ House eat baby.
6. _____ I used to live in Denver.
7. _____ I hear that you don't like it.
8. _____ Daddy sit chair.
9. _____ Daddy sit baby chair.
10. _____ {Give the bone to Dingo.} (The child knows that these sentences have the {Give Dingo the bone. } same meaning.)

SOME TRAITS OF LANGUAGE 2

EXERCISE 1: Language Is Patterned Behavior

A Pattern of English Word Order

The linguist approaches language as a set of patterns or rules. In the phrase *several young Canadian girls,* the order of the words is not random or at the pleasure of the speaker, but is determined by the rules of English. Linguists have not ferreted out all the rules of such phrases, but any native speaker of English follows them automatically: he would know how to put *violin, Italian, old,* and *the* into the most common English order—*the old Italian violin.*

The object of this exercise is to call your attention to a rule of English that you already know but are probably not aware of using. This rule specifies the order of words in some simple phrases similar to the two above.

The procedure is this: first you are to apply the knowledge of English phrases that you have as a native speaker, and then you are to discover and write out explicitly the rule you applied so easily and automatically.

A. Rewrite each of the following lists of words into natural English order. The rule for this section is already written out below.

   1. American/new/astronauts/the _____ *the new American astronauts* _____

   2. latest/the/fashions/French _____

   3. lasses/Scottish/the/young _____

The rule or pattern that you followed to change the order is this: you put *the* first, then the word giving the age of what is being talked about, and then the nationality of what is being talked about. To check this rule, give one new example of a similar four-word phrase and see if the rule applies.

_____

B. Rewrite each list of words into natural English order.

   1. five/the/freshmen/beginning _____ *the five beginning freshmen* _____

   2. recent/the/accident/third _____

3. peaches/fresh/the/three _____

What system did you follow in reordering these lists?

_____

_____

To check this rule, write one new example of a similar four-word phrase below.

_____

C. We are now ready to combine these rules into one more useful rule. In the phrases we discussed in A, we noted that the native speaker of English places age first, and then nationality. In B, we noted that when age and number occur in one phrase, number comes first. In what order would age, number, and nationality come in a single phrase? Where would you insert *three* in *the old Spanish guitars?*

Between _____ and _____ .

Where would you insert *French* in the phrase *the third new girl?*

Between _____ and _____ .

Give the order in which words giving age, nationality, and number come in many English noun phrases.

_____ , _____ , _____ .

Check this rule by giving two new phrases of your own to which it applies.

_____

_____

This rule you have uncovered gives the most common word orders for such phrases. There are occasions when you would not order them this way. For example, if there were several young girls in a classroom and two were Canadian, you might have occasion to speak of *the Canadian young girls* rather than *the young Canadian girls,* according to the rule above. You would be speaking of the young women who were Canadian, not the Canadian women who were young. *Canadian* would be the new information and *young women* the old, already known from the context.

Patterns of Negation and Interrogation

All languages have patterns that show that some sentences are related. This exercise is concerned with uncovering a little of what you know about the relationships between affirmative and negative sentences, and affirmative and interrogative sentences.

A. *Negative Sentences.* Rewrite each of the following affirmative statements as a negation.

1. He could drive. _____ *He could not drive.*

2. He could have driven. _____

3. He has gone. _____

The rule that you followed might be stated thus: Positive statements are turned into negative statements by adding **not** after the first of the helping verbs (such as **could** or **has**).

This rule works well enough when there is a helping verb in the sentence, but what happens when there isn't one? To find out, change the following sentences into negative sentences. (Be sure you have not added any new ideas to the sentence besides negation, such as 'ability' in **could**.)

1. They drive to town. _____ *They don't drive to town.* _____

2. We drive to town. _____

3. You walk to town. _____

State the rule you used.

_____

_____

B. *Interrogative Sentences.* Rewrite each of the following statements as a question.

1. He could drive. _____ *Could he drive?* _____

2. He could have driven. _____

3. He has been teaching. _____

4. He is talking. _____

State the rule.

_____

_____

This rule, like the first rule for negation, works well enough when the statements contain words such as **could, have,** and **is.** As a first step toward finding out the transformation you use in sentences without such words, change the following sentences into questions.

1. They drive. _____ *Do they drive?* _____

2. We drive. _____

3. You walk. _____

State the transformation.

_____

_____

C. *Negative-Interrogative Sentences.* Rewrite the following sentences according to the models.

1. He was going home at noon. _____*Wasn't he going home at noon?*_____

2. He works on his car Saturdays. _____*Doesn't he work on his car Saturdays?*_____

3. He walked to town. _____

4. He always went home weekends. _____

5. He has seen it already. _____

State the pattern you followed.

_____

_____

Make up another pair of sentences, and check to see if the pattern works.

_____

_____

Rules of Pronunciation in English

A. In the first two exercises you were made aware of word order and of how some English sentences are related. This exercise is devoted to uncovering some of the rules of English pronunciation that you know implicitly. The process will be the same as before: you will apply the rules, using your skill as a native speaker, then write out explicitly what you have done. Read the following two sentences aloud.
1. Did you convict him of the crime?
2. Where was the convict taken?

Which syllable of *convict* did you emphasize in the first sentence? _____

In the second? _____

The following pairs of words show the same pattern as *convict.* Underline the emphasized syllable of each of the words in dark type.

1. I *combine* them regularly.
   The *combine* is good for business.
2. He won't *permit* it.
   Do you need a *permit?*
3. Did the *contract* give you trouble?
   Did you *contract* German measles?
4. How do you *combat* the common cold?
   The *combat* took place near Gettysburg.

State the pattern you followed in changing the stress in these words. Ask several other people whether they pronounce **combat** according to this pattern.

_____

_____

B. The native speaker knows where the stress occurs in words and how it changes when the word endings change. Read each of the following lines aloud, and consider how you change the position of the primary stress as you change the endings of the words.

provoke   provocative   provocation
repeat   repetitive   repetition
derive   derivative   derivation

Where is the stress placed in the words of the first column? _____

Of the second column? _____ Of the third column? _____

EXERCISE 2: Language Is Systematic

Examine these columns of corresponding words and phrases written in four modern languages, and then follow the instructions given below. (In Persian the æ is pronounced somewhat like the *a* in **bat,** the *č* like *ch* in **church,** and the *x* like *ch* in German **Bach.** In Hebrew the *š* is pronounced like the *sh* in **shin.**)

English	German	Colloquial Persian	Hebrew
1. man	Mann	mærd	iš
2. a man	ein Mann	mærdi	iš
3. the man	der Mann	mærdé	haiš
4. the woman	die Frau	zæné	haiša
5. a good man	ein guter Mann	mærde xubi	iš tov
6. the good man	der gute Mann	mærde xubé	haiš hatov
7. a good woman	eine gute Frau	zæne xubi	iša tova
8. the good woman	die gute Frau	zæne xubé	haiša hatova
9. a good house	ein gutes Haus	mænzele xubi	bayit tov
10. the large house	das grosse Haus	mænzele bozorgé	habayit hagadol
11. a small house	ein kleines Haus	mænzele kučeki	bayit katan
12. a large book	ein grosses Buch	ketabe bozorgi	sefer gadol
13. a man's house	eines Mannes Haus	mænzele mærdi	beyt iš
14. the house of a man	das Haus eines Mannes	mænzele mærdi	beyt iš
15. the man's wife	des Mannes Frau	zæne mærdé	ešet haiš
16. the wife of the man	die Frau des Mannes	zæne mærdé	ešet haiš
17. The man is good.	Der Mann ist gut.	mærdé xube.	haiš tov.
18. The book is small.	Das Buch ist klein.	ketabé kučeke.	hasefer katan.
19. The woman is good.	Die Frau ist gut.	zæné xube.	haiša tova.
20. The house is small.	Das Haus ist klein.	mænzelé kučeke.	habayit katan.

A. Complete the following vocabulary list for each language. Give the words, leaving off the endings. For example, when you find *gute, guter, gutes,* and *gut* all translated as 'good,' insert *gut* as the vocabulary item.

English	German	Colloquial Persian	Hebrew
1. man	Mann	mærd	iš
2. woman			
3. good	gut		
4. house			bayit
5. small			
6. large	gross		
7. book			
8. is			(none)
9. a			(none)
10. the	der, die, das		

B. By constructing the vocabularies, you have already learned much about the grammars of small portions of these languages. The following statements are true of one or more of these languages. Basing your conclusions on the limited data given, circle the languages for which each statement is true.

1. There is an ending or word with the meaning of English *a.*	Eng	Ger	Per	Heb
2. The adjective follows the noun.	Eng.	Ger	Per	Heb
3. The adjective changes according to the noun.	Eng	Ger	Per	Heb
4. Possession is shown by endings.	Eng	Ger	Per	Heb
5. Possession is shown by a preposition.	Eng	Ger	Per	Heb
6. A separate word corresponds to *is.*	Eng	Ger	Per	Heb
7. A suffix corresponds to *is.*	Eng	Ger	Per	Heb
8. Nothing corresponds to *is.*	Eng	Ger	Per	Heb

C. Translate each expression into the three other languages.

English	German	Colloquial Persian	Hebrew
1. The small book			
2.	Das Buch ist gross.		
3.		mænzele kučeké	
4.			haiš hagadol

EXERCISE 3: Language Is Largely Arbitrary

A. There is generally no necessary connection between the sound of a word and its meaning, beyond the agreement of those who use the word. Two classes of words, however, have a closer connection than this. One class is made up of words that are thought to imitate some natural noise, such as the sound an animal makes. Speakers of Urdu, a language of Pakistan and India, think the words in the first column below imitate various natural sounds. First, without looking at the second column, try to guess what the words imitate. Write your guesses in the first blank column. Then match each imitative word with the words in the second column, writing the correct number in the second blank column. Check your answers with the key at the bottom of the page.

	vow vow		1. a cat
	myow		2. a horse
	ba		3. a slamming door
	sahee		4. a bell
	cuck-roo-coo		5. a cock
	bwack		6. a dog
	guwru guwrun		7. a sheep
	dhun		8. a clock
	tik		9. a pig
	ting-ting		10. a duck

B. The second class of words that have more than a simple arbitrary and conventional connection between sound and meaning consists of groups that are more arbitrary than the echoic words in Exercise A. Consider the words *rump, bump, lump, thump,* and *chump.* They have in common the sound *-ump* and the general meaning 'heaviness and bluntness.' In these words the sound itself suggests the meaning to an English speaker. Give other words that belong in this group.

_____

_____

Give the meaning held in common by the words in each group below, and add as many as you can to the list.

chew, chomp, munch, chaw _____

_____

Key: 6, 1, 7, 2, 5, 10, 9, 3, 8, 4

screech, squeak, scream, squeal _____

_____

flip, flop, flutter, flicker _____

_____

hiss, sizzle, swish, whish _____

_____

snuff, snore, snout, sneeze _____

_____

What sort of evidence must be presented before one can assert that each of the sound groups above has a special status in English? (This question will be dealt with more thoroughly in Chapter 9.)

_____

_____

_____

DISTINCTIVE SOUND 3

EXERCISE 1: The Articulation of Sounds

The diagram below shows the organs of speech that regulate the flow of air from the lungs to create the sounds of speech. (Speech almost always takes place only during exhalation.) As the air leaves the lungs, it is modified by muscular actions of the *vocal cords*, the *uvula*, the *tongue*, the *jaw*, and the *lips*.

Can you say **up, on,** or **do** while holding your breath? If not, why not? _____

_____

_____

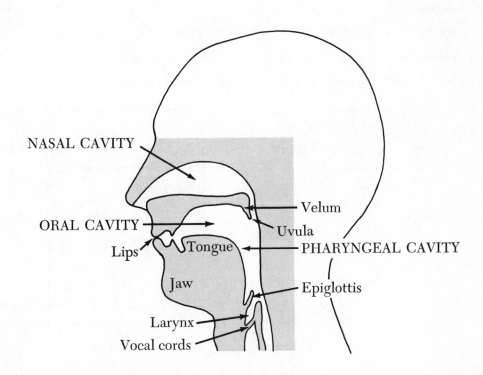

Vocal Cord Positions

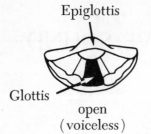

Epiglottis

Glottis

open
(voiceless)

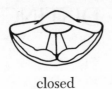

closed

Vocal cords

partially closed
(voiced)

Voiced and Voiceless Sounds

One modification of the air stream may take place at the vocal cords. When these muscles vibrate (see diagram), the sounds produced are called *voiced*. Compare the voiced sound *z* with the voiceless *s*. If you place your hands on your ears and pronounce *z* and then *s*, you will hear vibrations with the *z* but not with the *s*. Another test is to place your hand on your throat and repeat the sounds; you will *feel* the vibration with *z*. All sounds in English may be distinguished as voiced or voiceless in this manner.

Place **V** beside a voiced sound and **VL** beside a voiceless sound.

_V_ b   ____ v   ____ d   ____ r

____ p   ____ y (as in *yet*)   ____ th (as in ***thin***)   ____ l

____ f (as in ***feet***)   ____ t   ____ th (as in ***then***)   ____ m

Try the vowels *a, e, i, o, u.* Are they voiced or voiceless? _____

The sounds *m, n, l, r, y,* and *w* are all _____

Compare the representation of voiced-voiceless contrasts for sounds *b* and *p.*

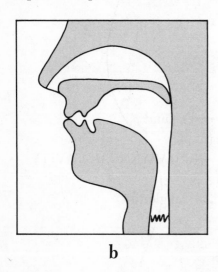

b

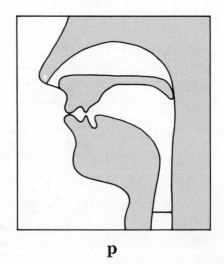

p

Now, given the representation of **s**, complete the diagram for **z**.

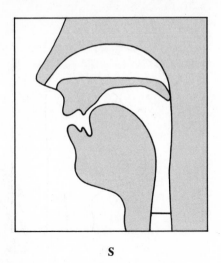

s

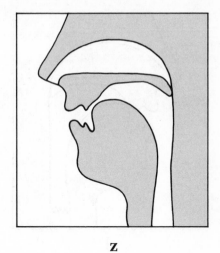

z

Nasal Versus Oral Sounds

Another modification may take place at the velum, the muscular flap at the back of the mouth. If the velum is lowered—allowing the air to pass through the nasal cavity—the sound produced by the organs of the oral cavity is nasal.

Which of these are nasal sounds? Place an *N* beside the nasal sounds.

_____ b   _____ n   _____ ng (as in *sing*)

_____ m   _____ t   _____ f

Note the contrast in the production of the oral sound *b* and the nasal *m*.

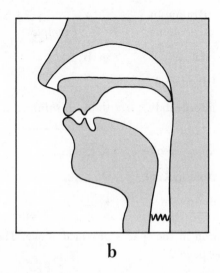

b

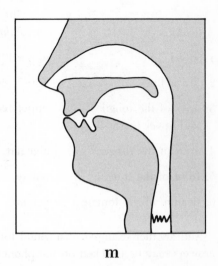

m

Now, given the representation of *d,* draw in that of *n.*

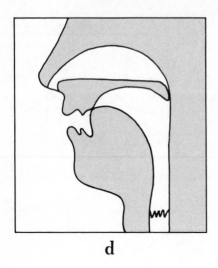

d

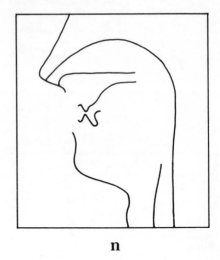

n

Positions of Articulation

Most of the contrasts in the sounds of speech are made by modifying the relation of the *lower jaw* and the *tongue* to the *upper jaw.* The generally stationary organs of the upper jaw are called *points of articulation.* They are the *upper lip* and *teeth,* the *alveolar ridge,* the (hard) *palate,* the *velum* (or soft palate), and the *uvula.* The uvula and the upper lip are the only organs in the upper jaw that move. The organs along the lower jaw are called *articulators.* They are the *lower lip* and *teeth,* and the *apex* (tip), *front,* and *dorsum* (back) of the tongue (see the diagram on p. 19). There are six major positions of articulation made by the relation of the articulator to the point of articulation. They are defined as follows:

Articulator	Point of Articulation	Position of Articulation	Examples
1. lower lip	upper lip	bilabial	m, b, _____
2. lower lip	upper teeth	labiodental	f, _____
3. apex of the tongue and lower teeth	upper teeth	interdental	th (as in *thin*), _____ (as in _____)
4. apex of the tongue	alveolar ridge	apicoalveolar	n, t, _____
5. front of the tongue	palate	frontopalatal	sh, _____
6. dorsum of the tongue	velum	dorsovelar	k, _____

Add another example of a sound for each position in the spaces provided above. The answers may be checked on the phonetic chart on page 22.

The seventh position of articulation, the *glottal* position, is described as follows: when no organs other than the vocal folds are used in producing a sound, the sounds are called glottal. The **h** in **he** and the sound heard between the two parts of the colloquial negative **hunh-uh** are examples of this position of articulation.

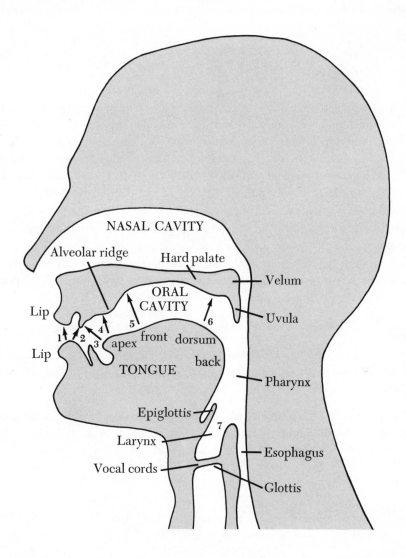

Name the positions of articulation signified by numbers 1 through 7 in the preceding diagram.

1. _____

2. _____

3. _____

4. _____

5. _____

6. _____

7. _____

Manners of Articulation

Further modifications of sound are determined by the distance between the articulator and the point of articulation. (Consult the phonetic chart on p. 22 as you read the following.) The two may touch and stop the air stream for a moment; these sounds are called *stops* (*p, t, k, b, d, g*). Non-stop sounds are called *continuants*. The continuants may be divided into *fricatives*, in which the air is constricted at one of the positions of articulation (*f, th, s, sh,* and *h*), and other sounds collectively called *resonants*. [Another group of sounds, *j* (*jet*) and *ch* (*chip*), is made by combining a stop and a fricative. Such sounds are called *affricates* and are not considered continuants.] The resonants (*m, n, ng* of *sing, l, r, y, w,* and all vowels) are either *nasal* (the first three) or *oral* (the others). In the articulation of the oral resonants the air stream may leave from the side of the mouth as in *l*, which is called a *lateral*, or it may leave through the more common *central* position. The central oral resonants are the *semivowels* (*r, y, w*) and the *vowels*. The jaw is lowest in the production of vowels. It is lower for some vowels than for others.

Vowels

When the air leaving the lungs is allowed to flow freely through the mouth, the resulting sound is a vowel. The position of the lower jaw, the tongue, and the lips determines the quality of the sound.

A. *Vowel height.* Number the following sets of sounds in the order of increasing jaw opening, starting with *1* for the highest position. The first set has been completed.

	I		II		III
_1_ pin	___ boon		___ ten		___ boot
_2_ pen	___ ban		___ tune		___ bait
_3_ pan	___ boat		___ tan		___ bought

Why does a doctor ask a patient to say *aaaah* instead of *iiiih?* _____

_____

B. *Degree of Frontness.* Determine the degree of frontness of the tongue in the vowels of the following sets of words. Use *1* to indicate the front sounds and *2* to indicate the non-front sounds (whether they be central or back), as shown in the example.

	I		II		III		IV
_1_	sat	___	put	___	Ben	___	beat	___	soot
_2_	sought	___	pit	___	bone	___	boat	___	sat

Are the lips rounded when any of the front vowels are produced? _____

Can you round your lips when you say any of these front sounds? _____

If so, are the sounds you are producing English sounds? _____

Can you say the vowel in *toot* without rounding your lips? _____

Does it sound like any English sounds you have heard? _____

Does it occur in any foreign language you know of? _____

C. *Full Versus Reduced Vowels.* Place *1* beside each word containing a full vowel and *2* beside the word in which the underlined vowel is reduced. See the example.

	I		II		III
_1_	each	___	chimpanzee	___	common	___	boot
_2_	basic	___	away	___	soap	___	a (as in *he's a dog!*)
_2_	Harry	___	borrow	___	sofa	___	but (as in *but of course*)

Do all monosyllabic words in English have full vowels? _____

Do all polysyllabic words in English have reduced vowels? _____

EXERCISE 2: A Classification of English Sounds

Since phonetics attempts to describe and classify all possible human language sounds, the phonetic chart on page 22 is only a subset of what would be included in a theoretically complete chart. Our concern here is only with the phones, or sounds, that are found in most dialects of English. Further modification of the symbols used in this chart will be discussed at the end of this chapter.

The Phonetic Chart

A. Why is the vowel chart placed where it is in relation to the consonants? _____

_____

B. It would be hard to find any language that does not have at least one of the sounds *p, b, m.* Why would this be the case? _____

_____

_____

The Phonetic Chart

Manner of Articulation		Position of Articulation →	Bilabial	Labiodental	Interdental	Apicoalveolar	Frontopalatal	Dorsovelar	Glottal
Stop	Stop	VL	p (*pit*)			t (*tip*)		k (*kit*)	ʔ
		V	b (*bit*)			d°(*dip*)		g (*get*)	
Affricate		VL					č (*chip*)		
		V					ǰ (*jet*)		
Fricative	Continuant	VL		f (*fit*)	θ (*thin*)	s (*sit*)	š (*ship*)		h† (*hit*)
		V		v (*vex*)	ð (*then*)	z (*zip*)	ž (*azure*)		
Nasal	Resonant	(V)	m (*moon*)			n (*noon*)		ŋ (*ring*)	
Lateral		(V)				l (*loom*)			
Semivowel	Oral / Central	(V)				r (*bar*)‡	y (*boy*)	w (*bow*)	

Vowel chart

	Front	Central	Back
High	i (beat)		u (boot)
Lower high	ɪ (bit)	i§	ʊ (put)
Mid	e (bait)	ə§ e§	o (boat)
Lower mid	ɛ (bet)	ʌ (but)	ɔ (bought)
Low	æ (bat)		a (pot)

← Tongue height →

— Degree of frontness —

Note: The vowel qualities in the examples will not match those of every speaker. You will have to find examples in your own speech that fit the definition of the vowels.

*The flap sound [ɪ] appears in words such as *butter* and *ladder* in American speech and in very in British speech.

†This is similar in articulation to an aspirated voiceless vowel.

‡The **r** is not pronounced in New England and much of the South. In this chart semivowel = semiconsonant.

§The three reduced vowels **i** (many), **ə**, often called *shwa* (sofa), and **e** (willow) represent vowels usually found in unstressed positions in words.

C. Why are there so few consonants in the labiodental column? _____

_____

D. In which position of articulation are the consonantal sounds most numerous? _____

_____

Would you guess that these sounds are frequent in English? _____ A recent statistical analysis of the English language provides the following figures for the relative frequency of each position of articulation:[1]

Bilabial	9.2%	Frontopalatal	2.4%
Labiodental	5.6%	Dorsovelar	13.7%
Interdental	4.2%	Glottal	4.1%
Apicoalveolar	60.8%		

E. The vowel chart is reproduced here so that you may represent the English diphthongs. A diphthong is a glide from one vowel to another. One indicates the movement of the tongue on a vowel chart by drawing an arrow with the base at the position where the tongue starts and the tip of the arrow where the tongue finishes. [y] symbolizes a movement to or from a high front position, and [w] to or from a high back position. Draw the diphthong arrows for these words: *boy* [ɔy], *yore* [yɔ], *wan* [wa], *high* [ay], *Yamaha* [ya], *you* [yu]. The diphthong of the word *how* [aw] is shown on the chart. Label each arrow with the phonetic spelling of the diphthong. (There are several other diphthongs in some varieties of American English. If you use any of them, mark them on the vowel chart.)

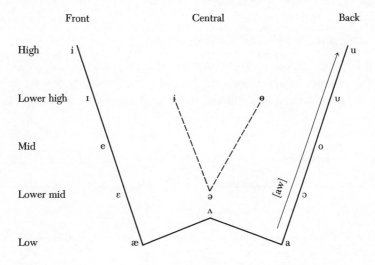

[1] These figures were arrived at by adding the frequencies of the individual sounds as found in A. Hood Roberts, *A Statistical Linguistic Analysis of American English* (= *Janua Linguarum, Series Practica* 8) (The Hague: Mouton & Co., 1965), Fig. 5, p. 41.

F. The phonetic chart can be expanded and modified to include all possible human sounds. Even within the limits of the simplified chart given here, there are empty spaces that represent possible sounds. Some of these are used in other languages; some, in fact, occur in English as variants of sounds found on the chart. Place the first five symbols defined below in the proper location on the phonetic chart:[2]

1. [c] as in *k* of Persian *yek* 'one,' a voiceless frontopalatal stop
2. [ß] as in *b* of Spanish *La Habana, Cuba,* a voiced bilabial fricative
3. [x] as in *ch* of German *lachen* 'to laugh,' a voiceless dorsovelar fricative
4. [ts] as in *ts* of Hebrew *Tsipór* 'bird,' an apicoalveolar affricate
5. [ɲ] as in *gn* of French *cognac,* a frontopalatal nasal
6. [y] as in *ü* of German *müde* 'tired,' a rounded high front vowel
7. [ã] as in *and* of French *quand* 'when,' a nasalized low back vowel

G. Most popular given names, especially when not abbreviated, have one or more resonant sounds other than vowels. Names such as *Mary* and *Wayne* are composed of only resonant sounds, whereas the names *Joseph* and *Edith* have no resonant sounds other than vowels. Names of the latter type are rare. Write your name and underline the resonant sounds in it, if any (see the rows for resonant sounds on the chart). _____

H. The sequence of sounds on the vowel chart may be remembered by comparing it to the *meow* of a cat. It begins with *m* and makes an arc stretching from high front to low central to high back: [miɪeɛæaɔɔʊu].

The Articulation of Vowels and Consonants

A. After studying the relationship between the English and phonetic alphabets (see chart), describe the *position of articulation* of the following sounds. (Consider the degree of frontness of a vowel—the position along a front-back axis—as its position of articulation.)

1. [p] _____*bilabial*_____   7. [f] _____

2. [ə] _____*central*_____   8. [ɔ] _____

3. [z] _____   9. [g] _____

4. [ɪ] _____   10. [w] _____

5. [š] _____   11. [l] _____

6. [n] _____   12. [θ] _____

---

[2] Brackets [ ] indicate that the enclosed letter is a *variation of a sound*. The *sound* is written in virgules / /. Later in this chapter, you will see many variations, or allophones, of the phoneme /k/.

B. Describe the *manner of articulation* of the following sounds.

1. [m] _____nasal_____   9. [t] _____
2. [æ] _____   10. [l] _____
3. [n] _____   11. [p] _____
4. [r] _____   12. [š] _____
5. [d] _____   13. [ə] _____
6. [ɪ] _____   14. [ŋ] _____
7. [s] _____   15. [z] _____
8. [k] _____

Articulatory Description of Sounds

A. Write the phonetic symbols of sounds defined as follows:

1. low back vowel	[a]	6. frontopalatal semivowel	[ ]
2. apicoalveolar semivowel	[ ]	7. mid central reduced vowel	[ ]
3. voiceless apicoalveolar stop	[ ]	8. apicoalveolar lateral	[ ]
4. lower high front vowel	[ ]	9. mid back vowel	[ ]
5. voiceless dorsovelar stop	[ ]	10. voiced interdental fricative	[ ]

B. Give a phonetic description, such as those in the preceding exercise, for each of the sounds below. Descriptions differ for consonants and vowels. For consonants the following order is used:
1. voicing (indicated in English for stops, fricatives, and affricates, where there is a voicing contrast)
2. position of articulation
3. manner of articulation

Vowels are described as follows:

1. tongue height
2. degree of frontness along the front-back axis
3. "reduced" (not indicated if vowel is not reduced)
4. "vowel" (always included)

1. [f]_____*voiceless labiodental fricative*_____
2. [ə]_____
3. [n]_____
4. [ɛ]_____

5. [t]_____

6. [ɨ]_____

7. [k]_____

8. [s]_____

Write one word in conventional spelling that has all eight sounds. _____

_____

Sound Relations

A. Compare the sounds that are represented by the darker letters in the following pairs of related words:

describe–description   defend–defense

thief–thieves   choice–chosen

absent–absence

Describe their similarities and differences on the basis of voicing, position, and manner of articulation.

Sounds	Voice	Position	Manner
1. [b p]	[b] *is voiced*	*both are bilabial*	*both are stops*
	[p] *is voiceless*		
2. [f v]	_____	_____	_____
	_____		
3. [t s]	_____	_____	_____
4. [d s]	_____	_____	_____
	_____		_____
5. [s z]	_____	_____	_____
	_____		

B. List the similarities and differences of the following pairs of sounds. Consider voicing (when applicable), position and manner of articulation for consonants, and tongue height and degree of frontness for vowels.

Sounds	Similarities	Differences
1. [p g]	*both are stops*	[p] *is voiceless,* [g] *is voiced*
	_____	[p] *is bilabial,* [g] *is dorsovelar*

	Sounds	Similarities	Differences
2.	[b t]		
3.	[n ŋ]		
4.	[č j]		
5.	[ž v]		
6.	[ð š]		
7.	[k s]		
8.	[g ǰ]		
9.	[i u]		
10.	[e o]		
11.	[ɪ ʊ]		
12.	[ɪ æ]		

Transcription for Reading Practice

Transcribe these words into conventional English spelling.

1. [kæt] *cat*
2. [trɪk]
3. [trit]
4. [tem]
5. [taym]
6. [hayt]
7. [hol]
8. [hawl]
9. [rɔy]
10. [bʊk]

11. [ǰʌǰ]
12. [rozəz]
13. [čɪp]
14. [čip]
15. [bʌtn]
16. [pæč]
17. [batl]
18. [yuθ]
19. [klæŋ]
20. [bɛt]

Transcription

A. Transcribe these words phonetically as you normally say them. How would you describe your predominant geographical dialect? _____

1. ban	[bæn]	14. horse	_____
2. bang	_____	15. blush	_____
3. hung	_____	16. chick	_____
4. ham	_____	17. suit	_____
5. hail	_____	18. soot	_____
6. pale	_____	19. rut	_____
7. dread	_____	20. note	_____
8. sting	_____	21. shave	_____
9. help	_____	22. scratch	_____
10. bee	_____	23. plague	_____
11. buy	_____	24. machine	_____
12. brought	_____	25. strength	_____
13. dog	_____	26. bugs	_____

B. Transcribe the following sentences phonetically.

1. The crew slept. _____

2. There they are! _____

3. The motorcade passed us. _____

4. Live a full life. _____

5. Singing is fun. _____

6. Harry wallowed in riches. _____

7. The police pursued the robbers. _____

8. The soldiers were fatigued. _____

9. Miss America was selected yesterday. _____

_____

10. Having exhausted all possibilities, he finally gave up. _____

_____

EXERCISE 3: Prosody

The major characteristics of intonation are range, direction, height, abruptness, and pattern. Apply these terms to the following examples:

A. How would a cheerleader's emotional expression of the results of a game differ in intonation if she were to report the following?

    1. We won 48 to 13. _____

    2. We lost 13 to 12. _____

B. Which characteristic distinguishes these two sentences in speech? _____
    1. If you are happy when you see me, smile!
    2. If you are happy, when you see me smile!

C. In the sentence *I won't play chess with you,* which characteristic of intonation is used to express the desire

    1. not to play chess, but another game. _____

    2. not to play with you, but with anyone else. _____

D. Using Bolinger's notation, write the following sentences showing pitch direction.

    1. He's hungry. Aren't you?

    2. Where did you find it? In my room?

    3. *Q.* Where did you find it? *A.* In my room.

E. Show the intonation pattern of *on the bus*

    1. as a command.

    2. as a reply to the question *Where did you hear that?*

F. Underline the accented syllables in the following sentences:
   1. He's right here!
   2. What is that?
   3. Is he dumb!
   4. I won't do it.
   5. Is that a fact?
   6. There you are.
   7. How do you do?
   8. Okay, I guess. (In response to "How are you feeling?")
   9. That was some movie!
   10. What do you expect from a guy like that?

G. Using Bolinger's system, show the pitch pattern of the first five sentences above.

   1. _____

   2. _____

   3. _____

   4. _____

   5. _____

EXERCISE 4: Acoustic Phonetics

Early phoneticians did not have machines to analyze sounds for them, but some were observant enough to detect the overtones, or formants, that make up the vowels. Try this double experiment. First *whisper* slowly the vowels [æ e i] (as in **bat, bait, beat**), in that order, and see if you can hear a sound that rises in pitch from one to the next. That is the second formant. Now, without whispering or saying anything but just setting your mouth and tongue in position for each of the three vowels, snap your middle finger just to the side of your Adam's apple. You should hear another pitch that goes *down* with each sound. That is the first formant. As you can observe, it is mainly the throat cavity that produces the first formant and the forward part of the mouth cavity that produces the second formant.

Answer the following questions as you look at Figure 3–2 (p. 55) in Bolinger.

A. Compare the first formants of the high vowels [i] and [u] with the other vowels. Do

   high vowels have a lower first formant? _____

   Is there any relationship between the height of the vowel and the frequency of the first

   formant? _____

Second formant? _____

B. Consider the difference in frequency of first and second formants for front and back vowels. Which has a greater frequency difference between the first and second formants?

_____ Do the high vowels [i] and [u] have a greater frequency difference between the first and second formants than the other vowels? _____

EXERCISE 5: The Syllable

The exercises in this section are limited to English monosyllables. The monosyllable is a frequent form in English.

English Syllables

Give two English words in phonetic transcription that exemplify each of the following monosyllable types:

C = consonants [p t k b d g č ǰ f v s š z ž m n ŋ l h]
S = semivowels = semiconsonants [y r w]
V = vowels

VC   [ʌp], [it] _____

CVC _____

CV _____

CVS _____

SVC _____

VS _____

SVS _____

SV _____

CVCC _____

V _____

SVSC _____

VSS _____

VSC _____

CVSC _____

CSVC _____

The CVC Pattern in English

Each of these patterns is further broken down according to positions of articulation. Let us consider the possible CVC words in English. For the sake of simplicity, let us use one symbol for a group of related sounds as follows:

B = bilabials and labiodentals [p b f v m]   D = dorsovelars [k g ŋ w]
I = interdentals [θ ð]   G = glottal [h]
A = apicoalveolars [t d s z l n r]   V = vowels [i ɪ e ɛ æ ʌ ɑ ɔ o ʊ u]
F = frontopalatals [š ž č ǰ y]

Note that the semivowels [r y w] are distributed in A, F, and D respectively. Thus, CVC also covers SVC, CVS, and SVS. Since in English [ž] and [ŋ] do not occur initially and [h] does not occur finally, the theoretically possible number of CVC words is $22 \times 11 \times 23 = 5566$ English words. Of the 10,000 most frequently used words examined in Ernest Horn's *A Basic Writing Vocabulary*, 307 words are reported by Roberts to be of the CVC type.[3] This number is only 6 per cent of the number of permissible words. Some of the permissible words exist but are rare in English. The following words may be found in larger dictionaries: *dap, duff, fid, gib, jus, beck, lall, luff, mel, motte, raff, rick, shim,* and *sudd.*

Give three English words to fit each CVC pattern below. The symbols are those which were defined above.

DVA _____ *cat, will, gun* _____

BVA _____

IVA _____

AVD _____

BVF _____

AVA _____

FVA _____

GVA _____

FVD _____

AVB _____

DVB _____

IVF _____

GVD _____

IVB _____

[3] Roberts, *Statistical Linguistic Analysis*, Table 4, p. 50.

There are thirty-six such possible sets. In Roberts' analysis no examples for eleven of the sets are found. Can you find any words that fit any of the patterns IVI, IVG, AVF, AVG, FVI, FVG, DVI, DVG, GVB, GVI, GVG? There are 568 words that fit these patterns. Check some of your hunches. You might find that some of the words that you considered non-words are actually words. They are often found in crossword puzzles. (An example of IVI is **Thoth.**)

_____

_____

When *countless* and *loveless* are divided into syllables, are the *tl* and *vl* separated? _____ Are there native English words that start with [tl] or [vl]? _____ How would you class the proper name **Vladimir?** Is it difficulty of pronunciation that makes [vl] unusual in English?

_____ Think of other unusual combinations of consonants in English, and see if you can account for them. _____ Do [šl šn šm] have a special status? (Think of **schnook,** for example.)

_____

Initial Consonant Clusters—Two Consonants

In the chart below give examples of words that begin with the sound given at the left followed by the sound provided above each column. If you find no words that fit, draw a line in the appropriate intersection. Place fairly common foreign words in parentheses.

	1	r	w	y	Others
p	*please*	*pray*	*(pueblo)*	*pure*	
b					
t					
d					
k					
g					
f					
v					
θ					
s					
š					
h					
m					

A. In the words above how did you spell /kl-/ _____, /kr-/ _____, /kw-/ _____, /ky-/ _____, and /fr-/ _____? How else might the last one be spelled? _____

B. From the chart above determine which consonant phonemes occur in English before /l/ _____, before /r/ _____, before /w/ _____, and before /y/ _____. The last one differs from one dialect to another on the basis of pronunciation of words such as *stupid* (/styúpid/ or /stupid/).

Initial Consonant Clusters—Three Consonants

Complete the chart below as you did in the previous exercise. Ø in the first column indicates that you are to add no consonants. (These are words with two-consonant initials, which share some features with the others.)

	Ø	l	r	w	y	Others
sp	speak	splash	spray	——	spew	
st						
sk						
sf						
sm						
sn						

A. How did you spell /skØ-/ _____, /skl-/ _____, /skr-/ _____, /skw-/ _____, and /sky-/ _____?

B. Using the chart above, do the following: in the cases where three-consonant clusters occur, name the first phoneme /_____/, describe the voicing and manner of articulation of the second _____, and describe manners of articulation of the third consonant _____.

C. Write five words that begin with [sn-]. _____

_____

Do they have any semantic notions in common? In Brightland and Gildon's *A Grammar of English Tongue*,[4] published in 1711, we find this interesting quip: [sn-] "is an ending [sic] that generally implies the nose, or something belonging to it, which are deriv'd

[4] P. 127.

from it, and have a great Relation to it; as, *snout, sneeze, snore, snort, sneer, snicker, snot, snivil, snite, snuff, snuffle, snaffle, snarl, snudge,* to hold your Nose into your Bosom."

What does your list show, if anything? _____

"Fuzzy Borders" Between Syllables

The "fuzzy borders" between syllables have been the cause of some changes in words. For example, the word *apron* in Middle English was *napron. A napron* was interpreted as *an apron.* Below are a few phrases that might lead to misunderstanding.

A. Identify the features that can distinguish these.

a gray train / a great rain _____ *(released vs. unreleased /t/)* _____

I scream / ice cream   _____

a tall / at all   _____

a name / an aim   _____

for getting / forgetting   _____

frontier / front tier   _____

Bett's bread / bedspread   _____

B. Listen carefully as you say the following aloud, and decide what the audible clues are that enable you to tell one from the other:

1. Professor Black's in SANE. Professor Black's insane. _____

_____

2. It won't make any difference to Hiram. It won't make any difference to hire 'em.

_____

3. I want another smaller one. I want another, smaller one. _____

_____

4. Are there sorority houses in all-girls schools? Are there sorority houses in all girls' schools? _____

5. Now he has all the wine that he wants to drink (two meanings). _____

_____

6. They'll get there in time (two meanings). _____

_____

7. They don't live right here (two meanings). _____

_____

EXERCISE 6: The Allophone

It may be claimed that no two representations of a sound are ever exactly alike. Although this is technically correct, as one can see by examining sound spectrograms (electronic visual reproductions of sounds), we perceive like sounds as the same sound. But these like sounds may be construed as different sounds by the speakers of another language. Two such like sounds are the /k/ in *keep* and *cool.* The first is frontopalatal, phonetically represented as [c]; the second is dorsovelar, symbolized as [k]. The various sounds perceived as one sound in any given language are the *allophones* of the sound. The "one" sound is the *phoneme.* The phoneme /k/ has the two allophones [c] and [k] in *keep* and *cool.* Let us consider the major articulatory variations of the phoneme /k/.[5]

Consider the following words: *cat, keep, cool, stack, scat!, act,* and *tack.* In order to perceive the similarities and differences of the allophones more clearly, a feature grid will be used. The symbols used in the grid will denote the following:

+ the feature in the column is *present* in that row
− the feature in the column is *absent* in that row

Check your pronunciation of the words with the phonetic transcription given on the chart. Most of the features are quite apparent. A few minutes of concentration on the variations in pronunciation will aid you in mastering the notion of allophones. You might find that your own speech is not represented here. In any case, the questions on k that follow are based on this chart.

Major Allophones of /k/

Word	Phonetic representations of /k/	Aspirated°	Released†	Frontopalatal [c]	Dorsovelar [k]
cat	[cʰæt]	+	+	+	−
keep	[cʰip]	+	+	+	−
cool	[kʰul]	+	+	−	+
stack	[stæk⌐]	−	−	−	+
scat!	[scˀæt]	−	+	+	−
act	[æk⌐t]	−	−	−	+
tack	[tæk⌐]	−	−	−	+

°*Aspirated* means that the sound is released with an outrush of air. If you hold a lighted match a couple of inches in front of your mouth, it will be blown out when you pronounce **pin.** The aspirated /p/ in **pin** is symbolized [pʰ].

†In *released* sounds, the articulator is sharply withdrawn from the point of articulation. In this case, the dorsum of the tongue is withdrawn from the velum. Compare the release of /k/ in **scat** and **act.** The released sound is symbolized by [⌐], the unreleased by [ˀ]. Aspirated sounds, for example [kʰ], are released. In final positions, release is optional.

---

[5]Virgules / / indicate phonemic transcription, and brackets [ ] indicate phonetic transcription.

Some Allophones of English

A. On the chart on page 36, are all cases of initial /k/ aspirated? _____

   Final /k/? _____

B. Are all aspirated sounds released? _____ Are all released sounds

   aspirated? _____

C. Is the frontopalatal allophone [c] used before a front or a back vowel? _____

D. When is the dorsovelar allophone [k] used? _____

E. Are there any cases of final [c]? _____

F. Aside from intonation, one of the ways the speech of nonnative speakers differs from that of native speakers is in the use of allophones. When we hear a foreign accent, we recognize differences, but they are difficult to pinpoint. Native speakers are not generally aware of the allophones that cause this difference. On the basis of the above information, explain why you would hear a foreign accent in the word [tæcʰ] for **tack**. This is the pronunciation of the word for 'lone' in Persian. Examine the distribution of [cʰ]. Does it appear in the final position of any word on the chart? _____

G. Holding the palm of your hand in front of your mouth, try to estimate the aspiration of the initial /k/ in the following sets of words:

I		II	
cóntract	cóllege	contráct	collégiate
cáncel	córporate	canál	coóperative
cátalogue	kiln	catástrophe	kinétic
call		collíde	

   The /k/'s in column II are followed by reduced vowels. Are they aspirated? _____

   Under what condition do you find a weakening of aspiration in initial stops? _____

   _____

H. Just as no initial /k/ before a full vowel (column I in G) is unaspirated, no /k/ following /s/ is aspirated. Each position, initial and medial, has its own characteristics. These two positions are said to be in *complementary distribution*. Find the distribution of the two allophones of the phoneme /l/ given below by examining the sets of words in which they occur.

[l]	[ɫ]
lip	bulk
loot	full
link	milk
lie	cool

Distribution: _____   _____

I. Consider [tæk˥] and [tæk⌐]. Can final /k/ be released? _____

Unreleased? _____ When two allophones can fill the same
position, they are said to be in *free variation*. Allophones are either in complementary
distribution or in free variation.

J. Given the phonetic representations for /p/, fill in the "aspirated" and "released" columns
for the words *pin, pun, spin, spun,* and *nip.*

Major Allophones of /p/

Word	Phonetic representations of /p/	Aspirated	Released
pin	[pʰɪn]	+	+
pun	[pʰʌn]		
spin	[sp⌐ɪn]		
spun	[sp⌐ʌn]		
nip	[nɪp⌐]		
nip!	[nipʰ]	+	+

1. In what position (initial, medial, or final) do the possibilities of aspirated, unaspirated,
   released, and unreleased allophones of /p/ occur? _____ These allo-
   phones are said to be in _____
   (see *I*).
2. On the other hand, no [pʰ] follows /s/ and no word begins with [p⌐]. They are
   said to be in _____ _____ (see *H*).

K. What practical applications to foreign language learning does the study of allophones
   have? _____

   _____

   _____

   _____

   _____

   _____

   _____

   _____

EXERCISE 7: The Phoneme

Determining Vowel Phonemes

The study of phonemics includes features other than just the ones touched on in the previous exercise. It also includes features such as length and nasalization—any feature, in fact, that *could* be distinctive in a speech sound whether or not it happens to be distinctive in English. If, on studying the environment of a sound (such as /p/ before a full vowel in English, as in *pie*), we discover that the feature of aspiration is automatic, then that feature is nondistinctive: it does not serve to tell one phoneme from another. What the linguist does is to state the rule by which the feature can be predicted (sound *x* in environment *y* always has feature *z*) and then eliminate it from the description of the phoneme in question. He must then look for some other feature or features that characterize that phoneme. The following exercise illustrates this technique by applying it to the vowels of Persian. You are to decide whether such features as length and stress are needed to characterize them— that is, are needed in making a phonemic transcription of the Persian vowels. The solution should become obvious as you answer the questions. (The dot following the vowel means extra length. The consonant and vowel sounds are phonetic—those described in the previous chapter—plus [x], which is a voiceless dorsovelar fricative, as in German **Bach.** The stress in a word of more than one syllable is indicated by ′ above the vowel in the stressed syllable.)

1. i·n	'this'	u·d	'lute'		
ɛsm	'name'	ɔmr	'life' (time)	}	vowel initial
æz	'from'	a·z	'greed'		
2. bi·d	'willow'	bu·d	'was'		
sɛr	'insensible'	sɔr	'slide'	}	vowel medial
sær	'head'	na·m	'name'		
3. si·	'thirty'	bu·	'smell'		
sɛ	'three'	dɔ	'two'	}	vowel final
dæ	'ten'	ba·	'with'		
4. ni·st	'isn't'	gu·št	'meat'		
zešt	'ugly'	košt	'killed'	}	before consonant cluster
dæšt	'plain'	ka·št	'planted'		
5. di·vá·r	'wall'	ku·zé	'jug'		
pɛsǽr	'son'	mɔtór	'engine'	}	unstressed
kæbí·r	'great'	ta·zé	'fresh'		
6. kæbí·r	'great'	æknú·n	'now'		
na·mé	'letter'	šɔtór	'camel'	}	stressed
æsǽr	'result'	kɛtá·b	'book'		

A. Find minimal pairs (pairs of words that are similar in all respects but one) in this list to distinguish the following Persian vowel phones from each other. The difference in meaning is attributable to that single difference in sound. The two sounds are thereby established as separate phonemes. (To do this exercise, you will also need the words xu·d 'helmet' and xɔd 'self'.)

[i· u·]	[bi·d]	[bu·d]
[ɛ ɔ]	_____	_____
[æ a·]	_____	_____
[i· ɛ]	_____	_____
[ɛ æ]	_____	_____
[u· ɔ]	_____	_____
[ɔ a·]	_____	_____

B. Which vowels are consistently long? _____ _____ _____

C. Which ones are consistently short? _____ _____ _____

D. Look at group 4. Is vowel length affected by final consonant clusters? _____

E. In group 5, all six vowels appear in an unstressed position (the first syllable). In group 6, all six vowels appear in a stressed position. Does stress affect the length of the vowels?

_____

F. Is the stress predictable from the data given? _____ If so, give the rule. ____

_____

G. Is length predictable? _____ If so, give the rule. _____

_____

H. If stress and length are predictable, is it necessary to write them? _____

I. Write the simplified phonemic vowels of Persian in the chart below.

Front   Back

High

Mid

Low

J. Group 5 would appear as follows phonemically:

/divar/	/kuze/
/pesær/	/motor/
/kæbir/	/taze/

Write group 6 phonemically.

_____	_____
_____	_____
_____	_____

EXERCISE 8: Segmental Phonemes of English

Minimal Pairs

For the following sets of segmental phonemes of English, find pairs of words that are similar in all features but the sounds noted here. Find two pairs of words: one pair should contrast the initial position, another the final. Write them phonetically. The sounds are in the order of decreasing frequency of occurrence in English. If you cannot find examples, go on to the next pair. The pair /t r/ is illustrated here.

Pairs	Initial	Final
1. /t r/	[tʌn], [rʌn]	[tut], [tur]
2. /r n/	_____	_____
3. /n s/	_____	_____
4. /s l/	_____	_____
5. /l d/	_____	_____
6. /d h/	_____	(no example)
7. /h m/	_____	(no example)
8. /m k/	_____	_____
9. /k ð/	_____	_____
10. /ð z/	_____	_____
11. /z v/	_____	_____
12. /v f/	_____	_____
13. /f b/	_____	_____

Pairs	Initial	Final
14. /b p/		
15. /p ŋ/	(no example)	
16. /ŋ g/	(no example)	
17. /g š/		
18. /š č/		
19. /č θ/		
20. /θ ǰ/		
21. /ǰ ž/	(no example)	
22. /i ɪ/		
23. /ɪ e/		
24. /e ɛ/		
25. /ɛ æ/		
26. /æ ʌ/		
27. /ʌ a/		
28. /a ɔ/		
29. /ɔ o/		
30. /o ʊ/		
31. /ʊ u/		

Some phonemic contrasts are not much exploited—for example, the contrast between /u/ and /ʊ/, as in *cooed-could, pool-pull, gooed-good, hood(lum)-hood, fool-full, Luke-look.* Can you give three other pairs with these two phonemes? _____

_____

The extent to which a contrast is exploited is called its *functional load:* /u/ versus /ʊ/ obviously has a light functional load. Can you guess why? _____

_____

What is apt to happen eventually to this contrast? _____

_____

_____

SOUNDS AND WORDS 4

EXERCISE 1: Systematic Phonemes

Some Morphophonemes in English

Below are lists of pairs of English phonemes. Although they have been established to be different from each other, they alternate with each other under certain conditions. In most cases, a change in word class accompanies the change in sounds. For example, the list contains pairs of words that consist of a noun and a verb, a noun and an adjective, or a verb and an adjective. Give another example of the alternation for each pair of phonemes.

		half	*halves*
/f v/	life, lives		
/θ ð/	breath, breathe		
/s z/	house, houses		
/t d/	bucked /t/, bugged /d/		
/t č/	rite, ritual		
/t š/	implicate, implication		
/t s/	celibate, celibacy		
/k š/	electric, electrician		
/k s/	public, publicize		
/d s/	deride, derisive		
/d ž/	provide, provision		
/d ǰ/	grade, gradual		
/ǰ s/	individual, divisive		
/s ž/	derisive, derision		
/z ž/	please, pleasure		
/g ǰ/	esophagus, esophageal		

/e i/	reception, receive	_____	_____
/ɪ ay/	linear, line	_____	_____
/æ e/	audacity, audacious	_____	_____
/o ɔ/	verbose, verbosity	_____	_____
/aw ʌ/	pronounce, pronunciation	_____	_____

Underline the two principal alternations in the consonant pairs above:

1. palatalization   2. nasalization   3. voicing   4. labialization

Underline the two principal alternations in the vowel pairs:

1. lip rounding   2. tongue height   3. dipthongization   4. degree of frontness

EXERCISE 2: Distinctive Features

Distinctive Features

A. Look at the distinctive feature chart of the consonants of English on page 79 of Bolinger. Answer the following questions by comparing that chart with the phonetic chart of this book.

    1. To which positions of articulation does [+grave] correspond? (Give in the order of front to back.) _____ , _____ , _____

    If [ŋ] were on the chart, would it be [+ grave] or [− grave]? _____

    2. To what positions of articulation do [+ diffuse] sounds belong? (Give in the order of front to back.) _____ , _____ , _____ ,

    _____

    3. To what manners of articulation do [+ strident] sounds belong? _____ ,

    _____

    Why are [θ, ð] not [+ strident]? Check the definition of **strident** in your text.

    _____

    4. To what manner of articulation do [+ continuant] sounds belong? _____

B. Answer the following questions by checking the distinctive feature chart of English in Bolinger. Find all sounds that are defined by the combination of the following sets of features.

1. [− vocalic, + consonantal, + grave, + nasal] __[m]__ , __[ŋ]__

2. [− vocalic, + consonantal, + nasal] _____ , _____ , __[ŋ]__

3. [−vocalic, + consonantal, + grave, + strident] _____ , _____

4. [− vocalic, + consonantal, + strident] _____ , _____ , _____ , _____ ,

_____ , _____ , _____ , _____

Compare the number of sounds defined in 1 and 2 and in 3 and 4. Note that 1 and 3 have one feature more than 2 and 4. Does the addition of a feature increase or decrease the number of sounds defined? _____ The fact that generalizations may be represented by fewer symbols than the same number of unrelated sounds is one of the advantages of using distinctive features in descriptions, even though for specific sounds they are more cumbersome than the phonetic symbols of the previous chapter.

C. Indicate the distinctive features for the sounds listed in the sentence

/ðə kɔw ǰʌmpt ovər ðə mun/

	ð	k	w	ǰ	m	p	t	v	r	n
consonantal	+	+	−	+	+	+·	+	+	+	+
vocalic										
high										
low										
back										
anterior										
coronal										
continuant										
voiced										
nasal										
strident										
sonorant										

D. In the first exercise of this chapter, we noted a relationship among certain pairs of phonemes of English: *life-lives, breath-breathe, rite-ritual, implicate-implication, provide-provision, public-publicize,* among others. Check the distinctive feature chart in the Bolinger text and determine what features separate each member of the pair from the other.

	[− voice]	[+ voice]
/f v/	_____	_____
/θ ð/	_____	_____
/t č/	_____	_____
	_____	_____
	_____	_____
/t š/	_____	_____
	_____	_____
	_____	_____
	_____	_____
/d ž/	_____	_____
	_____	_____
	_____	_____
/k s/	_____	_____
	_____	_____
	_____	_____
	_____	_____
	_____	_____

What can be said about the pair /f v/ compared to /k s/? _____

_____

By what phonetic features are /k/ and /s/ distinguished in manner of articulation? _____

In position of articulation? _____

How do you account for the fact that six distinctive features are needed to make a generalization for /k s/ compared to one for /f v/? _____

_____

_____

Distinctive Features in Pairs

The first pair of each set of phonemes below is different from the second in one or two features. After determining common features in each pair of a set, compare the two pairs and find the feature or features that separate them. Mark the + or − distinction in the space provided as shown on line 1. Doing this exercise will increase your awareness of the differences between phonemes and groups of phonemes.[1]

1. b d / v ð   *− continuant*   *− continuant*   *+ continuant*   *+ continuant*

2. p t / v s   _____   _____   _____   _____

      _____   _____   _____   _____

3. p t / č k   _____   _____   _____   _____

4. t č / p k   _____   _____   _____   _____

5. f θ / v ð   _____   _____   _____   _____

6. p b / f v   _____   _____   _____   _____

      _____   _____   _____   _____

7. m / n   _____   _____

8. š č / ž ǰ   _____   _____   _____   _____

9. č ǰ / s z   _____   _____   _____   _____

      _____   _____   _____   _____

10. p b / k g   _____   _____   _____   _____

EXERCISE 3: Word Shapes

Word Shapes in English

Place an **E** beside any word on the left that when pronounced could be a native English word, an **N** beside any word that could not, and explain why those words you mark with **N** could not be native English words.

Explanation (for non-English cases only)

__N__ Vladivostok   *No initial vl- consonant clusters in English*   _____

____ truft   _____

____ bishphelt   _____

[1] We are indebted to Professor Meri Lehtinen of the University of Minnesota for the form of this exercise.

_____ ngew   _____

_____ zlota   _____

_____ peptor   _____

_____ azhta   _____

_____ Zsa Zsa   _____

_____ vraiment   _____

_____ shprom   _____

_____ bnigmatic _____

_____ lamga   _____

_____ lozh   _____

_____ stlength   _____

Word Boundaries

Some terms are frequently encountered in incorrect forms. Examine the following lists, and comment on what they reflect about our sense of what a word is.

Correct Form	*Incorrent Form*
men-o'-war	man-o'-wars
notaries public	notary publics
attorneys general	attorney generals

_____

_____

_____

EXERCISE 4: Morpheme Identification

Modern Hebrew

Determine the morphemes in the following list of Hebrew words. Proceed by isolating the one that means 'wrote'.

1. katávti   'I wrote'
2. katávta   'you (masculine singular) wrote'
3. katávt   'you (feminine singular) wrote'
4. katáv   'he wrote'
5. katvá   'she wrote'
6. katávnu   'we wrote'

7. kətavtém   'you (masculine plural) wrote'
8. kətavtén   'you (feminine plural) wrote'
9. katvú   'they wrote'

A. What are the morphemes for the following words?

_____	I	_____	we
_____	you (m. s.)	_____	you (m. pl.)
_____	you (f. s.)	_____	you (f. pl.)
_____	he	_____	they
_____	she		

B. What are the three allomorphs of *wrote*? _____

_____

C. Given the Hebrew word *yašáv* 'he sat,' translate the following:

she sat _____

you (m. pl.) sat _____

I sat _____

they sat _____

yašávnu _____

yašávt _____

Classical Arabic

1. yáktubu   'he writes'
2. yaktúbuhu   'he writes it (m.)'
3. yaktúbuha   'he writes it (f.)'
4. yáktubu lahu   'he writes to him'
5. yáktubu laha   'he writes to her'
6. yaktúbuhu laha   'he writes it (m.) to her'
7. yaktúbuhu lahu   'he writes it (m.) to him'
8. yaktúbuhu lahum   'he writes it (m.) to them (m.)'
9. yaktúbuhu lii   'he writes it (m.) to me'
10. yaktúbuhu lana   'he writes it (m.) to us'
11. yaktúbuhu laka   'he writes it (m.) to you (m. s.)'
12. yaktúbuhu laki   'he writes it (m.) to you (f. s.)'
13. yaktúbuhu lakum   'he writes it (m.) to you (m. pl.)'
14. yaktúbuhu lakúnna   'he writes it (m.) to you (f. pl.)'
15. yaktúbuhu lahúnna   'he writes it (m.) to them (f.)'

A. Write the morphemes for the following words:

_____ me	_____ us
_____ you (m. s.)	_____ you (m. pl.)
_____ you (f. s.)	_____ you (f. pl.)
_____ him (it)	_____ them (f.)
_____ her (it)	_____ to (give the allophones)

B. Is stress predictable? If so, give the rule. (Omit *lakúnna* and *lahúnna.*)

_____

_____

C. Given the word *yúrsilu* 'he sends,' translate the following:

yursíluhu _____

yursíluha lahu _____

yursíluhu lakunna _____

He sends it (m.) to us. _____

He sends it (f.) to them (f.). _____

EXERCISE 5: Conditioning

English Plural Morphemes

Suppose the words on the chart on the following page were introduced into the noun class of English. Your knowledge of English will help you predict whether /s/, /z/, or /əz/ would be used in forming the plural. Write the word in the proper column.

1. What determines the choice of /əz/? _____

_____

2. What determines the choice of /z/? _____

_____

3. What determines the choice of /s/? _____

_____

4. What kind of conditioning is at work here? _____

_____

	/s/ (as in **bucks**)	/z/ (as in **bugs**)	/əz/ (as in **ashes**)
[šæb]			
[foš]			
[ima]			
[šuk]			
[heyf]			
[lož]			
[bibi]			
[sæg]			
[bɛš]			
[gæč]			
[hɛs]			
[bɔrǰ]			
[bɔz]			
[bu]			

Some Negative Prefixes in English
Which negative prefix (*ir-*, *il-*, *im-*, *in-*) is used with each of the following words?

Prefix	Word	Prefix	Word	Prefix	Word
1. *ir-*	relevant	5. _____	adequate	9. _____	possible
2. _____	logical	6. _____	movable	10. _____	admissible
3. _____	modest	7. _____	legal	11. _____	reversible
4. _____	equitable	8. _____	regular	12. _____	literate

im- is used before _____

ir- is used before _____

il- is used before _____

in- is used before _____

Circle the term that describes the conditioning process:

dissimilation   assimilation

Some Special Noun Morphemes

Transcribe phonemically the singular and plural allomorphs of your own speech for the following words:

	Singular Allomorph	Plural Allomorph
1. life	/layf/	/layv-/
2. thief		
3. path		
4. knife		
5. booth		
6. wolf		
7. leaf		
8. sheaf		
9. loaf		
10. sheath		
11. house		
12. truth		

1. Give examples of English nouns ending in /f θ s/ that do not change to their voiced counterparts before adding plural suffixes. _____

_____

2. What kind of conditioning is this? _____

_____

3. In Costa Rica, the Spanish verb meaning 'to go' has an imperative form based on another verb that means 'to walk'. A somewhat similar situation is found in the past form of the English verb *to go*. What kind of conditioning is it?

_____

4. What special term is applied? _____

EXERCISE 1: Idiom and Collocation[1]

Some Common Idioms in English
Place the number of the idiom on the right beside the corresponding definition on the left.

__8__ 'dominated by wife'		1. apple-polish
_____ 'empty talk'		2. birdbrained
_____ 'to flatter a teacher'		3. black gold
_____ 'to extort'		4. blackmail
_____ 'to sell or make liquor illegally'		5. bootleg
_____ 'to be the brains behind a scheme'		6. down-to-earth
_____ 'practical and realistic'		7. egghead
_____ 'deceitful and hypocritical'		8. henpecked
_____ 'stingy'		9. highhanded
_____ 'overly romantic or idealistic'		10. hot air
_____ 'stupid'		11. mastermind
_____ 'oil'		12. old maid
_____ 'overbearing, arbitrary'		13. starry-eyed
_____ 'a quarter of a dollar'		14. tightfisted
_____ 'an intellectual'		15. two bits
_____ 'a spinster'		16. two-faced

[1]The exercises in this section are based on information from Adam Makkai's *Idiom Structure in English* (The Hague: Mouton, 1972).

EXERCISE 2: Collocation

Collocation I

Complete the following phrases and indicate those that are idioms.

Phrase		Idiom?
in sickness and in	_____health_____	_yes_
yes or	_____	_____
dead or	_____	_____
life and	_____	_____
law and	_____	_____
assets and	_____	_____
deaf and	_____	_____
each and	_____	_____
sticks and	_____	_____
this and	_____	_____
his and	_____	_____
nuts and	_____	_____
bread and	_____	_____
in black and	_____	_____
assault and	_____	_____
cash and	_____	_____

A. In what ways do the idioms differ from the other phrases?

_____

_____

_____

B. As phrases become institutionalized, they often reflect the values of the society. Below are a few phrases involving names or titles of females and males.

1. Fill in as many other examples as you can.

Male Mentioned First	Female Mentioned First
Mr. and Mrs.	_ladies and gentlemen_
his and hers	_aunts and uncles_

Male Mentioned First	_Female Mentioned First_
_____	_____
_____	_____
_____	_____
_____	_____
_____	_____
_____	_____
_____	_____

2. Which type is more prevalent? _____

   Why? _____

   _____

3. In Persian there is no gender distinction in the third person pronoun. **He** and **she** are

   represented as [u]. Does that necessarily reflect a less sexist society? _____

   _____

   _____

Collocation II

Complete the second half of each phrase.

A. Intensifiers:

sly as _____ _a fox_ _____	neat as _____
quick as _____	sharp as _____
fit as _____	strong as _____
happy as _____	sober as _____
poor as _____	clean as _____
hungry as _____	stubborn as _____
slow as _____	good as _____
old as _____	blind as _____

B. Manners:

drink like _____	sleep like _____
work like _____	eat like _____
live like _____	laugh like _____

Collocation III

A. Every seventh word of this text adapted from *Aspects of Language* has been omitted. Read it through once. On the second reading, write in the words you feel would be appropriate.

In the last chapter we defined _____ as the smallest elements that are
_____ coded—an abstruse way of saying _____ they are the
$\overline{2}$ $\overline{3}$
pawns in the _____, the common pieces that are constantly _____
$\overline{4}$ $\overline{5}$
_____ and sometimes used alone to convey _____ message. The one-
$\overline{6}$
to-one or one-to-many relationship _____ words and meanings is under-
$\overline{7}$
stood by _____ speaker. It is the one thing _____ the
$\overline{8}$ $\overline{9}$
practical use of language that _____ know children can be effectively
$\overline{10}$
taught. _____ it is not quite at the _____ level of awareness
$\overline{11}$ $\overline{12}$
as the relationship _____ a hammer and hitting a nail, _____
$\overline{13}$ $\overline{14}$
can nevertheless be brought to that _____ very easily. The person strug-
$\overline{15}$
gling with _____ idea who says *I can't think* _____ *the right*
$\overline{16}$ $\overline{17}$
word is never heard _____ say °*I can't think of the* _____
$\overline{18}$ $\overline{19}$
prefix or °*I can't think of* _____ *right sound* (though he may say
$\overline{20}$
_____ *can't think of the right way* _____ *put it,* which has
$\overline{21}$ $\overline{22}$
to do _____ something higher up on the scale _____ words).
$\overline{23}$ $\overline{24}$

Now check your guesses against the words that appeared in the text.[2]

B. How many of the seven words in the group 4, 7, 16, 19, 20, 22, 23 did you guess correctly?

_____

C. How many of the seven words in the group 1, 2, 5, 9, 11, 14, 15 did you guess correctly?

_____

D. You probably had more correct in *B* than *C.* Why? _____

_____

_____

_____

[2] 1. words   2. independently   3. that   4. game   5. reassembled   6. a   7. between   8. every   9. about
10. we   11. if   12. same   13. between   14. it   15. level   16. an   17. of   18. to   19. right   20. the   21. I
22. to   23. with   24. than

EXERCISE 3: The Make-up of Words

Compounding

A. Are all idioms compounds? _____

B. Consider these compounds:

brick red	snow-white	sky blue	ice-cold
jet-black	pitch-dark	red-hot	lukewarm

1. Are all compounds idioms? _____

2. Do the elements of compounds qualify as collocations? _____

C. Consider the following idiomatic compounds consisting of an adjective and a noun:

I		II	
blácklist	hóthead	Black Déath	hot aír
blúenose	rédcoat	blue móon	red ápples
gréenhorn	yéllowbelly	green thúmb	yellow féver

1. List two ways in which group I is different from group II. _____

_____

_____

2. List three more type I compounds. _____, _____,

_____. Are these idioms? _____.

3. Now read group I with the same emphasis as occurs in group II (for example, **black list,**

blue nóse, green hórn, and so on). Are these still idioms? _____

4. In what other way, then, is group I different from group II? _____

_____

_____

5. Which list, I or II, has the normal Adjective + Noun intonation? _____

The Spelling of Compounds

A. Some of the following compound nouns are spelled as one word, some as two words, and some are hyphenated. Write these words correctly in the space beside each compound. Check your answers in your desk dictionary.

1. launch pad _____	3. jet port _____
2. blast off _____	4. free way _____

5. free loader _____   8. side kick _____

6. feather bedding _____   9. side light _____

7. sit in _____   10. high light _____

B. Whether a compound is spelled as two words, hyphenated, or made into a single word, appears to depend on _____.

C. All the major categories of words can be part of the process of compounding. Give another example of each of the types described below:

	Example I	*Example II*
Preposition + Preposition	along with	_____
Conjunction + Conjunction	whenever	_____
Adverb + *and* + Adverb	high and low	_____
Adjective + Adjective	red-hot	_____
Noun + Noun	skylab	_____
Noun + Noun + *-ed*	pigeon-toed	_____
Adjective + Noun	greenhouse	_____
Adjective + Noun + *-ed*	highhanded	_____
Verb + Noun	kill-joy	_____
Noun + Verb	toothpick	_____
Noun + Verb + *-er*	man-eater	_____
Verb + Verb	make-believe	_____
Verb + Adverb	takeover	_____
Adverb + Verb	downpour	_____
Noun + Verb + *-ing*	heartwarming	_____
Adjective + Verb	deep-fry	_____

EXERCISE 4: Derivation

Some Prefixes in English

A. In the space provided beside each prefix, place the numbers of the stems that combine with that prefix to form a word.

_1, 3, 10_ de-	1. -bug	
_____ extra-	2. -curricular	
_____ inter-	3. -ference	
_____ micro-	4. -organism	
_____ out-	5. -run	
_____ pre-	6. -mature	
_____ post-	7. -doctorate	
_____ pseudo-	8. -sophisticate	
_____ super-	9. -natural	
_____ trans-	10. -form	

B. List these prefixes on the basis of the number of unions entered to form words.

3 or less   _4 or more_

de-
_____ _____   _____
_____ _____   _____
_____ _____   _____
_____ _____   _____

C. A *free morpheme* is one that can occur by itself, whereas a *bound* morpheme occurs only in the company of another morpheme. List the free and bound morphemes of the following sentence. (Words consisting of more than one morpheme have been divided.)

The make/up of the derivative/s can be high/ly com/plex.

	Free Morphemes		_Bound Morphemes_
The	_____		-s
_____	_____		_____
_____	_____		_____
_____	_____		_____

D. In the following pairs of sentences, indicate whether there is a word in one that is more affix-*like* (A) than the corresponding word (N) in the other. Would any be written solid? Underline expressions that would be written solid.

<u>N</u> 1. We've got to give him his money's value.

<u>A</u> 2. We've got to give him his money's worth.

_____ 3. This is truly the composer's master opus.

_____ 4. This is truly the composer's master work.

_____ 5. Stop acting like a crazy man.

_____ 6. Stop acting like a crazy fool.

_____ 7. I'm doing it for Cecily's welfare.

_____ 8. I'm doing it for Cecily's sake.

EXERCISE 5: Compound or Derivation?

Are words that contain the element *-man* compounds, derivatives, or both? Place **C** or **D** beside each of the following words to indicate whether you feel it is a compound or a derivative. (Pay special attention to whether or not there is a full vowel [æ] in each one.)

_____ woodsman	_____ postman	_____ garbage man	_____ lineman
_____ chairman	_____ mailman	_____ fireman	_____ salesman
_____ milkman	_____ workman	_____ oilman	
_____ trashman	_____ repairman	_____ gasman	

How do you feel about the substitution of *-person* for *-man* in certain of these, for example, *chairperson, salesperson?* What does the fact that some are reduced to *-m'n* mean to you?

_____

_____

EXERCISE 6: Morphemes

Morphemes

Divide the following words into their morphemes, placing a slash between each morpheme and the next. Some of the words are composed of only one morpheme.

1. *aw/ful*
2. breakfast
3. crystallization
4. deformity
5. evangelical
6. forgetfulness
7. gyroscope
8. honesty
9. insincere
10. jargon
11. knockabout
12. lovely
13. miraculous
14. nowhere
15. obstinate
16. periodical
17. query
18. restaurant
19. satisfied
20. trimmings

A. The word *apparently* can be divided as *apparent/ly* or *appar/ent/ly.* What is the rationale for dividing it the second way? _____

_____

Can you find other words that change in the same way as *appear* and *appar-* do?

_____

B. Some linguists analyze *made* as *make* + past. If this kind of analysis is used, what information about words is needed in order to decide what a morpheme is? _____

_____

C. In the word *their,* one might say that *thei* is a morpheme (as in *they*) and *-r* is a morpheme (as in *your*). Do you agree or disagree with this justification of *their* as two morphemes?

_____

_____

D. Divide the words in the following sentences into their morphemes by placing a slash between each morpheme and the next. Read the sentences through before dividing them into morphemes.

1. *The/ organ/ic/ function/ of/ language/ is/ to/ carry/ mean/ing.*
2. The apparently meaningful bits that are smaller than words are termed morphemes.
3. What are words?
4. A word is evidently something that is not to be broken up.
5. The morpheme is semi-finished material from which words are made.
6. Semi-finished means second-hand.
7. Practically all words that are not imported bodily from some other language are made up of old words or their parts.
8. The only thing a morpheme is good for is to be melted down and recast in a word.
9. The meanings of morphemes can vary as widely as their forms.
10. Almost no morpheme is perfectly stable in meaning.
11. When morphemes are put together to form new words, the meanings are almost never simply additive.

EXERCISE 7: Lexical Morphemes
and Grammatical Morphemes

On the following page, list the lexical morphemes and the grammatical morphemes in sentences 3, 4, 6, and 9 of the preceding exercise. Use each morpheme only once.

Lexical Morphemes		Grammatical Morphemes	
3. _____	_____	_____	_____
4. _____	_____	_____	_____
_____	_____	_____	_____
_____	_____	_____	_____
_____	_____	_____	_____
_____	_____	_____	_____
6. _____	_____	_____	_____
_____	_____	_____	_____
9. _____	_____	_____	_____
_____	_____	_____	_____
_____	_____	_____	_____
_____	_____	_____	_____
_____	_____	_____	_____
_____	_____	_____	_____

A. Which group is more numerous? _____

B. Which group is repeated more frequently? _____

C. Would you expect a different result for A and B if there were more sentences? _____
_____

EXERCISE 8: Word Formation

Noun Formation by Derivation

Add one or more of the suffixes in the list below to each numbered word to create new nouns. In some cases the form of the new noun is quite different from its elements; for example, *pope + cy = papacy.*

-age	-cy	-ics	-ist	-ness
-al	-ee	-ing	-ity	-or
-an	-ence	-ion	-let	-ship
-ance	-er	-ions	-ling	-ster
-ce	-ian	-ism	-ment	-th

1. distinct _____+ -ion, + -ness_____
2. elegant _____
3. lenient _____
4. senile _____
5. fresh _____
6. young _____
7. democrat _____
8. member _____
9. library _____
10. magic _____
11. violin _____
12. gang _____
13. lecture _____
14. alcohol _____

15. marry _____
16. refer _____
17. accept _____
18. write _____
19. build _____
20. train _____
21. dismiss _____
22. retire _____
23. elect _____
24. dear [dar] _____
25. home [ham] _____
26. warm _____
27. communicate _____
28. phoneme _____

Check your list and answer the following questions.

A. Which suffixes are added to adjectives to make nouns? _____
_____

B. Which suffixes may be added to verbs to make nouns? _____
_____

C. Which suffixes may be added to nouns to create new nouns? _____
_____

D. What is the common form of 'unableness'? _____
_____

Some Common Words Derived from Proper Names
Identify the source of the following words by checking your dictionary.

1. bantam _____
2. guillotine _____
3. hooligan _____
4. leotard _____

5. museum _____

6. palace _____

7. philander _____

8. quisling _____

9. sideburns _____

10. silhouette_____

11. spa _____

12. syphilis _____

13. vaudeville _____

EXERCISE 9: Initialism and Acronym

A. Identify the titles or terms the following initials stand for.

   1. F.B.I. _____

   2. UFO _____

   3. ESP _____

   4. L.A. _____

B. Identify as many of the following acronyms as you can.

   1. NATO _____

   2. UNESCO _____

   3. NOW _____

   4. NASA _____

   5. PUSH _____

C. Identify the following imaginary groups (answers given at bottom of page).

   1. WAGE (a labor organization favoring secure salaries) _____

   _____

   2. SPEL (a group dedicated to the defense of our native tongue) _____

   _____

1. Workers Advocate Guaranteed Earnings 2. Society for the Preservation of the English Language 3. Organization of Pessimistic Stockbrokers 4. Free Universities Now

3. OOPS (a Wall Street group with a dim view of the economic future) _____

_____

4. FUN (a militant student organization advocating immediate liberation of insti-

tutions of higher learning) _____

EXERCISE 10: Reduplication

Supply the first element in the following reduplicated words and then give the source and definition of the word. A dictionary will be needed for most.

1. *hodge* podge   *Variation of **hotchpot** (from Old French **hochepot**), meaning*

                          'a bringing together and mixing of property for the purpose

                          of dividing it evenly'. At present, 'a mess'.

2. _____ nilly   _____

_____

_____

3. _____ chat   _____

_____

_____

4. _____ flop   _____

_____

_____

5. _____ panky   _____

_____

_____

6. _____ raff   _____

_____

_____

7. _____ zag   _____

_____

_____

8. _____ shape _____

_____

_____

_____

9. _____ dally _____

_____

_____

_____

EXERCISE 11: Zero-derivation

For each of the words below, write two sentences, using the word as a different part of speech in each sentence.

1. run _____ *How fast can he run the mile?* _____

_____ *He had a run of good luck.* _____

2. shift _____

_____

3. act _____

_____

4. catch _____

_____

5. trick _____

_____

6. feature _____

_____

7. up _____

_____

8. while _____

_____

9. slow _____

_____

SYNTAX 6

EXERCISE 1: The Essence of Syntax Is Freedom

Write as many sentences as you can using the words *go, can, you, today.* Use punctuation marks as needed. (Note: In statements, *today* can appear at the beginning or at the end, with or without the main verb *go.*)

Examples:
1. Go!
2. You can.
3. Can you?

4. _____
5. _____
6. _____
7. _____
8. _____
9. _____
10. _____
11. _____
12. _____

Given a fifth word, *not,* how many new sentences are you able to construct? (Note: Use *can't* in place of *can not.*)

13. You can't.
14. Can't you?
15. You can't go.

16. _____
17. _____

18. _____

19. _____

20. _____

21. _____

22. _____

Adding *she, and, tomorrow, or, come* (making a total of ten words) would yield several hundred additional possible sentences. Considering the large vocabulary of English, it is not surprising that the number of possible sentences approaches infinity. By one estimate, the total number of sentences that are *between one and twenty words long* is 1×10^{30}. (Compare this with the number of seconds in a century: 3×10^9.) These are all sentences that one can understand and might use, as communication requires it. What does this suggest

about the scope of learning a foreign language? _____

_____

_____

_____

_____

_____

Some Limitations on Syntactic Freedom

Once we begin to use compound and complex sentences, content or syntax may dictate the order of the simple sentences of which they are composed. In the pairs of sentences that follow, indicate with *N* those that need not follow a particular order when they are joined by *and.* Indicate with *O* those that need to be ordered. Aside from the examples

below, in your opinion, which type is more prevalent? _____

_N_	1. The sun is shining.	The wind is blowing.
_O_	2. Susie went to sleep.	She had a dream.
_____	3. John came in.	He closed the door.
_____	4. He came in.	John closed the door.
_____	5. She felt embarrassed.	She blushed.
_____	6. The sky is blue.	The grass is green.
_____	7. He walked away.	He got up.
_____	8. He enjoyed the meal.	He loved the pickles.

EXERCISE 2: Operators

How do content words and operators serve to inform the reader/listener of the intentions of the speaker/writer? In the first sentence below, the operators have been garbled, and in the second sentence the content words have been changed. After you read both, describe the function and relative importance of content words as opposed to operators.

Ef example illustratem yorkel kind fa relatednim, quile sie yim fundamental noy thorel raum syntax.

This Sploze graums another lurve of spartness, which is more vardal than anything with frax.[1]

_____

_____

_____

_____

_____

EXERCISE 3: Analysis by Immediate Constituents[2]

One of the methods of sentence analysis used by American structuralism is called Immediate Constituent (IC) analysis: a sentence is divided into adjacent parts, then each of these parts is in turn divided into adjacent parts, and so on until no further division is possible. This sort of analysis allows one to see the sentence in terms of layers of syntactic structures.

A. The first task is to make a division between modifiers of the sentence and the sentence itself. A sentence can be modified by either words or groups of words.

Usually	*the train comes on time.*
Modification	

When the morning train comes late,	*most of the men take the bus.*
Modification	

---

[1] This sentence, from Bolinger's Chapter 6, is "This example illustrates another kind of relatedness, which is more fundamental than anything within syntax."

[2] *An Introductory English Grammar*, by Norman C. Stageberg (New York: Holt, Rinehart and Winston, 1965), is the model for the IC analysis in this exercise.

Separate the sentence modifiers from the rest of the sentence below. Follow the model.

1.

When she heard that, she slammed the door.
Modification

2. Since the car wouldn't start, I had to walk to work.

3. To make up for lost time, we skipped lunch.

B. When there is no sentence modifier, the first cut, or division, is made between the subject and the predicate.

The man	*walked in.*
Predication	

The old woman in the gray suit	*walked over to the counter.*
Predication	

The old man who had lost his glasses	*had to walk into town for a new pair.*
Predication	

Make a cut between the subject and the predicate in these sentences. You might have to cut off the sentence modifier first.

1.

Usually	he	walked
	Predication	
Modification		

2. The old farmer went to the market.

3. The brown cow in the pasture walked along the fence.

4. On Tuesday, most of the students attended the lecture.

C. The first cut in a subordinate clause is made after the conjunction that subordinates. The following example is one kind of *structure of subordination.*

whenever	he	comes to town
	Predication	
Subordination		

Some subordinating conjunctions are *after, although, because, before, until, since, when, whenever.*

Identify the structures of predication and subordination below by making the appropriate cuts.

1.

because	you	brought your guitar
	Predication	
Subordination		

2. after he drove the car

3. once the concert was over

D. The first cut in a prepositional phrase comes immediately after the preposition. A prepositional phrase is another kind of subordination.

in	*the car that Joan bought*
	Subordination

Make the first cut in these phrases.

1.

under	the rug
Subordination	

2. across the blue meadow

3. into the old white house that he had just sold

E. A noun phrase is a noun with words or groups of words modifying it. The subjects of most of the sentences we have studied were noun phrases. Some modifiers come after the noun, but most come before. First cut off the modifiers that come after the noun, beginning with the last, then the next-to-last, and so on to the noun.

the old red car	*in the garage*	*with the rusted cylinders*
Modification		
Modification		

the old red car	*in*	*the garage*	*with the new cement floor*
		Modification	
		Subordination	
Modification			

Note that *with the new cement floor* does not modify *the old car* but *the garage.* The whole phrase *in the garage with the new cement floor* modifies *the old red car.* After you cut off the modifiers that come after the noun, cut off those that come before, beginning with the first modifier.

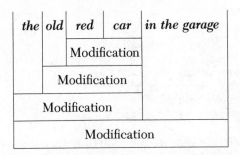

Cut off all the modifiers from the main noun in each of these noun phrases.

1.

2. the hunter who was sneaking up on the crow

3. the hunter in the red jacket who was sneaking up on the crow

4. the hunter who was sneaking up on the crow on the dead branch

F. In the sentence *John hit the ball, the ball* is a complement of the verb. In *He gave John the ball,* both *John* and *the ball* are complements of the verb. A complement is a word or phrase that in some sense completes the meaning of the verb. Complements are cut off from the verb just as modifiers after the verb are cut off, beginning with the last.

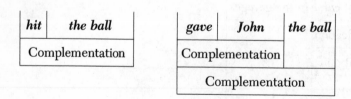

Complements and modifiers that come after the verb are cut off in turn when they occur together.

hit	the ball	hard
Complementation		
Modification		

Make the IC cuts for verbal modifiers and complements in the following verb phrases.

1.	usually	went	into spring training	with great eagerness
		Modification		
		Modification		
	Modification			

2. sullenly slouched in his chair

3. hit the ball hard to center field

G. Make a complete IC analysis of the following sentences. You should end up with a line between any two adjacent words (except for the verb with its auxiliaries, which are treated as units). Cut off the sentence modifier first, next cut the subject from the predicate, and then make any other cuts that apply.

1.

The	first	of	the	men	left	his	jacket	in	the	car.
			Modification		Modification			Modification		
Modification		Subordination			Complementation			Subordination		
Modification					Modification					
Predication										

2. When you are ready, you can get the equipment from the car.

3. When the trouble started, the police advised those who were present to leave.

EXERCISE 4: Word Classes

Clues to Word Classes

Some of the underlined words in the following paragraph may not be familiar to you. You will, however, know what part of speech each word is. As you read, look for the cues that help you determine the part of speech.

In the morning, after you get out of the <u>rack</u>, you will scrub the <u>deck</u>, the <u>bulkheads</u>, and the <u>overhead</u> before leaving the <u>billet</u>. You will clean the <u>portholes</u>, and sweep the <u>ladder</u>. After <u>headcalls</u>, you will go through the <u>hatch</u>, put your <u>cover</u> on your <u>gourd</u>, make sure you are wearing clean <u>skivvies</u>, and run to the <u>messhall</u>. You are not allowed to get <u>chow</u> from the <u>reefer</u> in the <u>galley</u> or to get <u>pogibates</u> at the <u>gedunk</u>. After you leave the <u>messhall</u>, the <u>smokinglamp</u> will be lit if there are no fights with the <u>Squids</u> and no one is <u>fatmouthing</u>. All <u>sickbay</u> <u>commandos</u> will report to the <u>Louie</u> or the <u>Gunner</u>. Don't listen to <u>scuttlebut</u>. I am the only one with the <u>skinny</u>.[3]

What part of speech are most of the underlined words? _____

List the clues you had for determining the part of speech. Consider word endings and the position of the word in relation to determiners, modifiers, and verbs. _____

_____

_____

_____

_____

_____

_____

A. Classify the following as mass or count nouns:

Word	Mass	Count	Word	Mass	Count
humor	X	_____	flare-up	_____	_____
joke	_____	X	leaf	_____	_____
laugh	_____	_____	foliage	_____	_____
laughter	_____	_____	fear	_____	_____
anger	_____	_____	scare	_____	_____

[3] From a paper by Merle N. Schneidewind, "Navy Slang."

B. In what way do the following sets of verbs differ as to the kind of object they require?

_____

_____

_____

_____

	A			B	
devalue	*cash*		*convince*	*amuse*	
varnish	*leach*		*persuade*	*anger*	
publish	*unfurl*		*convict*	*dishearten*	

Verbs

Below is a list of fifteen transitive verbs. Match them with the noun phrases found on the right to produce grammatical and acceptable sentences. You will note that although all the verbs are transitive, there are certain syntactic and semantic restrictions on what each one may be paired with. Match each verb with the appropriate numbers. (People differ in their attitudes as to the acceptability of some sentences.)

I consider _____*1, 3, 5, 6, 7, 10, 11, 13*_____   1. his abilities as a musician.

I know _____*1, 6, 10, 13*_____   2. the daylight out of him.

I admire _____   3. him impossible to comprehend.

I find _____   4. very little fish.

I keep _____   5. her trustworthy.

We prefer _____   6. her to be trustworthy.

You terrify _____   7. him president.

You eat _____   8. it in the garage.

I force _____   9. him stealing bread.

We'll try _____   10. him to be a scholar.

We'll elect _____   11. fighting policemen.

We caught _____   12. myself to eat liver.

We avoid _____   13. the truth.

I want _____   14. to persuade him to stay.

I take _____   15. no credit for this.

In what way do the verbs *consider* and *know* differ syntactically in their choice of objects? (Consider their combinations with 5, 6, 7, and 10.) _____

_____

_____

_____

Semantic Compatibility

In the passage below, called "Political Speech," the choice of words to fill the blanks is rather predictable if the context is known. However, if the context is unknown and one fills the blanks with random words of the proper parts of speech, the passage becomes nonsensical and sometimes funny. Games such as "Mad Libs" depend on this principle of semantic incompatibility for their humor. For the passage below, ask someone to provide you with words of the specific parts of speech that you name (written below the lines). Do not let the person see the paragraph until he or she has finished. How do you account for the fact that if this exercise were done by a number of people who saw the passage

as they filled in the words, they would agree on their choice of many of the words? _____

_____

_____

_____

POLITICAL SPEECH[4]

Ladies and gentlemen, on this _____ occasion it is a privilege to address such
                                  1   adjective

a _____ looking group of _____. I can tell from your smiling
  2 adjective   *3 plural noun*

_____ that you will support my _____ program in the coming
  4 plural noun   *5 adjective*

election. I promise that, if elected there will be a _____ in every
                                           6 noun

_____. And two _____ in every garage. I want to warn you
  7 noun   *8 plural noun*

against my _____ opponent, Mr. _____. This man is nothing
    9 adjective   *10 name of person*
                                         in room

[4] Roger Price and Leonard Stern, *Son of Mad Libs* (Los Angeles: Price/Stern/Sloan Publishers, 1959). Copyright 1959 by Price/Stern/Sloan Publishers, Inc. Reprinted by permission of the publisher.

but a _____ _____. He has a _____ charac-
  11 adjective   *12 noun*   *13 adjective*

ter and is working _____ in glove with the criminal element. If elected, I
              14 noun

promise to eliminate vice. I will keep the _____ off the city's streets. I will
                        15 plural noun

keep crooks from dipping their _____ in the public till. I promise you
                  16 plural noun

_____ government, _____ taxes, and _____
  17 adjective   *18 adjective*   *19 adjective*

schools.

Consider any five "wrong" answers. What semantic rules are violated? For example,
if for the third blank, "plural noun," you have *lamps,* the problem is that this sense of the
verb *address* requires a human object.

_____

_____

_____

_____

_____

_____

_____

_____

EXERCISE 5: Classes and Functions

Embedding

A. In the following sentence identify as many embedded sentences as you can:

"An underground magazine called *Metanoia,* conceived by several former university
students, has evolved from a one-page Xerox sheet to a polished thirty-five-page magazine
in less than a year."

1. _____ *The magazine is called* Metanoia. _____

2. _____

3. _____

4. _____

5. _____

6. _____

7. _____

8. _____

9. _____

10. _____

EXERCISE 6: Semantic Distinctive Features

Classes as Features

The business of distinguishing one word from another is made much easier by dividing the meanings of words into elements, much as a chemist lists the elements present in his chemical compounds. These elements are called *semantic distinctive features*. To see how this works, look at the grid below. A plus sign for a particular word at a particular feature means that that feature is present in the word's meaning, and a minus means that that feature is not present. For example, the grid defines *piano* as 'a keyboard instrument that produces sound when its strings are hit'. The chart makes clear that the harpsichord differs from the piano in that its strings are plucked, not hit.

	String	Percussion	Plucked	Keyboard		
1. piano	+	+	−	+		
2. harpsichord	+	−	+	+		
3. _____						
4. _____						
5. _____						

How could the harp be fitted in here so that it would be neatly distinguished from the piano and the harpsichord? Enter *harp* on line 3 and fill in the grid. Note that the features already present can do the job of defining the harp. Now put *harmonium* on line 4. You will need a new feature, for the harmonium is a reed instrument. Fill in the new feature and the plus and minus symbols in the grid. Note that when a new feature is added, the previous words, as well as the new word, have to be marked plus or minus for that feature. Now put the word *accordion* on line 5, and fill in the grid. The harmonium and the accordion are not distinguished on the grid; there are not enough features. Both instruments, being reed instruments, are operated by blowing air past the reeds. They could be differentiated by the type of power driving the bellows: the harmonium is a foot-bellows instrument, and the accordion is a hand-bellows instrument. Fill in the grid so that these words are differentiated by these two features.

Fill in the names of musical instruments that fit the feature descriptions, or invent new instruments. Choose among an aeolian harp, dulcimer, harp, harpsichord, and piano for those choices for which a specific musical instrument exists.

	Percussion	Plucked	Keyboard
None such exists. Perhaps a combination piano and harpsichord, with a foot pedal giving the player his choice, or two keyboards.	+	+	+
	+	+	−
	+	−	+
	+	−	−
	−	+	+
	−	+	−
	−	−	+
	−	−	−

EXERCISE 7: Syntax

Syntactic Differences

Of the three sentences given for each set below, one sentence is syntactically different from the other two. Circle the letter before the sentence that is different. Be ready to explain your choice in each case. Consider the following example:

A. She was driven to the airport.
B. She was flown to Cuba.
C. She was opposed to the plan.

C is different because one can say that "X drove her to the airport," "X flew her to Cuba," but not "X opposed her to the plan."

1. A. Mary is anxious to graduate.
   B. Mary is eager to eat.
   C. Mary is easy to tease.

2. A. John impresses Bill as incompetent.
   B. John regards Bill as incompetent.
   C. John identifies Bill as incompetent.

3. A. They're afraid to run.
   B. They're able to play.
   C. They're ready to use.

4. A. The doctor's house was surprising.
   B. The doctor's arrival was surprising.
   C. The doctor's departure was surprising.

5. A. The king's banishment was unjust.
   B. The committee's appointment was unjust.
   C. The patient's complaint was unjust.

6. A. John promised his mother to drive carefully.
   B. John persuaded his mother to drive carefully.
   C. John expected his mother to drive carefully.

Syntactic Ambiguities

The following sentences are ambiguous as they stand. Rewrite them to remove the ambiguity, preserving one of the meanings. For example, in *The jockey dismounted from the horse with a smile,* the ambiguity is removed if *with a smile* is replaced by an adjective and the adjective is placed between *the* and *jockey,* as in *The smiling jockey dismounted from the horse.*

1. John was angry at the time. _____

2. Mary likes music better than Susan. _____

_____

3. John and Mary visited me. _____

_____

4. My father drag races with red and gold convertibles. _____

_____

5. That girl's cooking made me sick. _____

_____

6. John enjoys entertaining women. _____

_____

7. The dress comes in pink, yellow, and green on white. _____

_____

8. Draw more simple designs. _____

_____

9. He composed music for a play that is hard to understand. _____

_____

10. Certain reactions to given stimuli are inherent in the human animal. _____

_____

_____

11. The boy feels strange. _____

_____

12. They're ready to eat. _____

_____

13. John was injured by the tractor in the field. _____

_____

14. It was too hard for me to cut. _____

_____

15. That horse is hard to beat. _____

_____

EXERCISE 8: Transformational-Generative Grammar (TGG)[5]

In the following brief discussion of Transformational-Generative Grammar, three generative rules, that is, phrase structure rules, and eight transformational rules are introduced. Be sure to do each exercise before going on to the discussion that follows.

Constituents of a Sentence[6]
Consider the sentence

   (a) *Columbus discovered America.*

If you were to break this sentence into two parts, you would probably break it as

    Columbus   *discovered America.*

rather than

    Columbus discovered   *America.*

These two basic *constituents*, ***Columbus*** and ***discovered America***, correspond to the following rule in the *phrase structure* (PS) *rules* of TGG:

$$\text{PS 1. S} \longrightarrow \text{NP} + \text{VP}$$

PS 1 is read: A sentence (S) consists of a noun phrase (NP) followed by a verb phrase (VP). Usually the VP can also be divided into two parts—as in the sentence given above, in which there is a verb (V) ***discovered***, and an NP, ***America***, giving the rule

$$\text{VP} \longrightarrow \text{V} + \text{NP}$$

In the sentence ***Columbus died***, the VP consists of only a verb, ***died***.

$$\text{VP} \longrightarrow \text{V}$$

We can write this rule as part of PS 2 by modifying the rule to specify that the NP may or may not occur. This option is shown by enclosing the NP in parentheses. (This convention will be followed in the rest of the chapter.)

$$\text{PS 2. VP} \longrightarrow \text{V} + \text{(NP)}$$

Do PS 1 and PS 2 hold in the following complicated sentence?

   (b) *Columbus, who was one of the most prominent explorers of the fifteenth century, discovered the land that would one day lead the other nations of the world in man's exploration of the universe.*

To answer the question, we must know more about the NP.

---

[5] We are indebted to Professor Larry Hutchinson of the University of Minnesota for his comments, suggestions, and guidance in the preparation of this section.

[6] In preparing this discussion we have gained many insights from Jacobs and Rosenbaum's *Grammar 1* and *Grammar 2* (Boston: Ginn and Co., 1967).

The Noun Phrase

Rather than listing what constituents may be considered as noun phrases, let us note some interesting properties of noun phrases. Consider what happens to the NP's of the sentence *Columbus discovered America* when the sentence is transformed to its passive counterpart.

$$\textit{Columbus discovered America.} \overset{\text{passive}}{\Longrightarrow} \textit{America was discovered by Columbus.}$$

A transformation is symbolized by $\Longrightarrow$. We note that the positions of the NP's *Columbus* and *America* have been interchanged. Since only the NP's interchange, the *passive transformation* can determine the NP constituents of sentences. This is a helpful guide in the case of those sentences that undergo the passive transformation. Some sentences do not. Underline the sentences in which the passive transformation applies.

Columbus suppressed a mutiny. (A mutiny was suppressed by Columbus.)

1. Columbus died a happy man.
2. Columbus died happy.
3. Columbus greeted the Indians.
4. Columbus was a lucky man.
5. Columbus ignored the sailors.

Underline the NP's in the following sentences. If you are not sure, use the passive transformation as a guide.

1. The emotional actress divorced the movie magnate.
2. Webster's III heralded a new age of lexicography.
3. The strikers demanded better working conditions.

Now consider the sentence

(c) *Beauty is in the eye of the beholder.*

The passive transformation does not apply to this sentence. The NP, however, can be isolated by means of another transformation, which turns the statement into a question taking *yes* or *no* as an answer, as in *Is beauty in the eye of the beholder?* The shift of the verb *be* has isolated the NP.

Beauty (is) *in the eye of the beholder.*
(NP)

Thus, the *yes-no question transformation* also identifies the NP, in this case *beauty.* Underline the NP's in the following sentences with the aid of the passive and the yes–no question transformation guides.

1. The clerk at the third counter was happy to cash the check.
2. His discourteous manners and unkempt look could annoy many persons.
3. Winter arrives early in Minnesota.

To apply a yes-no question transformation to the third sentence, you had to supply a form of the auxiliary *do* to the sentence. *Does* is the word that moves around the NP. Where does *does* belong in sentence 3? Transform the sentence to an emphatic sentence, **Winter *does* arrive early in Minnesota,** or to the negative sentence **Winter doesn't arrive early in Minnesota.** The position of *does,* and therefore the NP constituent that functions as the subject, becomes obvious.

There are other transformations that can be used to isolate the NP. The *cleft transformation* identifies the NP as follows:

$$\textit{John lacks sincerity.} \overset{\text{cleft}}{\Rightarrow} \textit{It is } \underline{\textit{sincerity}} \textit{ that John lacks.}$$
$$\text{NP}$$

or

$$\textit{John lacks sincerity.} \overset{\text{cleft}}{\Rightarrow} \textit{It is } \underline{\textit{John}} \textit{ who lacks sincerity.}$$
$$\text{NP}$$

This transformation does not apply to NP's immediately after a form of *be* that is a main verb, such as

$$\textit{He is the chairman.} \Rightarrow \textit{°It is the chairman who he is.}$$

But we do have ***It is he who is the chairman,*** where the NP (***he***) is predicted. Now go back to sentence (b). Can you identify the two NP's, the VP, and the V?

More About the Constituents of a Sentence

Consider the sentence

(d) ***The police denounced the students in Lincoln Park.***

Were the students who were being denounced present in Lincoln Park or not? Did the police voice the denunciation in the park or elsewhere? The sentence would permit either of the possibilities. Sometimes we can ascertain the intention by the intonation. But it is not always helpful in resolving ambiguities. Sentence (d) may be paraphrased as sentences (e) or (f).

(e) ***The police denounced the students who were in Lincoln Park.***
(f) ***In Lincoln Park, the police denounced the students.***

Transformational grammarians claim that since a speaker of the English language knows that sentences (e) and (f) are different from each other and yet related to (d), the grammar must account for this relationship. The explanation given by some is that at an abstract level, sentences (e) and (f)—that is, the different senses of (d)—are distinct. Each sentence in the abstract level then undergoes a series of transformations. As a result of these transformations, some sentences that had different structures at the abstract level come to resemble each other. In sentence (d), the different structures at the abstract level can be represented as follows:[7]

(g) *The police denounced the students (the students were in Lincoln Park).*
(h) *The police denounced the students in Lincoln Park.*

Notice that (h) is just like our original ambiguous sentence (d). The difference is that (h) is structured so as to have only one semantic interpretation, so that *in Lincoln Park* only modifies the sentence *The police denounced the students.* It is imperative that this structure be known. The structure is shown in two ways: by means of rules such as the PS rules you have already seen and graphically by means of tree structures that are generated by the rules. Each of these will be explained below for sentences (g) and (h).

The PS 1 rule given earlier can be expanded to include an Adverbial (Adv) such as *in the field.* Since the adverbial is optional—that is, it may or may not occur in any given sentence—it is placed within parentheses.

$$\text{PS 1. S} \longrightarrow \text{NP + VP} \quad \text{(Adv)}$$

Graphically, rule PS 1 generates tree structure (TS) 1 (if the Adv is selected).

TS 1

```
              S
          ___/|\___
        NP   VP   Adv
```

Adding rule PS 2, described earlier, and PS 3, which expands the NP, the tree structure becomes TS 2.

$$\text{PS 2. VP} \longrightarrow \text{V + NP}$$
$$\text{PS 3. NP} \longrightarrow \text{Det + N} \qquad \text{(Det = determiner, N = noun)}$$

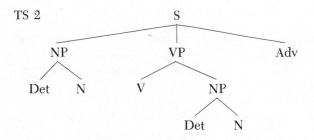

TS 2

```
                     S
         _____|_____
        NP          VP            Adv
       / \         / \
     Det  N       V   NP
                     / \
                   Det  N
```

---

[7] Technically, the abstract level, the level that is the seat of meaning, is represented differently from what is given here. In the following representations, a number of phenomena, such as agreement, tense, and so on, are included in the abstract structure for the sake of simplicity. They are properly treated by transformations.

There will be other rules in the grammar that specify that *police* is an N, *denounced* is a V, and so forth, so that the structure TS 3 will be generated.

TS 3

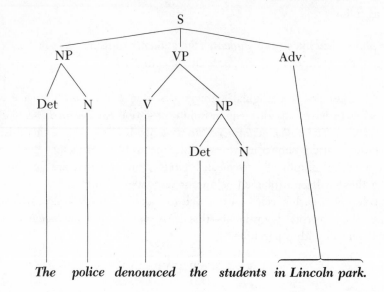

The police denounced the students in Lincoln park.

The structure of sentence (h) and similar sentences was shown by rules PS 1, PS 2, and PS 3. What is the structure of sentence (g)? In this sentence, we need to explain the fact that the police denounced the students, that the students were in Lincoln Park, and that the students who were in Lincoln Park were the ones who were denounced. The phrase-structure (PS) rules that show this relationship are as follows:

$$\text{PS 1. S} \longrightarrow \text{NP} + \text{VP}$$
$$\text{PS 2. VP} \longrightarrow \text{V} + \text{NP}$$

PS 3, given earlier, needs to be modified. An NP can also consist of a noun phrase (NP) followed by a sentence (S).

$$\text{PS 3. NP} \longrightarrow \text{NP} + \text{S}$$

PS 3 corresponds to *the students* (*the students were in Lincoln Park*). We can show that it is an NP by applying one of the three guidelines for determining NP's developed in section B. If we apply the passive transformation, we note that all of the NP + S is interchanged with the other NP.

The police denounced the students (the students were in Lincoln Park).
passive ⇓
The students (the students were in Lincoln Park) were denounced by the police.

The tree structure of sentence (g), resulting from the application of rules PS 1, PS 2, and PS 3 shown above, is found in TS 4.

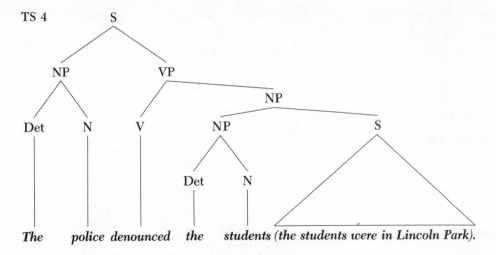

TS 4

The police denounced the students (the students were in Lincoln Park).

We have seen that sentence (d) is ambiguous. The transformational grammarians propose a model of description that claims that the sentence should be represented at an abstract level by as many structures as the sentence has ambiguous interpretations. The ambiguity found in sentences is then due to a coming together of some of these distinct abstract structures as transformations are applied to them. Let us now see how the two distinct abstract structures, sentences (h) and (g) and diagrams TS 3 and TS 4, come together in sentence (d).

First, we must distinguish between the structure of the abstract sentence generated by the phrase-structure rules and the structure of written and spoken sentences. We will call the former *deep structures* and the latter *surface structures*. More will be said about this in the section "The Function of Transformations."

In sentence (g), the following changes take place from the given deep structure to the surface structure. The *relative clause transformation* changes the second identical NP, *the students,* to a relative pronoun, in this case *who.*

(g) ***The police denounced the students (the students were in Lincoln Park).***
⇓ relative clause
The police denounced the students who were in Lincoln Park.

The result of the relative clause transformation is a sentence that occurs in English; the ***who were*** in it may be removed optionally by the *relative **BE** deletion transformation to* yield

$\xrightarrow{\text{rel } BE \text{ del}}$ ***The police denounced the students in Lincoln Park.***

This sentence is identical to (d).

Looking back at the ambiguous sentence (d), we note that its ambiguity resulted from the fact that it may be traced back to two different structures: ***in Lincoln Park*** is a reduced relative clause in (g) and an adverbial in (h). To some readers sentence (d) might not have appeared ambiguous at first. Transformational grammar forces one to recognize and account for such facts about language.

Apply the following transformations to the sentences given.

1. The students (the students were in the hall) harassed the dean.

Relative clause _____

Relative **BE** deletion _____

Passive _____

Yes–no question _____

2. The FBI questioned the students (the students harassed the dean).

Relative clause _____

Passive _____

Write the deep structure sentence and the transformations that have resulted in the following sentences.

3. _____

_____ A fish was swallowed by a man.

_____ Was a fish swallowed by a man?

Draw the tree structure diagram of the deep structure of 3.

There are at least eight interpretations of the following sentence. How many can you find?

The seniors were told to stop demonstrating on campus.

_____

_____

_____

_____

_____

_____

_____

_____

_____

_____

_____

The Adjective

The adjective is treated as the result of a relative clause transformation. Consider the sentence

(i) *The police used dangerous weapons.*

with the deep structure

The police used weapons (weapons are dangerous).

By relative clause transformation, we obtain

The police used weapons that are dangerous.

By relative **BE** deletion transformation, we obtain

* The police used weapons dangerous.

The *adjective transformation* changes the position of what remains of the relative clause to the front of the noun, giving us the sentence

The police used dangerous weapons.

Apply the transformations listed to the following sentence:

The men brought the children (the children were hungry) food.

Relative clause transformation _____

Relative **BE** deletion _____

Adjective transformation _____

Now consider the two seemingly similar phrases *the under-the-counter sale, * the on-the-shelf book.* Why is one acceptable and the other not? On inspection we note that the phrase *under-the-counter sale* is an idiom, referring to an illegal sale, not to a sale that actually takes place *under* the counter. The contrast, then, is between the adverbial phrase *on the shelf* and the adjectival idiom *under-the-counter.* The fact that *under-the-counter* takes the adjective transformation emphasizes that it is an example of a fusion; that is, it is considered as one unit.

The difference between the two phrases becomes clear when we examine their PS rules and tree diagrams. Other words that can be substituted for the phrases are used to clarify the difference between the two structures.

$$\text{PS 1. S} \longrightarrow \text{NP} + \text{VP}$$

$$\text{PS 2. VP} \longrightarrow \textbf{be} + \begin{Bmatrix} \text{Adj} \\ \text{Loc} \end{Bmatrix}$$

$$\text{PS 3. NP} \longrightarrow (\text{Det}) + \text{N}$$

In PS 2, the braces are used to combine two rules into one. It means Verb Phrase (VP) consists of a form of the verb *to be* followed by *either* an adjective (Adj) *or* a locative (Loc) (an adverb of location).

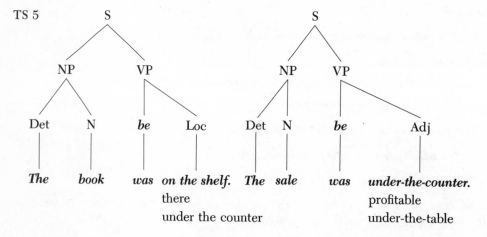

In one case we cannot use the adjective transformation since it does not apply to the Loc, an adverb—a fact that explains the starred forms ** the on the shelf book, * the there book,* and ** the under the counter book* (as opposed to *the under-the-counter book*). The adjective transformation applies to the other case, forming *under-the-counter sale, profitable sale,* and *under-the-table sale.*

There are numerous other examples of the latter, all having the process of fusion in common. Some others are *an up-and-coming young man, a tried-and-true friend, a here-is-your-hat-what-is-your-hurry hostess, an easy-come-easy-go attitude.*

Give a few more examples of phrases that accept the adjective transformation.

_____

_____

_____

_____

More About the Noun Phrase

Let us consider another manifestation of the NP. The sentence

(j) *It was unforgivable for the police to arrest the students*

is represented by the following derivation (application of PS rules) and tree diagram:

1. S $\longrightarrow$ NP + VP
2. VP $\longrightarrow$ *be* + Adj
3. NP $\longrightarrow$ N + S
4. N $\longrightarrow$ *it*
5. S $\longrightarrow$ NP + VP
6. VP $\longrightarrow$ V + NP
7. NP $\longrightarrow$ Det + N

TS 6

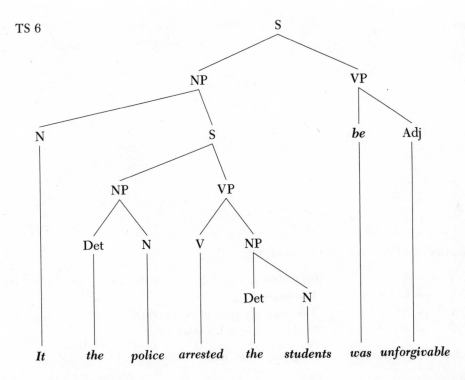

Here we find that the NP consists of an N followed by an S. We say that the S is *embedded* in the NP. How is the sentence represented by the tree structure related to the sentence *It was unforgivable for the police to arrest the students?* Note the position of *for . . . to.* *For* and *to* surround the NP of the sentence embedded in the NP. Applying this *infinitive complementizer transformation* to the result of the tree structure diagram, we obtain

°*It for the police to arrest the students was unforgivable.*

A quick inspection of the phrase-structure tree will reveal that (*for*) *the police* (*to*) *arrest the students* has been moved around *was unforgivable* to yield sentence (j). The moving of the S around the VP is called the *extraposition transformation.*

In the space below, draw the diagram and list the transformations applied to the sentence given to arrive at *It was unusual for Bill to please John.* Start with °*It* (*Bill pleased John*) *was unusual.*

In summary, we have seen four types of NP:

1. NP ⟶ N   (Columbus . . .)
2. NP ⟶ Det + N   (The mouse . . .)
3. NP ⟶ NP + S   (The man, the man is in his office)
4. NP ⟶ N + S   (It, the man is in his office)

(Some other determiners (Det) are: *my, no, some, any.*)

All four rules may be collapsed into one rule; we will call it PS 3.

$$\text{PS 3. NP} \longrightarrow \begin{Bmatrix} \text{(Det)} + \text{N} + \text{(S)} \\ \text{NP} + \text{S} \end{Bmatrix}$$

PS 3 generates Det + N + S as well. This new structure occurs in English and corresponds to NP's such as

The fact that the war continues is disheartening.

The fact is Det + N and **_the war continues_** is S. Had we not included the Det + N + S possibility, the rule would have been longer. Try writing the four rules above without allowing the Det + N + S possibility. Here is another case, similar to the situation with the distinctive features in Chapter 3, in which greater generalizations require simpler rules.

More About the Verb Phrase

So far we have considered the VP's of the form

1. **_died,_** as in **_Columbus died_** (VP $\longrightarrow$ V)
2. **_discovered America,_** as in **_Columbus discovered America_** (VP $\longrightarrow$ V + NP)
3. **_was easy,_** as in **_It was easy_** (VP $\longrightarrow$ be + Adj)
4. **_was there,_** as in **_He was there_** (VP $\longrightarrow$ be + Loc)

Consider the sentence

(k) **_Walter is the chairman._**

The VP consists of **_be_** and NP.

5. VP $\longrightarrow$ be + NP

The tree diagram is
TS 7

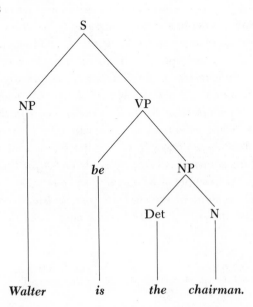

Give another example of each of the five VP types presented so far.

1. _____

2. _____

3. _____

4. _____

5. _____

Rules 1–5 may be abbreviated as follows:

$$\text{PS 2. VP} \longrightarrow \left\{ \begin{array}{l} be + \left\{ \begin{array}{l} \text{Adj} \\ \text{NP} \\ \text{Loc} \end{array} \right\} \\ \text{V (NP)} \end{array} \right\}$$

The structure of the VP is very complex. There is some controversy over the representation of the VP in a sentence such as **They elected him president.** We have not accounted for this or for sentences such as **John appeared nervous, John chose to leave,** and **John hates himself.** Current research will hopefully shed light on these complexities.

The Function of Transformations

The transformational grammarian has as his goal not only the description of structures in language but also the explanation of relations among structures that are known to the speakers of the language. The relations are shown by means of transformations, which are statements of relations between structures. Transformations apply to deep structures or to structures that have already undergone transformations.[8] The transformations we have examined show four qualities: change in order; deletion; addition; and substitution. An example of *change in order* is the extraposition transformation. It changed the order in *It for the police to arrest the students was unforgivable* to **It was unforgivable for the police to arrest the students.** An example of *deletion* is the relative **BE** deletion transformation, which changes **the students who were in the hall** to **the students in the hall.** An example of *addition* is the infinitive complementizer transformation, in which *for . . . to* is added around the NP of the embedded sentence. In our earlier example, it showed the relation of *It the police arrested the students was unforgivable* to *It for the police to arrest the students was unforgivable.* An example of *substitution* is the relative clause transformation. In our example, **The police denounced the students (the students were in Lincoln Park),** **who** was substituted for **the students,** as in **The police denounced the students who were in Lincoln Park.**

---

[8] For full treatment of deep and surface structures, see Paul Postal, "Underlying and Superficial Linguistic Structure," in *Harvard Educational Review* 34, no. 2 (1964): 246–66. Note especially pages 249–58. We consider this article to be one of the finest examples of TGG methodology.

The transformations discussed in this section are listed below. Briefly describe what each does.

Passive _____

_____

_____

Yes–no question _____

_____

_____

Cleft _____

_____

_____

Relative clause _____

_____

_____

Relative **BE** deletion _____

_____

_____

Adjective _____

_____

_____

Infinitive complementizer _____

_____

_____

Extraposition _____

_____

_____

EXERCISE 9: Hidden Sentences: The Performatives

Rewrite the following sentences into two or more constituent sentences.

1. She is truly wonderful.   *I truly declare. She is wonderful.*

2. He was incidentally misled.   _____

3. I am frankly bored.   _____

4. Happily, the man was not home.   _____

5. The man was definitely remorseful.   _____

6. He was supposedly in Chicago.   _____

7. She had apparently overslept.   _____

8. I don't suppose he is cured.   _____

9. I really think he is over it.   _____

10. Todd must be lonesome.   _____

MEANING 7

EXERCISE 1: Antonyms and Semantic Features

Semantic feature analysis worked well in isolating the differences among the musical instruments in Chapter 6; this is why that group was chosen for analysis. The entire vocabulary of a language cannot be analyzed at once; one must proceed with a small group of words that contrast with one another. For this reason, antonyms are very convenient for analysis. (Two words are antonyms when the negative of either can replace the other in a significant number of contexts, as *plural*, for example, can replace *not singular*.) Consider the following semantic grid of the antonyms *adult* and *minor*, and note how the + and − are used to show antonymy.

Figure 7–1

	Human being	Over 21
adult	+	+
minor	+	−

Now fill in the feature specifications for the word *youth* below.

Figure 7–2

	Male human being	Adult	Pre-pubescent
man	+	+	−
boy	+	−	+
youth			

99

Note that **man** and **boy** are antonymous only in certain contexts; the negative of the one does not really cover the meaning of the other. **Man, boy,** and **youth** together, however, form a relatively well-defined group; a male human being must be one or another, as we have defined the terms here, and there is no overlap. There are many such groups, and some are of indefinite size. One group that is limited but difficult to enumerate is the words for young mammals: **child, pup, kitten, fawn,** and so on. Construct a grid for these four.

Figure 7–3

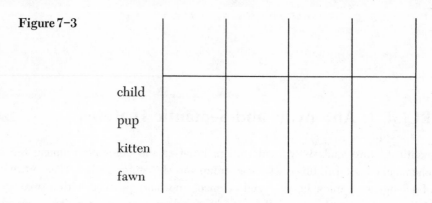

Many words that are usually considered antonyms are not complete antonyms. For example, **decry** and **praise** come close, but **decry** has an element of appeal to public opinion that is not necessarily present in **praise.** Fill in the chart below for **decry, praise,** and **extol,** after looking the words up in a good desk dictionary, such as the *Standard College Dictionary* or *Webster's Seventh New Collegiate Dictionary.* (Not all desk dictionaries mention the element of appeal to public opinion in **decry.** Dictionaries do not usually give all the important elements of words.)

In order to fill in this grid, you will need a new symbol, ±, which signifies that for the relevant word the feature thus marked can be either present or absent.

Figure 7–4

	To present strong, polarized opinion about			Public statement
decry				
praise				
extol				

Wet and **dry** are antonyms that appear to cover the field and to have no middle term. **Moist** or **damp,** however, is used when the two antonyms are not sufficiently precise. A noise can be **loud, soft,** or **moderate,** and even these three words do not cover all the possibilities. There are many antonyms in English that have middle terms. Write some of them in the left-hand column below, and add a middle term in the right-hand column.

1. _____*wet–dry*_____ _____*moist*_____

2. _____ _____

3. _____ _____

4. _____ _____

Construct grids for the following pairs of words that will show in what ways they are antonyms and what extra features they have that make them incomplete antonyms, like *decry* and *praise.*

sophisticated–immature   *weak–courageous*   *tardy–fast*   *faithful–disobedient*

Notice how much more difficult these words are to control than are words for manufactured objects, such as musical instruments.

EXERCISE 2: Synonyms

Two words are synonyms when one can be used in place of the other. *Urchin* and *brat* are synonyms; they have their most important feature in common, and the one can often be used in place of the other.

Figure 7-5

	Human child	Ragged	Ill-behaved
urchin	+	+	±
brat	+	±	+

Complete this grid for the words *callow* and *immature.*

Figure 7-6

	Not mature	
callow	+	+
immature	+	±

Can you say with assurance that these words are synonyms? Not synonyms? They might be in one circumstance, and not in another.

The following grid has four verbs that are not close synonyms but still can be studied together. Most words have several meanings. The words used here are to be considered as used in a sentence such as **John exiled Jim.** This will limit us to one meaning or to a group of closely related meanings for each word.

The three features given in Figure 7-7, with their three possible values, are capable of discriminating as many as twenty-seven words, but more features will be needed to deal with the six synonyms that remain to be filled in.

Begin by giving the values of the three existing features for each of these words. You will need to make extensive use of a dictionary to do this.

What word is **reproach** similar to? _____ You will need to add another feature to distinguish the two. To find out what it is, look in a dictionary for a synonym list with these words in it. Words considered to be synonyms are often carefully discriminated from one another in a list of synonyms that follows the entry of one of the words in the synonymy. The *Standard College Dictionary* discusses the noun forms of **reproach** and **admonish** after the entry for **reproof:** "**Reproach** expresses personal hurt or displeasure, as at thoughtlessness or selfishness. **Admonition** is warning or counsel, looking to future conduct rather than to past misdeeds." *Webster's Seventh New Collegiate Dictionary* says this: "**Admonish** suggests earnest or friendly warning and counsel; **reproach** and **chide** suggest displeasure or disappointment expressed in mild reproof or scolding." What feature do both

dictionaries attribute to **reproach** that they do not attribute to **admonish?** _____

Figure 7-7

	Official	Membership or personal relationship lost	Wish or hope that the object will change			
1. excommunicate	+	+	+			
2. exile	+	+	±			
3. reprimand	+	±	+			
4. censure	+	±	±			
5. dun						
6. condemn						
7. admonish						
8. dislike						
9. reproach						
10. blame						

Write this new feature at the top of the fourth column, and fill in the +, −, or ± for each word.

The grid says little about the meanings of *dislike* and *blame* except that they belong with a group of words expressing disapproval. What feature can you find that will distinguish

these two words? _____

Enter that feature in the fifth column, and fill in the grid.

These five features adequately discriminate these words, but by no means do they give an adequate definition of the words. As an example, consider the feature "superiority." It is not needed to distinguish between any two of these words, but it is an essential feature of *excommunicate, exile, reprimand, censure,* and *dun* and a possible but not necessary feature of the others.

Besides being inadequate as a description of the full meanings of these words, the semantic grid does not give other kinds of information necessary to a user of the language in building sentences with these words. For example, some of the ten words can occur with a following infinitive (although none require it): *The judge condemned him to die.* A native speaker of English would not use a following infinitive with *reproach* in a parallel structure: *John reproached him to leave.* In the sixth column in Figure 7-7, give a ± to each word that occurs with or without a following infinitive in a sentence parallel in structure to that above. Give a minus to each word that cannot occur with a following infinitive.

EXERCISE 3: Selection Information

An ordinary dictionary gives at least three kinds of information in describing a word: it gives pronunciation, grammatical classification, and meanings. For example, the *Standard College Dictionary* entry for **extensile** is "(ik·sten'sil) *adj*. **1.** Capable of being protruded, as the tongue **2.** Extensible." The second part, the grammatical classification, is devoted to helping a user of the language build sentences. The sixth column in Figure 7–7 gives such information.

In a dictionary of the future, the third part of an entry, the meaning, might give semantic features. It might also give means of determining what kinds of words the word being defined can occur with. This would help explain how English speakers use the word in building sentences. For example, the verb *gallop* has as its core meaning a certain gait of a quadruped. The selection information in a dictionary of the future would specify that this word cannot be used unless there is some reference in the sentence to a quadruped capable of this gait. The sentence *The boy galloped up the drive* in a context that makes it clear that he has no horse is deviant although possibly quite effective. Its deviance and possible effectiveness depend upon the speaker's not following the selection information of *gallop.* The selection information would look like this: < + quadruped>. It would follow the other parts of the dictionary entry. A phrase that lacked a word with a meaning including this semantic feature could not include the word *gallop.* A dictionary could thus tell us in what way the sentence above is deviant.[1]

Consider the sentence *The dog laid an egg.* This is clearly deviant. For the meaning of *lay* as it pertains to birds, the selection information is < + egg-bearing animal>. *Lay* with this meaning must occur in a phrase in which some other word has this feature present. The sentence *The dog laid an egg* would not follow the selection information of its verb. Using an encyclopedia if you need to, work out the selection information of the verbs listed below enough to avoid any nonsensical sentences with animal names as subjects. You can check your correctness by making a sentence for each of the verbs with *turtle, dog, robin, lizard, mayfly,* and *bass.* If your selection restrictors keep you from making nonsense sentences, then they are correct.

engender _____   suckle _____

brood _____   gestate _____

lay _____   spawn _____

For the following words write out the selection restrictors that will keep them from combining with the wrong kind of living creatures. For simplicity's sake, think of the *habitual* action characteristic of a particular kind of creature.

---

[1] For some of the ideas of this exercise, see Jerrold J. Katz, *The Philosophy of Language* (New York: Harper & Row, 1966), Chapters 4 and 5.

rack _____   slither _____

hike _____   fly _____

The selection information indicates which meaning of a word can be properly used in a particular sentence, as well as which words can be properly used. For example, the noun *needle* has several different meanings. The selection information automatically assigns the meaning that is relevant to each particular use of the word.

needle (noun)   1. 'hypodermic syringe' $<+ \text{medicine}>$
                  2. 'a steel instrument with a hole $<+ \text{sewing}>$
                     at one end used in sewing'
                  3. 'a narrow pointed crystal' $<+ \text{crystallography}>$

When the word *needle* is used in a sentence, the presence of one of these three semantic features attached to one of the words in the sentence or in the immediate context will automatically assign the relevant meaning to *needle*. The sentence ***That is a nice tourmaline needle*** automatically assigns meaning 3, "a narrow pointed crystal," to *needle* because the semantic features of ***tourmaline*** include "crystal."

With the aid of your dictionary, write out three other meanings with selection information for *needle* (noun).

4. _____

   _____

5. _____

   _____

6. _____

   _____

Do the same for two or three meanings of each of the following words.

flat (adjective)   1. _____

                       2. _____

                       3. _____

negative (noun)   1. _____

                       2. _____

                       3. _____

referee   1. _____

                       2. _____

MIND IN THE GRIP OF LANGUAGE 8

EXERCISE 1: Affective Dimensions of Words

In Chapters 6 and 7, semantic-feature analysis was used to describe the meanings of words. The existence of a feature was inferred from the existence of a difference in meaning between two or more related words. The principal difference between *harp* and *harpsichord,* for example, was shown to be the feature "keyboard," while the difference between *reproach* and *admonition* was the feature we termed "personal disappointment."

Besides this analytical meaning, other kinds of meaning are important. The word *lion* does not simply represent the list of objective characteristics a zoologist would come up with. We must also consider such subjective associations as "king of beasts," a traditional reputation for bravery, and the friendly neighborhood pussycat image projected in the film *Born Free.* The meaning of the word *violin* includes our reactions to the sound and appearance of the instrument, to concerts or recordings we have heard in the past, and even to violinists we have known—among other things. Typically, the people in a community tend to agree on a group of associations that cluster around a concept. Such is the case with the associations around *lion,* although they may not be the same in New York and Nairobi.

The semantic-feature technique can be extended to present some of the affective, or emotional, meanings of words. This exercise represents one way to do this.[1]

The immediate object of this exercise is to examine the various clusters of associations that have become a part of certain political terms. In each of the seven sections below you will find one of these terms followed by a series of scales. The first term, *statesman,* was rated by the authors of this workbook. Try rating it yourself and see if your understanding of the term differs from theirs. In rating each of the remaining six terms, you will have to decide which of the two words on the scale is more closely related to the term to be rated. If, for example, you feel that *politician* is very closely related to a word at one end of the scale, place a mark on the line next to that word:

good _X_:____:____:____:____:____:____ bad

or

good ____:____:____:____:____:____: _X_ bad

---

[1] This exercise is based on the work of Charles Osgood, George Suci, and Percy Tannenbaum in *The Measurement of Meaning* (Urbana, Ill.: University of Illinois Press, 1957).

If it is quite closely related, place a check on the line one step farther in:

good ＿＿＿:＿X＿:＿＿＿:＿＿＿:＿＿＿:＿＿＿:＿＿＿ bad

or

good ＿＿＿:＿＿＿:＿＿＿:＿＿＿:＿＿＿:＿X＿:＿＿＿ bad

If it is only slightly related, place the mark like this:

good ＿＿＿:＿＿＿:＿X＿:＿＿＿:＿＿＿:＿＿＿:＿＿＿ bad

or

good ＿＿＿:＿＿＿:＿＿＿:＿＿＿:＿X＿:＿＿＿:＿＿＿ bad

If you associate a term equally with each word of the pair or if you have no associations, check the center space. Your word associations are the important thing, not your sense of logic. Fill in the scales first, then read the instructions telling you how to handle the data.

1. Statesman

a.   good ＿＿:＿＿:＿X＿:＿＿:＿＿:＿＿:＿＿ bad

b.   hard ＿＿:＿X＿:＿＿:＿＿:＿＿:＿＿:＿＿ soft

c.   passive ＿＿:＿＿:＿＿:＿＿:＿＿:＿X＿ active

d.   stable ＿＿:＿＿:＿X＿:＿＿:＿＿:＿＿ changeable

e.   defensive _X_:＿＿:＿＿:＿＿:＿＿:＿＿ aggressive

f.   optimistic ＿＿:＿X＿:＿＿:＿＿:＿＿:＿＿ pessimistic

g.   calm ＿＿:＿X＿:＿＿:＿＿:＿＿:＿＿ excitable

h.   colorful ＿＿:＿＿:＿X＿:＿＿:＿＿ colorless

i.   negative ＿＿:＿＿:＿＿:＿＿:＿＿:＿X＿ positive

j.   masculine ＿＿:＿＿:＿X＿:＿＿:＿＿ feminine

k.   cold ＿＿:＿＿:＿X＿:＿＿:＿＿ hot

l.   sane _X_:＿＿:＿＿:＿＿:＿＿:＿＿ insane

m. competitive ＿＿:＿X＿:＿＿:＿＿:＿＿ cooperative

n.   insensitive ＿＿:＿＿:＿＿:＿＿:＿X＿ sensitive

o.   severe ＿＿:＿X＿:＿＿:＿＿:＿＿ lenient

p.   rash ＿＿:＿＿:＿＿:＿＿:＿X＿ prudent

q.   humble ＿＿:＿X＿:＿＿:＿＿:＿＿ proud

r.   interesting ＿＿:＿X＿:＿＿:＿＿:＿＿ boring

2. Politician

a. good ____:____:____:____:____:____ bad

b. hard ____:____:____:____:____:____ soft

c. passive ____:____:____:____:____:____ active

d. stable ____:____:____:____:____:____ changeable

e. defensive ____:____:____:____:____:____ aggressive

f. optimistic ____:____:____:____:____:____ pessimistic

g. calm ____:____:____:____:____:____ excitable

h. colorful ____:____:____:____:____:____ colorless

i. negative ____:____:____:____:____:____ positive

j. masculine ____:____:____:____:____:____ feminine

k. cold ____:____:____:____:____:____ hot

l. sane ____:____:____:____:____:____ insane

m. competitive ____:____:____:____:____:____ cooperative

n. insensitive ____:____:____:____:____:____ sensitive

o. severe ____:____:____:____:____:____ lenient

p. rash ____:____:____:____:____:____ prudent

q. humble ____:____:____:____:____:____ proud

r. interesting ____:____:____:____:____:____ boring

3. Congressman

a. good ____:____:____:____:____:____ bad

b. hard ____:____:____:____:____:____ soft

c. passive ____:____:____:____:____:____ active

d. stable ____:____:____:____:____:____ changeable

e. defensive ____:____:____:____:____:____ aggressive

f. optimistic ____:____:____:____:____:____ pessimistic

g. calm ____:____:____:____:____:____ excitable

h. colorful ____:____:____:____:____:____ colorless

i. negative ____:____:____:____:____:____ positive

j. masculine ____:____:____:____:____:____:____ feminine

k. cold ____:____:____:____:____:____:____ hot

l. sane ____:____:____:____:____:____:____ insane

m. competitive ____:____:____:____:____:____:____ cooperative

n. insensitive ____:____:____:____:____:____:____ sensitive

o. severe ____:____:____:____:____:____:____ lenient

p. rash ____:____:____:____:____:____:____ prudent

q. humble ____:____:____:____:____:____:____ proud

r. interesting ____:____:____:____:____:____:____ boring

4. Legislator

a. good ____:____:____:____:____:____:____ bad

b. hard ____:____:____:____:____:____:____ soft

c. passive ____:____:____:____:____:____:____ active

d. stable ____:____:____:____:____:____:____ changeable

e. defensive ____:____:____:____:____:____:____ aggressive

f. optimistic ____:____:____:____:____:____:____ pessimistic

g. calm ____:____:____:____:____:____:____ excitable

h. colorful ____:____:____:____:____:____:____ colorless

i. negative ____:____:____:____:____:____:____ positive

j. masculine ____:____:____:____:____:____:____ feminine

k. cold ____:____:____:____:____:____:____ hot

l. sane ____:____:____:____:____:____:____ insane

m. competitive ____:____:____:____:____:____:____ cooperative

n. insensitive ____:____:____:____:____:____:____ sensitive

o. severe ____:____:____:____:____:____:____ lenient

p. rash ____:____:____:____:____:____:____ prudent

q. humble ____:____:____:____:____:____:____ proud

r. interesting ____:____:____:____:____:____:____ boring

5. Dictator

a.   good ____:____:____:____:____:____:____ bad

b.   hard ____:____:____:____:____:____:____ soft

c.   passive ____:____:____:____:____:____:____ active

d.   stable ____:____:____:____:____:____:____ changeable

e.   defensive ____:____:____:____:____:____:____ aggressive

f.   optimistic ____:____:____:____:____:____:____ pessimistic

g.   calm ____:____:____:____:____:____:____ excitable

h.   colorful ____:____:____:____:____:____:____ colorless

i.   negative ____:____:____:____:____:____:____ positive

j.   masculine ____:____:____:____:____:____:____ feminine

k.   cold ____:____:____:____:____:____:____ hot

l.   sane ____:____:____:____:____:____:____ insane

m.   competitive ____:____:____:____:____:____:____ cooperative

n.   insensitive ____:____:____:____:____:____:____ sensitive

o.   severe ____:____:____:____:____:____:____ lenient

p.   rash ____:____:____:____:____:____:____ prudent

q.   humble ____:____:____:____:____:____:____ proud

r.   interesting ____:____:____:____:____:____:____ boring

6. Strongman

a.   good ____:____:____:____:____:____:____ bad

b.   hard ____:____:____:____:____:____:____ soft

c.   passive ____:____:____:____:____:____:____ active

d.   stable ____:____:____:____:____:____:____ changeable

e.   defensive ____:____:____:____:____:____:____ aggressive

f.   optimistic ____:____:____:____:____:____:____ pessimistic

g.   calm ____:____:____:____:____:____:____ excitable

h.   colorful ____:____:____:____:____:____:____ colorless

i.   negative ___:___:___:___:___:___:___ positive

j.   masculine ___:___:___:___:___:___:___ feminine

k.   cold ___:___:___:___:___:___:___ hot

l.   sane ___:___:___:___:___:___:___ insane

m. competitive ___:___:___:___:___:___:___ cooperative

n.   insensitive ___:___:___:___:___:___:___ sensitive

o.   severe ___:___:___:___:___:___:___ lenient

p.   rash ___:___:___:___:___:___:___ prudent

q.   humble ___:___:___:___:___:___:___ proud

r.   interesting ___:___:___:___:___:___:___ boring

7. Ruler

a.   good ___:___:___:___:___:___:___ bad

b.   hard ___:___:___:___:___:___:___ soft

c.   passive ___:___:___:___:___:___:___ active

d.   stable ___:___:___:___:___:___:___ changeable

e.   defensive ___:___:___:___:___:___:___ aggressive

f.   optimistic ___:___:___:___:___:___:___ pessimistic

g.   calm ___:___:___:___:___:___:___ excitable

h.   colorful ___:___:___:___:___:___:___ colorless

i.   negative ___:___:___:___:___:___:___ positive

j.   masculine ___:___:___:___:___:___:___ feminine

k.   cold ___:___:___:___:___:___:___ hot

l.   sane ___:___:___:___:___:___:___ insane

m. competitive ___:___:___:___:___:___:___ cooperative

n.   insensitive ___:___:___:___:___:___:___ sensitive

o.   severe ___:___:___:___:___:___:___ lenient

p.   rash ___:___:___:___:___:___:___ prudent

q.   humble ___:___:___:___:___:___:___ proud

r.   interesting ___:___:___:___:___:___:___ boring

Osgood, Suci, and Tannenbaum, the authors of *The Measurement of Meaning,* have worked extensively with the pairs of words in this exercise and have found that college under-graduates tend to score some of the pairs alike, as if they had much the same associations. Such a group is **good–bad, optimistic–pessimistic,** and **positive–negative.** The students rated a concept such as "foreigner" about the same on each of these three pairs. The investigators studied many pairs and tried to discover how the students grouped them. On the basis of this information, the eighteen pairs of this exercise appear to fall into six groups with three pairs each. The names for the groups are strictly intuitive.

1. Evaluation
   a. good–bad;   f. optimistic–pessimistic;   i. positive–negative

2. Potency
   b. hard–soft;   j. masculine–feminine;   o. severe–lenient

3. Activity
   c. active–passive;   g. excitable–calm;   k. hot–cold

4. Collectedness
   d. stable–changeable;   l. sane–insane;   p. prudent–rash

5. Tautness
   e. aggressive–defensive;   m. competitive–cooperative;   q. proud–humble

6. Receptivity
   h. colorful–colorless;   n. sensitive–insensitive;   r. interesting–boring

We will investigate how you rate each political term by using these groups of pairs.

1. Evaluation

Following the example given for the term **statesman,** fill in the chart below for the three pairs of the first group: a. **good-bad;** f. **optimistic-pessimistic;** i. **positive-negative.** You can do this by assigning numbers to the spaces on each scale:

$$\text{good } \underline{+3}:\underline{+2}:\underline{+1}:\underline{0}:\underline{-1}:\underline{-2}:\underline{-3} \text{ bad}$$

Notice that for the pairs **good** and **bad, optimistic** and **pessimistic,** the more dynamic or positive word of the pair is on the left. But for **negative** and **positive** and for certain other pairs, the position is reversed. This is to keep the positive words of the pairs from consistently being associated with the plus side of the chart. Consequently, you must reverse the score of such pairs as **negative-positive.** If it was $+3$, it will become a -3. The pairs of words to be reversed are marked on the following charts.

Figure 8-1

Political terms

Pairs	1	2	3	4	5	6	7
a	+1						
f	+2						
Reverse i	+3						
Sums of the columns	+6						

2. Potency

Fill in this chart the same way you filled in the last one. The relevant pairs are *b*, *j*, and *o*. None are reversed.

Figure 8-2

Political terms

Pairs	1	2	3	4	5	6	7
b	+2						
j	0						
o	+1						
Sums	+3						

3. Activity

Pairs *c*, *g*, and *k*. Reverse the scores of all three. (It might be easier for you to add them all first and then reverse the sums.)

Figure 8-3

Political terms

Pairs	1	2	3	4	5	6	7
c	−3						
g	+2						
k	0						
Reverse sums	+1						

4. Collectedness

Pairs d, l, and p. Reverse the scores of p.

Figure 8–4   Political terms

Pairs	1	2	3	4	5	6	7
d	0						
l	+3						
Reverse p	+3						
Sums	+6						

5. Tautness

Pairs e, l, and q. Reverse the scores of e and q.

Figure 8–5   Political terms

Pairs	1	2	3	4	5	6	7
Reverse e	−3						
l	+1						
Reverse q	−2						
Sums	−4						

6. Receptivity

Pairs h, n, and r. Reverse the scores of n.

Figure 8–6   Political terms

Pairs	1	2	3	4	5	6	7
h	0						
Reverse n	+2						
r	+1						
Sums	+3						

Now combine your sums into one chart.

Figure 8-7

	Statesman	Politician	Congressman	Legislator	Dictator	Strongman	Ruler	Totals
Evaluation	+6							
Potency	+3							
Activity	+1							
Collectedness	+6							
Tautness	−4							
Receptivity	+3							

After filling in this table, add up your scores in each row and place the totals in the last column. These totals give your overall reactions to this set of political terms. Examine the last column. Did you rate the first three terms lower on the potency and activity groups than the last three? Consider how the choice of terms influenced the totals of the last column. What might have happened if the list had included more specific terms such as *president* and *governor* and not *politician* and *congressman?*

_____

_____

Inspect your scores for each term. They show your reactions to each separate term. How did you differ on *politician* and *dictator?* Which is the most potent term? Which is the least potent? Why?

_____

_____

_____

What are the similarities among the terms? _____

_____

Have you tended to put the political terms into two groups? If so, what are they? _____

_____

_____

Can you use the results to suggest what it is that you want from politicians? _____

_____

_____

_____

EXERCISE 2: Favorable and Unfavorable Naming

Words embody attitudes. The charts in Exercise 1 are one way of investigating these attitudes. In *Language in Thought and Action,* S. I. Hayakawa made use of an idea of Lord Bertrand Russell's to show clearly how words embody attitudes. Consider the following "conjugations":

> *I* may not know much about art, but I know what I like.
> *You* could profit by a course in art history.
> *He* is an uncultured ignoramus.

Or: *My* son is rambunctious and high-spirited.
       Your son is maladjusted and deprived.
       His son is a little hoodlum.[2]

"Conjugate" the following statements in a similar way.

1. I am pleasingly plump.

_____

_____

2. This is my collection of antique furniture.

_____

_____

3. I want a girl just like the girl who married dear old Dad.

_____

_____

[2] S. I. Hayakawa, *Language in Thought and Action,* 3rd ed. (New York: Harcourt Brace Jovanovich, 1972), p. 73.

4. Our dog is of a very unique breed.

_____

_____

5. Unaccustomed as I am to public speaking . . .

_____

_____

6. I believe that the government should not meddle in economic affairs.

_____

_____

7. I haven't called her lately.

_____

_____

8. Please excuse the way things look. Our maid was ill this week.

_____

_____

9. Sorry I haven't written sooner.

_____

_____

EXERCISE 3: Perceptions of Color

Different cultures tend to perceive the visual world differently. Such factors as climate, geography, and social customs inevitably affect the way in which each group must live, and language both reflects and shapes these variations. One of the more striking examples of linguistic diversity is found in the division of the color spectrum. Each culture makes its own divisions at different points along the spectrum. In the Navaho language, for example, the area of the spectrum that English speakers divide into yellow and orange overlaps, and a single word covers the whole range of hues that we call green, blue, and purple. American schools, of course, usually teach students to divide the spectrum into a six-part color wheel, and it is taken for granted that these particular hues are universally accepted. Recent research, however, suggests that there may be as many as eleven color categories universally basic to human perception.[3]

Using a bilingual dictionary for English and a non-Western language, such as that of Thailand, find the foreign words for the six colors given below. Then look up the English equivalents of each of these foreign words.

English spectrum	Equivalent in _____	English words used to translate the foreign words
blue		
green		
orange		
purple		
red		
yellow		

[3] Brent Berlin and Paul Kay, *Basic Color Terms: Their Universality & Evolution,* Berkeley: University of California Press, 1969).

Write the foreign terms on the color wheel shown below, locating them as accurately as you can. Consider the center of each segment of the wheel to be the "purest" example of the English term.

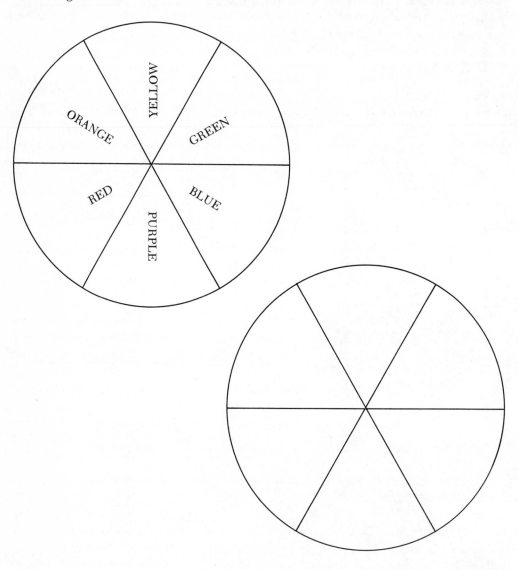

Which areas of the spectrum seem to dominate? _____

Can you think of any reasons for this? _____

_____

_____

_____

PSYCHOLOGY AND LANGUAGE LEARNING 9

EXERCISE 1: The Phonestheme: A Quantitative Approach

Most ways of studying language do not involve the examination of large samplings of words. Many language patterns can be discovered by methods that require only a few examples, but some patterns can only be demonstrated by using a quantitative approach.

A *phonestheme* is a similarity in sound that a group of words have in common, along with a semantic feature. For example, one suspects that the words *dump, lump,* and *thump* are evidence for a phonestheme, the /ʌ/ sound, with the semantic features of "heaviness" or "bluntness." Bolinger introduced the phonestheme in his discussion of meaning in Chapter 7; it is important in Chapter 9 as well because some phonesthemes are so common among the language families of the world that they may possibly constitute evidence for a type of linguistic inheritance.

Tracking down a phonestheme in a large number of languages requires a good deal of counting, and the effort is certainly beyond the scope of an exercise. For this reason we will confine our efforts to English and to a single phonestheme. The question to be considered in this exercise is whether the high and lower-high front vowels in English, /i/ and /ɪ/, are associated with the semantic features "smallness," "shortness," and "quickness," thus forming a phonestheme. Examples might be such words as *bit, little,* and *fleet.*

How does one determine whether or not a particular phonestheme exists? Are a few words of similar sound and meaning proof of a phonestheme when dozens of words without that sound express similar meanings and when many words with that sound express different meanings?

To discover the relationship between the presumed phonestheme and the general vocabulary of a language, it is imperative to study a broad sampling of words. There are any number of possible sources for such a sample, but some are clearly better than others. Some of the sources suggested below will lead you to a large number of unusual words; others will offer the more commonly used words of a language. Which of the items in the following list do you think would be the most useful for compiling this type of sample?

unabridged dictionary	grade school dictionary
encyclopedia	transcript of a presidential speech
newspaper story	transcript of a telephone conversation
thesaurus	dictionary of American slang

_____

Why? _____

Which would be least useful? _____

Why? _____

   The first step, then, is to make a list of words on which to base your calculations. Once you have made this list, the next step is to count those that have the sound in question. If 20 percent of the words on your list have a high or lower-high front vowel, one might reasonably expect that any other random list of words would also have about 20 percent with those vowels. If you now make a list of those words having one of the three semantic features in question and a phonestheme exists, it is likely that this figure will be significantly higher; if there is no phonestheme, the 20 percent figure will be maintained.

   Therefore, you must first establish the actual percentage of words in English that have a high or lower-high front vowel. To begin, turn to a page at random in your desk dictionary. Count the total number of words, ignoring names. Enter this number in the first column below. Now go over these same words again and count those that have an /i/ or an /ɪ/. Enter this number in the second column. Do this for six pages chosen at random.

Name of dictionary _____

Total Words	*/i/ and /ɪ/ Words*
_____	_____
_____	_____
_____	_____
_____	_____
_____	_____
_____	_____
▬▬▬▬	▬▬▬▬

Now divide the sum of the second column by the sum of the first column and multiply by 100. This will give you the percentage of words that have high or lower-high front vowels.

Write the percentage here. _____

The next thing to do is to establish the percentage of /i/ and /ɪ/ sounds among words with the semantic features in question. Using a thesaurus, make a list of fifty words that you believe represent the semantic features "small," "short," or "quick." Count those words that have high or lower-high front vowels, and list a dozen of them below.

/i/		/ɪ/	
_____	_____	_____	_____
_____	_____	_____	_____
_____	_____	_____	_____

How many of the fifty words have the right vowels? _____ Divide that number by fifty and multiply by 100 to obtain the percentage. Enter it here. _____ How does it compare with the percentage obtained from the random list? _____

If the first result is significantly larger than the second—and if your work was done carefully—it suggests that such a phonestheme exists. Exactly how great the difference between the two ratios should be to be considered significant is difficult to determine, but anything less than 20 or 30 percent is probably insufficient.

Before attempting to reach a conclusion based on the difference in percentage, you must ask several questions. First, was the original sample large enough? One way to answer this is to increase the size of the original sample. If the new percentage does not differ much from the percentage you originally calculated, then the sample would appear to be large enough. Try this with two more pages. What is your new percentage? _____

There were probably more than fifty words in your thesaurus with one of the appropriate semantic features, so you had to make judgments concerning which to leave out. These judgments will affect your percentage. For example, ignoring slang will lower your percentage, because people tend to use the phonestheme in forming new slang words. What sorts of words did you leave out and why? _____

_____

Could you have made the phonestheme stand out more clearly by adjusting the list of semantic features? For example, would leaving "short" out create a better list of fifty from the thesaurus? _____ Look over your list for other possibilities of adjusting the semantic features.

What conclusion have you come to concerning the existence of this particular phones-theme in English? Be sure to qualify your conclusion. _____

_____

_____

_____

_____

_____

_____

_____

EXERCISE 2: The Two-Word Sentences of Children

After the holophrastic stage, children speak in two-word sentences (with some three-word sentences as well) for some time. Table 9–1 of *Aspects of Language* shows the structure of some of these in terms of the semantic and grammatical role and the function of the words. Describe the following utterances according to the word classes of that table; assume that a full utterance is agent-action-dative-object-locative, and indicate which classes are present and which are absent.

Utterance	Present	Absent
Ball go? (Has the ball gone?)	_____	_____
I see.	_____	_____
See train.	_____	_____
Boot off. (Take my boots off.)	_____	_____
Papa away. (Papa has left.)	_____	_____
Airplane allgone. (The airplane has gone.)	_____	_____
Allgone boy.	_____	_____
More milk.	_____	_____
Dry pants.	_____	_____

EXERCISE 3: Syntactic Regularities in Children's Speech

After the two-word stage, children begin to acquire grammatical morphemes and the rules for their use. Negations and questions begin to take more complex shapes. Consider the following sentences, which are typical of the utterances of three children, each studied at three levels of development beyond the two-word stage.[1]

Negative Sentences

Level 1	Level 2	Level 3
1. No singing song.	I can't catch you.	I didn't did it.
2. No the sun shining.	We can't talk.	I can't see it.
3. No money.	You can't dance.	I don't want cover on it.
4. No sit there.	I don't like him.	You didn't caught me.
5. No play that.	Book say no.	Donna won't let go.
6. No fall!	Touch the snow no.	I am not a doctor.
7. No heavy.	That no fish school.	This not ice cream.
8. No want stand head.	He no bit you.	I not crying.
9. No Mom sharpen it.	That no mommy.	That not turning.
10. No Fraser drink all tea.	I no taste them.	They not cold.

Questions

Level 1	Level 2	Level 3
1. Fraser water?	See my doggie?	Does the kitty stand up?
2. Mommy eggnog?	That black too?	Does lions walk?
3. See hole?	Mom pinch finger?	Is Mommy talking to Robin?
4. I ride train?	You want eat?	Did I saw that in my book?
5. Have some?	Where baby Sarah rattle?	Oh, did I caught it?
6. Sit chair?	Where me sleep?	Where's his other eye?
7. Who that?	What book name?	What did you doed?
8. What cowboy doing?	What me think?	Why Paul caught it?
9. Where Ann pencil?	What the dollie have?	Which way they should go?
10. Where horse go?	Why you smiling?	What I did yesterday?

[1] Edward S. Klima and Ursula Bellugi-Klima, "Syntactic Regularities in the Speech of Children," in *Modern Studies in English*, ed. D. Reibel and S. A. Schane (Englewood Cliffs, N.J.: Prentice-Hall, 1969), p. 448–66.

Morphology

Describe the patterns of use of articles and possessives at each level. _____

_____

_____

_____

At the second level, the children used **don't** and **can't,** but not **do** and **can.** By the third level, they were using **do** and **can.** Describe the patterns of use of auxiliary verbs at each

level. _____

_____

_____

Describe the patterns of use of tense at each level. Be sure to weigh carefully the evidence

for the existence of the present tense at the first two levels. _____

_____

_____

Describe the person and number agreement and the plural morphemes, at each level.

_____

_____

_____

Describe the pronoun forms manifested at each level. _____

_____

_____

Syntax

What is the growth of length of sentence from stage to stage? _____

_____

What rule of negative placement did the children apply at the first level? _____

_____

What rules did they apply at the second level?_____

_____

_____

_____

At the third level, the children were using *n't* attached to auxiliaries that they also used in the affirmative form. What rules of negative placement did the children apply at the third level? _____

_____

_____

_____

What rule of questioning did the children appear to be applying at the first and second levels for yes–no questions? _____

For question-word questions? _____

_____

_____

What rules are used at the third level for question-word questions? _____

_____

_____

_____

For yes–no questions? _____

_____

_____

What do the uses of *do* for questions and for negatives have in common at the third level? _____

_____

_____

Take the sentences *I didn't did it* and *You didn't caught me.* What is the difference between these sentences and the same sentences translated into adult English? _____

_____

_____

THE ORIGIN OF LANGUAGE 10

STUDY QUESTIONS: How Language Began

A. The concept of the origin of language, taboo for a long time in linguistics, has re-emerged. It returns in a much more sophisticated form of research than those that led to the "bow-wow," "ding-dong," and similar theories. List five lines of investigation that have begun to make possible a meaningful study of when and how humans began to speak.

1. _____
_____

2. _____
_____

3. _____
_____

4. _____
_____

5. _____
_____

B. What were the three barriers in animal communication that had to be overcome in order to arrive at what we call human language? Give an example of each.

1. _____
_____
_____
_____

2. _____

   _____

   _____

   _____

3. _____

   _____

   _____

   _____

C. Bolinger refers to the overcoming of the three barriers as a "further gain in recursiveness." What does he mean?

   _____

   _____

   _____

   _____

   _____

   _____

   _____

   _____

   _____

   _____

D. What steps may we assume occurred in the millions of years from the time that the forelimb structure made tree climbing possible to the time when a wide range of vocal sounds became available to early humans?

   _____

   _____

   _____

   _____

   _____

   _____

_____

_____

_____

E. What feature of American Sign Language makes impossible its use as a means of communication in a prelanguage period?

_____

_____

_____

_____

_____

_____

_____

_____

_____

_____

F. You have already noted that the physiological stage was set by the increasingly erect posture and raised head of human beings, and the effects on the shape of the vocal tract. What set the *intellectual* stage for the transfer from gesture to speech?

_____

_____

_____

_____

_____

_____

_____

_____

_____

_____

G. What role did social interdependence play in decreasing reliance on instinctive behavior and in increasing "intelligent" activity?

_____

_____

_____

_____

_____

_____

_____

H. What do you think were some of the advantages of giving names to objects?

_____

_____

_____

_____

_____

_____

_____

_____

_____

_____

I. What analogies does Bolinger draw between the specialization in the brain and the *topic* and *comment* of a propositional sentence?

_____

_____

_____

_____

_____

_____

_____

_____

_____

_____

J. How did the use of tools pave the way for transfer from gesture to speech?

_____

_____

_____

_____

_____

K. What argument can be offered against the following statement? "Speech is merely an *overlaid* function, making artificial use of the organs that were designed by nature for the intake of food."

_____

_____

_____

_____

_____

_____

_____

L. What reason do we have to believe that the syllable preceded the phoneme as a unit?

_____

_____

_____

What fact may have accounted for a need to shift to the phoneme as the subconscious unit?

_____

_____

_____

_____

_____

_____

M. How would you support the statement, "Human beings evolved as speakers"?

_____

_____

_____

_____

_____

_____

_____

_____

_____

_____

_____

_____

_____

_____

_____

_____

_____

_____

VARIATION IN SPACE

11

EXERCISE 1: Regional Dialects

Regional dialect boundaries are drawn on the basis of information gathered from speakers of the region. Field workers interview informants who learned to speak in the area to be studied and who are still living there, and the resultant data are entered on maps. Map 1 is such a map. Each circle means that one speaker in that area used the form indicated. Maps 2 and 3 show the common next step: the area of predominance of a form is marked off by a line. Map 4 shows several such lines on one map and gives some idea how a number of lines can reinforce each other. When enough of these lines are sufficiently close to one another, they can mark off a dialect area. That is the goal of this exercise—to use the information contained in the first four maps to draw a dialect boundary on the fifth map. The dialect boundary in question separates what traditionally has been called the Northern and Midland speech areas. A line that shows the extent of use of a word is called an *isogloss;* if it deals with a sound, it is called an *isophone.*

First, draw the isogloss of *see* on Map 1. You need be concerned only with that part of the map where the isophone of Map 2 lies. Then, combining the isoglosses and isophones from the first four maps, draw the Northern-Midland dialect boundary on Map 5.

Note that the eastern boundary of the northern area where *see* is used for the preterite *saw* follows the Hudson River. Can you explain this?

_____

_____

_____

What might account for the lack of consistency of the data offered here in support of the Northern-Midland dialect boundary? (Reread "Areal communities," beginning on page 345 of *Aspects of Language.* Note Bolinger's comments on the origin of dialect differences in the eastern United States and the mechanism of dialect blending.)

_____

_____

_____

_____

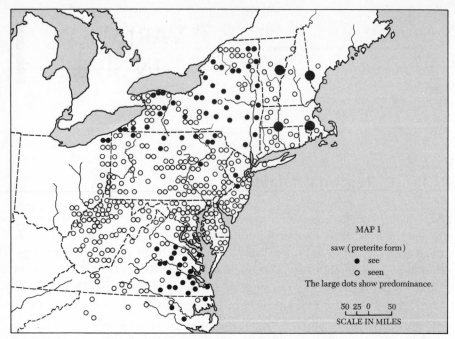

Adapted from E. Bagby Atwood, *A Survey of Verb Forms in the Eastern United States* (Ann Arbor, Mich.: University of Michigan Press, 1953), Fig. 17. Copyright 1953 by University of Michigan Press. Reprinted by permission of the publishers.

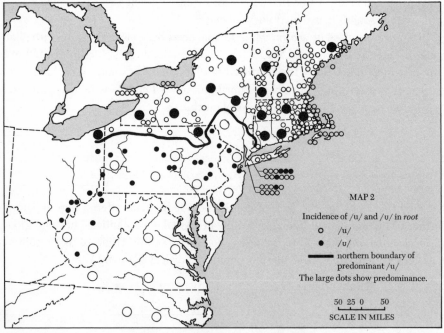

Adapted from Hans Kurath and Raven I. McDavid, Jr., *The Pronunciation of English in the Atlantic States* (Ann Arbor, Mich.: University of Michigan Press, 1961), Map 113. Copyright 1961 by University of Michigan Press. Reprinted by permission of the publishers.

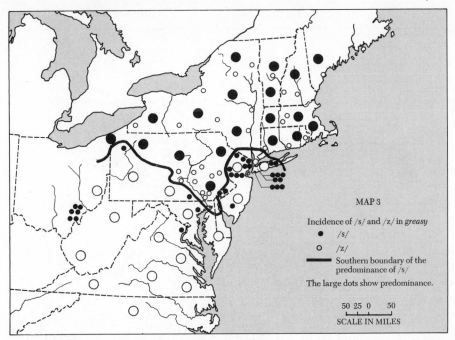

MAP 3

Incidence of /s/ and /z/ in *greasy*

● /s/

○ /z/

▬▬ Southern boundary of the
     predominance of /s/

The large dots show predominance.

50 25 0   50
SCALE IN MILES

Adapted from Hans Kurath and Raven I. McDavid, Jr., *The Pronunciation of English in the Atlantic States* (Ann Arbor, Mich.: University of Michigan Press, 1961), Map 171. Copyright 1961 by University of Michigan Press. Reprinted by permission of the publishers.

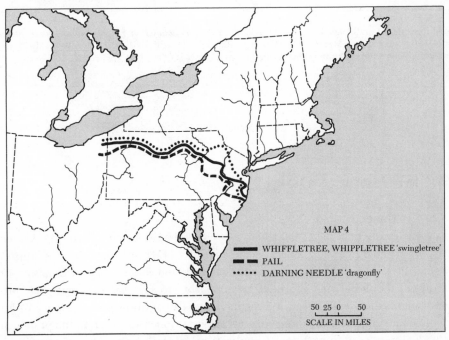

MAP 4

▬▬▬ WHIFFLETREE, WHIPPLETREE 'swingletree'
▬ ▬ ▬ PAIL
•••••• DARNING NEEDLE 'dragonfly'

50 25 0   50
SCALE IN MILES

Adapted from Hans Kurath, *A Word Geography of the Eastern United States* (Ann Arbor, Mich.: University of Michigan Press, 1949), Fig. 5a. Copyright 1949 by University of Michigan Press. Reprinted by permission of the publishers.

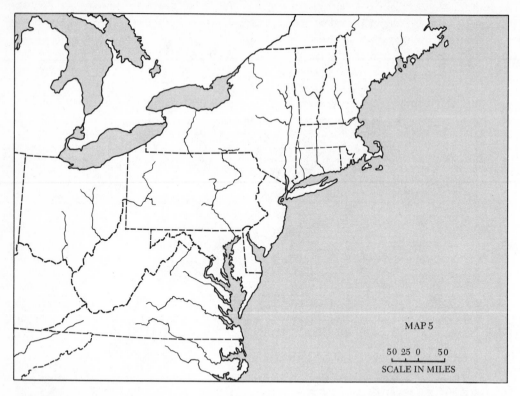

Adapted from Hans Kurath and Raven I. McDavid, Jr., *The Pronunciation of English in the Atlantic States* (Ann Arbor, Mich.: University of Michigan Press, 1961), Map 1. Copyright 1961 by University of Michigan Press. Reprinted by permission of the publishers.

EXERCISE 2: Social Dialects

A *Correct* Dialect?

It is a commonly held belief that there is such a thing as a single correct pronunciation of every word in the English language. Some manuals of English usage leave this impression, but in fact there is such a variety of accents and pronunciations used in English-speaking lands around the world that it would be impossible to say that one particular pronunciation—such as the British Received Pronunciation (RP) or Midwestern American—is more correct than any other. Even within a country there is much variation in the pronunciation of individual words, often with social implications for each variety.

The following is a summary of the regional and social variations in pronunciation of the word *aunt.*

aunt   In the Northern, Midland, and Southern speech areas, except for Eastern New England and a part of Tidewater Virginia, /æ/ is nearly universal at all social levels. The vowel /a/ as in *pot* is predominant in most of Eastern New England, though there are instances of /æ/ everywhere. "No social prestige seems to attach to /a/ in this area; in fact, some speakers regard /a/ as old-fashioned." This pronunciation is a prestige form in Connecticut, New York City, and Philadelphia, and is found only in cultured speech there. In a part of Tidewater Virginia dominated by Richmond, /a/ is the usual pronunciation at all social levels. Elsewhere in Virginia, this pronunciation is a prestige form "almost exclusively in cultivated city speech—as in Alexandria, Winchester, Charlottesville, and Roanoke. As a prestige pronunciation, it has also been adopted by better educated speakers on Albemarle Sound, N.C. The few instances of /a/ recorded in *aunt* from Charleston, S.C. southward occur in folk speech (four of the six in the speech of Negroes). Here cultured speakers avoid /a/."[1]

In the space below, answer either of the following two questions.

1. What is the correct pronunciation of *aunt?*
2. How would you rephrase the first question so that it could be briefly and reasonably answered?

_____

_____

_____

An *Irregular* Dialect?

A common myth about language in this country is that dialects other than the "establishment" dialects are erratic and disorderly, and thus lazy and inexpressive; but, in reality, they are consistent and patterned. Consider the following statements from one fourteen-year-old black in a Washington, D.C., poverty area.[2]

1. Every day last winter when they would come by to get me I would be busy.
2. Tomorrow morning when my mother get up I will be busy.
3. Every day, in the morning, when the others get up at my place I be busy.
4. Every day, in the morning, when you come I be busy.

He refused to substitute *I'm busy, I will be busy, I would be busy,* or (a dialect form) *I busy* for *I be busy* in 3 and 4. He would use these suggested substitutions knowledgeably at other times but said he would not use them in this context.

He would not say *I be busy right now;* for him the correct wording was *I'm busy right now.* If a person saw him on the street during the week and asked him why he had not been going to church Sundays, he might say, *Sunday I be busy.*

[1] Hans Kurath and Raven I. McDavid, Jr., *The Pronunciation of English in the Atlantic States*, p. 135. Copyright 1961 by University of Michigan Press. Reprinted by permission of the publishers.

[2] Marvin D. Loflin, "A Note on the Deep Structure of Non-standard English in Washington, D.C.," *Glossa* 1, no. 1 (1967): 26–32. Reprinted by permission of the publishers.

What does *I be* in *I be busy* in 3 and 4 mean in this dialect? Does it mean action in the present, action carried on from the past through the present, an action taking place occasionally, or what?

READING: The Language of the Ghetto Child[3]

Joan C. Baratz

What the psychologist who is studying the ghetto child and his learning patterns needs, among other things, is a sense of the child's language system. In this area the three major professions are the educators, the psychologists (mainly child-development types), and the linguists. The educators were the first to contribute a statement about the language difficulties of these children, a statement amounting to the fact that the children were virtually verbally destitute—they couldn't talk; if they did, it was deviant speech, filled with "errors." The next group to get into the fray, the psychologists, initially confirmed that the children didn't talk, and then added the sophisticated wrinkle that if they did talk, their speech was such that it was a deterrent to growth. The last group to come into the picture were the linguists, who, though thoroughly impressed with the sophisticated research of the psychologist, were astonished at the naiveté of his pronouncements concerning language. The linguist began to examine the language of black children and brought us to our current conception—that black children speak a well-ordered, highly structured, highly developed language system which in many aspects is different from standard English.

The linguist takes as basic that all human beings develop language. After all, there is no reason to assume that black African bush children develop a language and black inner-city Harlem children do not. Subsumed under this is that the language is a well-ordered system with a predictable sound pattern, grammatical structure, and vocabulary (in this sense, there are no "primitive" languages). The linguist assumes that any such verbal system used by a community *is* a language. The linguist also contends that children learn language in the context of their environment—that is to say, a French child learns French not because his father is in the home or his mother reads books to him but because that is the language he hears continually inside and outside the home and that is the language individuals in his environment respond to. Another assumption the linguist works with is that by the time a child is five he has developed language—he has learned the rules of his linguistic environment.

[3] *The Center Magazine*, a publication of the Center for the Study of Democratic Institutions, 2, no. 2 (January 1969): 32–33. Reprinted by permission of the publishers.

The syntax of low-income Negro children differs from standard English in many ways, but it has its own internal consistency. Unfortunately, the psychologist, not knowing the rules of Negro non-standard English, has interpreted these differences not as the result of well-learned rules but as evidence of "linguistic underdevelopment." He has been handicapped by his assumption that to develop language is synonymous with the development of the psychologist's own form of standard English. Thus he has concluded that if black children do not speak like white children they are deficient. One of the most blatant errors has been a confusion between hypotheses concerning language and hypotheses concerning cognition. For this reason, superficial differences in language structures and language styles have been taken as manifestations of underlying differences in learning ability. To give one example, a child in class was asked, in a test of simple contrasts, "Why do you say they are different?" He could not answer. Then it was discovered that the use of "do you say," though grammatically correct, was inappropriate to his culture. When he was asked instead, "Why are they different?" he answered without any hesitation at all.

There is a widespread notion among psychologists that some environments are better than others for stimulating language and learning growth. This assumption is, I believe, an outgrowth of the psychologist's confusion between general language development and the acquisition of standard English, which causes him to think that he must explain a "language deficit." According to researchers of this school, among the most detrimental factors is the "inadequacy" of the ghetto mothering patterns. The ghetto mother, they say, is so taken up with survival—"subsistence behaviors"—that she is too exhausted to talk to her children. Such a notion tells us more about the psychologist's lack of knowledge about the ghetto mother than it does about her real role. It also assumes that there is a minimal amount of language that must be present for language to be learned and that Negro mothers do not give this to their children. Part of this notion is that language is only learned from one's mother and that the language learned from her is underdeveloped. It is also presumed that the mother of a black child does not know how to stimulate or reinforce her child so that learning can occur. Under that assumption is the idea that such things as reading a book and singing to a child are essential behaviors in order for language to develop. Finally, it is presumed that she encourages passive, withdrawn behavior in her children because verbal ability is not highly valued in the ghetto community.

It seems as if all these assumptions have evolved because of misconceptions of what language is and how it functions. The psychologist has constructed elaborate environmental and psychological explanations of differences in language behavior but the elaborateness is unnecessary. The assumptions have been used after the fact to explain data erroneously —they have no experiential base.

★   ★   ★   ★   ★

A Dialect of Washington, D.C.

The data that Joan Baratz refers to in her last sentence can be explained by the hypothesis that there exist many different social *dialects*. The Center for Applied Linguistics has been studying urban dialects and dialectology. One of its projects was to tape the natural and spontaneous conversation of a number of blacks from Washington, D.C. The following exercise is constructed around the transcript of those tapes.[4]

The two people represented in the transcript below come from the same block and are of "a lower socioeconomic stratum."[5] Anita Porter (AP) and Jacqueline Drew (JD) are occasional playmates and are ten and eleven years of age. Sandy Barrett (SB) is a black research assistant, in her twenties.

The transcript is reproduced here in simplified form. Phrases in italics indicate that two people are speaking at once.

1. AP: Le' me tell you all a story.
2.   Jacqueline know it.
3. JD: *I cain'.*
4. AP: *See i' was dis* man.
5.   I' was a white man an' a colored man.
6.   Uh, how bout da' man hear da'?
7. SB: So wha'?
8. AP: An' nis, an' nis white,
9.   an' nis white man say:
10.   if you go in nere, an' eat dem beans,
11.   I gi' you ten thousan' dollars.
12. JD: I ma tell you . . . I ma tell . . .
13. AP: *An'so* . . . de white man wen' in *nere.*
14. JD: *Okay wait* a minute Anita.
15. AP: An' ne ghos' was . . . le' me tell i' . . .
16.   an' ne . . . *an' ne ghos' was in* nere.
17. JD: *I ain' go tell you da'.*
18.   I ma tell you another story about a . . . bout . . .
19.   a a . . . white man,
20.   a black man, an' de Chinese man.
21. AP: Da's de story I'm tellin'.
22. JD: An' mine's ain' bout no ghos'.
23. AP: An' all three o' dem men. An' so. So one
24.   de white man wen' in nere firs'.
25.   An' ne, an' ne ghos' scared him ou',
26.   an' so he ranned ou'.
27.   An' s- . . . an' so, um . . .
28.   an' de Chinese man wen' in nere.
29.   An' so he tried to eat dem beans
30.   an' de ghos' scared him ou',
31.   so de colored man wen' in nere. An' he say,

[4] Bengt Loman, *Conversations in a Negro American Dialect* (Washington, D.C.: Center for Applied Linguistics, 1967). pp. 21–22. Reprinted by permission of the publishers.
[5] *Ibid.*, p. ix.

32.   an' he scare', an' he was scarin' de colored man.
33.   Colored man say: I mo k- . . . I mo . . .
34.   No de ghos' say I ma kill you.
35.   An' ne ghos' say: . . . An' ne . . . an' ne . . .
36.   colored man say:
37.   I ma kill you if you mess wi' dese beans.
38.   Some'm like da'.

In reading over this transcript, keep in mind that most of the apparent irregularities are in fact the normal patterns of spontaneous and informal speech.

In what ways does this dialect differ from your own speech produced in similarly informal situations? Compare the speech of this transcript and your own speech with standard American English, as exemplified by network TV English. Go over the transcript line by line, entering in the spaces below the words that usually begin with [ð] in network TV English when pronounced alone. To check the phonetic environment, include the word that precedes each of these words.

Line	Words	Line	Words	Line	Words
4	was dis				
6	bout da'				

A. After what sounds (not letters) is a [d] used in the passage for the initial *th*-? _____

_____

_____

B. After what sounds is an [n] used for the initial *th*-? _____

_____

C. How do you account for this situation in terms of articulatory phonetics? _____

_____

_____

D. Now examine your own ideolect or that of a close friend who speaks like you. Listen and, if possible, record speech from as informal and relaxed a situation as Anita and Jacqueline were in. List your usage of [ð] below in the same way as you did theirs. Be sure to listen without preconceptions.

_____   _____   _____

_____   _____   _____

_____   _____   _____

_____   _____   _____

_____   _____   _____

_____   _____   _____

E. What sounds did you use for the initial *th-* in these words, and in what environments might they be expected?

Sound   *Environment*

_____   _____

_____   _____

_____   _____

_____   _____

How do you account for this situation in terms of articulatory phonetics?

_____

F. Pick out from the transcript those words that appear to be in the third person singular present form of standard American English. Include the subjects of the verbs.

Line	*Words*	*Line*	*Words*
____	_____	____	_____
____	_____	____	_____
____	_____	____	_____
____	_____	____	_____
____	_____	____	_____

G. Give the line numbers of those verbs that you would have expected to be in a past tense form in standard American English. _____

Which of these verbs is of doubtful use in the study of the children's choice of tense forms? _____ Why? _____

_____

_____

Note that these verbs have both the narrative use and phonetic environment in common. What is the phonetic environment these words have in common? _____

_____

What conclusions can you draw from this passage alone concerning whether **say** is meant as a past form? Why? _____

_____

_____

H. What does **ma** mean in the following examples?
   12. JD: I ma tell you, I ma tell
   18.   I ma tell you another . . .
   34.   No de ghos' say I ma kill you.
   37.   I ma kill you if you mess wi' dese beans.

_____

_____

Is the idea of necessity (**must**) expressed by **ma** in these examples? _____

_____

Is there an idea of determination or at least intention? _____

Could **I ma kill you** come from **I'm going to kill you?** By what process? _____

_____

_____

The purpose of the following essay, as Professor McDavid states in his introduction, is to "trace the chain of influence from the historical background to the sources of local speech patterns and the relationships of those speech patterns to the social order."

READING: Chicago: The Macrocosm[6]

Raven I. McDavid, Jr.

Northern Illinois—like northern Indiana, southern Michigan and southeastern Wisconsin—was first settled from the Inland Northern dialect region: western New England, by way of Upstate New York. In many of the small towns in Chicago's exurbia, the older families still show distinctly New England speech-traits, such as the centralized diphthongs [əu] and [əɪ] in *down* and *ride*, or /ʊ/ in *spoon* and *soon*. But the city of Chicago developed a more polyglot tradition from the beginning. The city was established at the time when the Erie Canal made it easy for the economic and political refugees from western Europe to reach the American heartland. The Irish brought reliable labor for the new railroads and a continuing tradition of lively politics; the Germans contributed their interest in beer, education, art, music and finance. Almost immediately Chicago also became a magnet for the younger sons of the agricultural settlements in southern Illinois and southern Indiana —Midlanders, whose speech patterns derived from western Pennsylvania. Scandinavians followed Germans and Irish; toward the end of the Nineteenth Century the population of the metropolitan area was swelled by mass peasant immigration from Southern and Eastern Europe—the strong backs and putatively weak brains on which Chicago's mighty steel industry was built. When this immigration tailed off during World War I, a new supply of basic labor was sought in the Southern Negro. Negro immigration has increased until Chicago is possibly the largest Negro city in the world. More recently the Negroes have been joined by Latin Americans (Mexicans, Cubans, Puerto Ricans), and last by rural whites from the Southern Appalachians. In response partly to the pressure of the increasing non-white population, partly to easy credit and slick promotion, Chicago whites like those in other cities have spread into the suburbs, many of which are at least informally restricted to a single economic and social (sometimes even an ethnic or religious) group.

In Chicago as in most large cities, the development of social dialects has been a byproduct of what might be called differential acculturation: differences in the facility and speed with which representatives of various social groups develop the ability to live alongside each other as individuals, without stereotyped group identification. In favor of the trend is the traditional American principle of individual dignity, and the belief that each man should be allowed to improve his lot as far as his ability and his luck permit. Against it is the tendency of people to flock together according to their nature and common ties—whether Filipinos, Orthodox Jews, Irishmen, hipsters or college professors—a tendency abetted by those with a stake in keeping the flock from scattering and by the tendency of each group to reject the conspicuous outsider. In the early Nineteenth Century, the Pennsylvanians and downstaters, with a few generations of Americanizing under their belts, soon mingled freely

---

[6] From "Dialect Differences and Social Differences in an Urban Society," in William Bright, ed., *Sociolinguistics, Proceedings of the UCLA Sociolinguistics Conference*, 1964 (The Hague: Mouton & Co., 1966), pp. 76–80. Reprinted by permission of the publishers. Professor McDavid ascribes much of the information of his essay to Professor Lee Pederson of Emory University in Atlanta.

with all but the wealthiest and most genealogically conscious Northerners. Acculturation was more difficult for the "clannish" Irish, Germans and Scandinavians.° The Irish were usually Roman Catholics; the Scandinavians spoke a foreign language; many Germans suffered from both handicaps, and all three groups had broken with their native cultures only recently and maintained many of their native customs. Nevertheless, all three of these groups had enough in common with the "Older American Stock"—all coming from north-western Europe—to make some sort of symbiotic assimilation easy, though all of these older immigrant groups were to suffer during the xenophobic hysteria of 1917–19 and after.† In general they managed to participate freely in the community, while retaining their cultural societies, newspapers and even foreign-language schools.

The later immigrants from Southern and Eastern Europe suffered, in general, from the twin disabilities of foreign language and Roman Catholicism. Moreover, they were largely peasants and illiterate, without the strong sense of their cultural tradition that the Germans and Scandinavians had brought.‡ All these groups found themselves at the focus of a complicated polyhedron of forces. In an effort to help their acclimatization—and no doubt to avoid the erosion of traditional ecclesiastical allegiance—the Roman hierarchy fostered the "ethnic parish," designed specifically for a single nationality or linguistic group. Whether or not this institution served its immediate purpose, it has the side effects of further identifying foreignness and Roman Catholicism, of separating the new groups from the American Protestants, from the "native Catholics" (chiefly of Irish and German descent), and from each other, and of fostering ethnic blocs in local politics.§ The blocs persist; but the common tendency of Chicagoans (as of Clevelanders) of Southern and Eastern European descent is to abandon their ancestral languages and turn their backs on their ancestral cultures, even in the first American-born generation. The notable exceptions are the Jews, with the attachment to the synagogue, to the synagogue-centered subculture, and to the family as a religious and culturally focused institution. But it is possible for an individual from any of these new immigrant groups to give up as much of his ethnic identity as he may wish, and to mingle relatively unnoticed in apartment building or housing development alongside members of the earlier established groups.

° It is obvious that only outsiders are clannish; in-groups are merely closely knit.

† Since the Germans were the largest functioning foreign-language group, and since their position in the cultural life of the community was so high, it is almost impossible to calculate to what extent the teaching of languages and literature, and the position of the scholar, suffered as a result of these witch-hunts. The abolition of Germanic studies at the University of Texas, as a gesture of patriotism, was only one of many such acts.

‡ Paradoxically, one of the most successful adaptations of native cultural traditions to the opportunities of the American setting—that of the South Italians of Chicago to the public demands during Prohibition—tended to stigmatize the whole group, whether or not they actively participated in the Syndicate's version of venture capitalism.

§ In the manuscript version of his *Language in the United States,* Joshua Fishman repeatedly attacks the heavily Irish American hierarchy of the Roman church for discouraging the ethnic parish in the past generation. In contrast, the late Msgr. John L. O'Brien, director of parochial education in the Charleston diocese, was outspoken in his belief (based on his home community in Pennsylvania) that the ethnic parish tended to prevent the development of a truly Catholic church in the United States. The Irish, after all, had found their ethnicity one of their greatest obstacles to full participation in American society.

In contrast to both of these groups of European immigrants, the American Negro in Chicago is a native speaker of American English, normally of at least five generations of residence in North America (cf. McDavid, 1951); little survives of his ancestral African culture, though undoubtedly more than American Caucasoids are generally willing to admit. Early Negro settlers in Chicago were able to settle as individuals—whether freemen or manumitted or fugitive before the Civil War, or emancipated migrants afterward; further-more, a large number of the earliest Negro immigrants were skilled craftsmen, who might expect to find a place in an expanding economy, and with some education to smooth off the rough corners of their dialects. However, even as an individual settler the Negro was more easily identified than any of the whites who had preceded him; and many Negroes exhibited traumata from slavery and mass discrimination. With the mass migrations of Negroes, other forces began to operate: the arrivals from 1915 on were largely a black peasantry, somewhat exposed to urban or small-town life but almost never actively partici-pating in the dominant culture. Their own American cultural traditions—gastronomic, ecclesiastical and everything between—often diverged sharply from those of middle-class Chicago. Their speech, though American English, was likewise sharply different from that of their new neighbors. Even an educated Mississippian has a system of vowels strikingly different from the Chicago pattern. An uneducated Mississippi Negro would have had his poor sample of learning in the least favored part of the Southern tradition of separate and unequal schools; his grammar would differ more sharply from the grammar of educated speech in his region far more than would the grammar of any Northern non-standard dialect differ from the local white standard. Furthermore, the easy identification of the Negro immigrant would provoke open or tacit pressure to reinforce the tendency of living with one's kind—a situation which, for the Chicago Negro, is likely to strengthen the linguistic and cultural features alien to the dominant local dialect pattern. Finally, the displacement of unskilled labor by automation has injured the Negroes—less educated and less skilled, on the whole—more than it has other groups. The specter of a permanently unemployable Negro proletariat has begun to haunt political leaders in Chicago as in other Northern cities, with inferior educational achievement and inferior employment opportunities reinforcing each other, and in the process strengthening the linguistic differences between whites and Negroes.

Of the Latin American, it can be said that he adds a language barrier to the problem of physical identification which he often shares with the Negro. Of the displaced Southern mountaineer, it has often been observed that he is even less acculturated to urban living than the Negro or the Latin; however, his physical traits will make it easy for his children to blend into the urban landscape, if they can only survive.

What then are the effects of this linguistic melting pot on the speech of metropolitan Chicago? And—since I wear the hat of English teacher as well as that of social dialectolo-gist—what are the implications for the schools?

First, the speech of the city proper has apparently become differentiated from that of the surrounding area, as the result of four generations of mingling of Inland Northern, Midland, and Irish, and the gradual assimilation of the descendants of continental European immigrants. The outer suburbs call the city /šikágo/, butcher /hagz/, and suffer from spring

/fag/; to most of its inhabitants the city is /šikógo/, quondam /hɔg/ butcher to the world, beset by Sandburg's cat-footed /fɔg/. To the city-bred, *prairie* and *gangway* and *clout* have connotations quite different from those they bear in the hinterlands.° Little if anything survives in the city of such Inland Northern speech forms as [əi] and [əu] in *high* and *how*, [ʊ] in *soon* and *spoon*, or /éjə/ as an oral gesture of assent. Even the second generation of Irish, lace-curtained or otherwise, have largely lost their brogue; such pronunciations as /ohérə/ for *O'Hare* Field seem to be socially rather than ethnically identifiable.†

Among the older generation with foreign-language backgrounds, one finds sporadic traces of old-country tongues, such as lack of certain consonant distinctions (e.g., /t/ and /θ/, /d/ and /ð/) that are regular in standard English. Among the younger generation of educated speakers some of the Jewish informants stand out, not only for the traditional American Jewish vocabulary, from *bar mitzvah* and *blintz* to *tsorris* and *yentz*, but for the dentalization or affrication of /t, d, n, s, z, r, l/. The former features have spread to other local groups, but the latter has not. The so-called Scandinavian intonation of English is rarely encountered, even among informants of Scandinavian descent; it has not been picked up by other groups as it has in Minneapolis.

Negroes born in Chicago before 1900 vary less from their Caucasoid contemporaries than the latter do among themselves, attesting to something like genuinely integrated residential patterns in the past. However, Chicago-born Negroes under 50 show many features of Southern and South Midland pronunciation, notably in the consistent use of /sikágo/ in outland fashion, in often having /griz/ and /grizi/ as verb and adjective,‡ in the frequent loss of postvocalic /r/ in *barn*, *beard* and the like, in contrasts between *horse* and *hoarse*, and in relatively greater length of stressed vowels. Such extralinguistic speech traits as wider spreads than Inland Northern usage offers between highest and lowest pitch or between strongest and weakest stress, or the quaver of ingratiation when speaking to someone presumed to be in authority, also survive and are generally recognized by Chicago-born whites and identified as characteristics of Negro speech. In grammar, the Chicago-born Negro who grows up in an environment of poverty and limited cultural opportunities—as most Chicago Negroes grow up—has a tendency to use forms that identify him easily and to his disadvantage, in writing as well as in speech. Most of these are forms of common verbs—absence of the third-singular present marker, as in *he do, it make;* old-fashioned preterites and participles, as *holp* "helped"; or the appearance of an *-s* marker in unexpected places as *we says, they does*—or in plurals of nouns, like *two postes* /-əz/. Many of these features of pronunciation and grammar, especially the lengthened stressed vowels, are also found among the recent immigrants from Appalachia, who have their own paralinguistic phenomena, such as strong nasalization, and a few grammatical peculiarities like the sentence-opening *used to:* "Used to, everybody in these-here hills made they own liquor."

° Evidence on these features is basically that of Pederson's dissertation and his unpublished lexical research.

† The pronunciation /ohérə/, definitely substandard in Chicago, is however the normal one for Mayor Richard J. Daley, probably the most powerful municipal politician in the United States. To urban Chicagoans a *prairie* is a vacant lot; a *gangway* is a passage between two apartment buildings; *clout* is political influence.

‡ *Grease* and *greasy* have been studied by Atwood, 1950 and previously by Hempl, 1896.

But because the recently arrived Appalachian whites are relatively few in number, because their residential patterns are not so rigorously segregated as those of the Negroes, and because they are not so readily identified as to physical type, their linguistic features do not seem to be perpetuated into the younger generation, and probably will never be.

★   ★   ★   ★   ★

READING: Is There a Negro Speech Pattern?[7]

William Labov

Is there a Negro speech pattern? This question has provoked a great deal of discussion in the last few years, much more than it deserves. At many meetings on educational problems of ghetto areas, time which could have been spent in constructive discussion has been devoted to arguing the question as to whether Negro dialect exists. The debates have not been conducted with any large body of factual information in view, but rather in terms of what the speakers wish to be so, or what they fear might follow in the political arena.

For those who have not participated in such debates, it may be difficult to imagine how great are the pressures against the recognition, description, or even mention of Negro speech patterns. For various reasons, many teachers, principals, and civil rights leaders wish to deny that the existence of patterns of Negro speech is a linguistic and social reality in the United States today. The most careful statement of the situation as it actually exists might read as follows: *Many features of pronunciation, grammar, and lexicon are closely associated with Negro speakers—so closely as to identify the great majority of Negro people in the Northern cities by their speech alone.*

The match between this speech pattern and membership in the Negro ethnic group is of course far from complete. Many Negro speakers have none—or almost none—of these features. Many Northern whites, living in close proximity to Negroes, have these features in their own speech. But this overlap does not prevent the features from being identified with Negro speech by most listeners: we are dealing with a stereotype which provides correct identification in the great majority of cases, and therefore with a firm base in social reality. Such stereotypes are the social basis of language perception; this is merely one of many cases where listeners generalize from the variable data to categorical perception in absolute terms. Someone who uses a stigmatized form 20 to 30 percent of the time will be heard as using this form all of the time. It may be socially useful to correct these stereotypes in a certain number of individual cases, so that people learn to limit their generalizations to the precise degree that their experience warrants: but the overall tendency is based upon very regular principles of human behavior, and people will continue to identify as Negro

[7] William Labov, "Some Sources of Reading Problems for Negro Speakers of Nonstandard English," in Alexander Frazier, ed., *New Directions in Elementary English* (Champaign, Ill.: National Council of Teachers of English, 1967), pp. 143–46. Revised and reprinted with the permission of the National Council of Teachers of English and William Labov.

speech the pattern which they hear from the great majority of the Negro people that they meet.

In the South, the overlap is much greater. There is good reason to think that most positive features of the Negro speech pattern have their origin in dialects spoken by both Negroes and whites in some parts of the South. Historically speaking, the Negro speech pattern that we are dealing with in Northern cities is a regional speech pattern. We might stop speaking of Negro speech, and begin using the term "Southern regional speech," if that would make the political and social situation more manageable. But if we do so, we must not deceive ourselves and come to believe that this is an accurate description of the current situation. The following points cannot be overlooked in any such discussion:

1. There are present in Negro speech patterns a small number of features which have not yet been plainly identified with any white Southern dialect: the deletion of the contracted *is*, as in *He crazy*, and the invariant *be* of *He be crazy* are the two prime examples. The persistence of these features, a number of irregular but strongly Creole patterns in the speech of young Negro children, and the historical evidence turned up by W. Stewart, all point to a possible Creole origin of Southern Negro speech patterns. This dialect may have passed through a process of "de-Creolization" before it became a regional or ethnic dialect of English.

2. For most Northern whites, the only familiar example of Southern speech is that of the Negro people they hear, and these Southern features function as markers of Negro ethnic membership, not Southern origin.

3. Many characteristic features of Southern speech have been generalized along strictly ethnic lines in Northern cities. For example, the absence of a distinction between /i/ and /e/ before nasals [*pin* equal to *pen*] has become a marker of the Negro group in New York City, so that most young Negro children of Northern and Southern background alike show this feature while no white children are affected.

4. In this merger of Northern and Southern patterns in the Northern Negro communities, a great many Southern features are being eliminated. Thus in New York and other Northern cities, we find the young Negro people do not distinguish *four* and *for*, *which* and *witch;* while monophthongization of *high* and *wide* is common, the extreme fronting of the initial vowel to the position of *cat* or near it, is less and less frequent; the back upglide of *ball* and *hawk,* so characteristic of many Southern areas, is rarely heard; grammatical features such as the perfective auxiliary *done* in *he done told me,* or the double modal of *might could,* are becoming increasingly rare. As a result, a speaker fresh from the South is plainly marked in the Northern Negro communities, and his speech is ridiculed. Negro speech is thus not to be identified with Southern regional speech. . . .

5. The white Southern speech which is heard in many Northern cities—Chicago, Detroit, Cleveland—is the Southern Mountain pattern of Appalachia, and this pattern does not have many of the phonological and grammatical features of Negro speech to be discussed below. . . .

6. Many of the individual features of Negro speech can be found in Northern white speech, as we will see, and even more so in the speech of educated white Southerners. But the frequency of these features, such as consonant cluster simplification, and their distribution

in relation to grammatical boundaries, is radically different in Negro speech, and we are forced in many cases to infer the existence of different underlying grammatical forms and rules.

We can sum up this discussion of the Southern regional pattern by saying that we are witnessing the transformation of a regional speech pattern into a class and ethnic pattern in the Northern cities. This is not a new phenomenon; it has occurred many times in the history of English. According to H. Kökeritz and H. C. Wyld, such a process was taking place in Shakespeare's London, where regional dialects from the east and southeast opposed more conservative dialects within the city as middle class and lower class speech against aristocratic speech. We see the same process operating today in the suburbs of New York City; where the Connecticut and New Jersey patterns meet the New York City pattern, in the overlapping areas, the New York City pattern becomes associated with lower socio-economic groups.

The existence of a Negro speech pattern must not be confused of course with the myth of a biologically, racially, exclusively Negro speech. The idea that dialect differences are due to some form of laziness or carelessness must be rejected with equal firmness. Anyone who continues to endorse such myths can be refuted easily by such subjective reaction tests as the Family Background test which we are using in our current research in Harlem. Sizable extracts from the speech of fourteen individuals are played in sequence for listeners who are asked to identify the family backgrounds of each. So far, we find no one who can even come close to a correct identification of Negro and white speakers. This result does not contradict the statement that there exists a socially based Negro speech pattern: it supports everything that I have said above on this point. The voices heard on the test are the exceptional cases: Negroes raised without any Negro friends in solidly white areas; whites raised in areas dominated by Negro cultural values; white Southerners in Gullah-speaking territory; Negroes from small Northern communities untouched by recent migrations; college educated Negroes who reject the Northern ghetto and the South alike. The speech of these individuals does not identify them as Negro or white because they do not use the speech patterns which are characteristically Negro or white for Northern listeners. The identifications made by these listeners, often in violation of actual ethnic membership categories, show that they respond to Negro speech patterns as a social reality.

★   ★   ★   ★   ★

READING: Society Dialects[8]

Stephen Birmingham

Then there is the Society voice. Trying to duplicate the American Society accent has provided the greatest stumbling block for the parvenu. Some say you must be born with

[8] Stephen Birmingham, *The Right People, a Portrait of the American Social Establishment* (Boston: Little, Brown & Co., 1968), pp. 9–10, 195. Copyright 1968 by Stephen Birmingham.

it to speak it properly and convincingly, but it is safe to say that graduates of such private schools as St. Paul's, Foxcroft, and Madeira, who may not have had the accent to begin with, can emerge with a reasonably close facsimile of it. It is a social accent that is virtually the same in all American cities, and it is actually a blend of several accents. There is much more to it than the well-known broad A. Its components are a certain New England flatness, a trace of a Southern drawl, and a surprising touch of the New York City accent that many people consider Brooklynese. Therefore, in the social voice, the word "shirt" comes out halfway between "shirt" and "shoit." Another key word is "pretty," which, in the social voice emerges sounding something like "prutty." There is also the word "circle," the first syllable of which is almost whistled through pursed lips, whereas the greeting, "Hi," is nearly always heavily diphthonged as "Haoy." This speech has been nicknamed "the Massachusetts malocclusion," since much of it is accomplished with the lower jaw thrust forward and rigid, and in a number of upper-class private schools, children are taught to speak correctly by practicing with pencils clenched between their teeth.

. . .

"My God!" said one young woman the other day. "My daughter's started talking with that Main Line accent. She's picked it up at school. She's started using Main Line words —words like 'yummy.' The other day I asked her how a certain party had been and she said, 'Oh, Mummy, it was such a giggle!'" Children attending the Main Line's private schools—Shipley, Agnes Irwin, or Baldwin for girls; Haverford or Episcopal for boys—seem to acquire the accent and language by osmosis, if they have not already acquired it from listening to their parents. The terminology is quaintly special, one might say precious. One is not startled on the Main Line to hear a businessman conclude a deal with a cheerful "All righty-roo!" Or to depart from a party with a bright "Nightie-noodles!" to his host and hostess. As for the accent, Barbara Best calls it "Philadelphia paralysis," or "Main Line lockjaw," pointing out that it is not unlike "Massachusetts malocclusion." Mrs. Best recalls that when she first moved to the area a native said to her, "My dear, you have the most beautiful speaking voice. I can understand every word you say!"

EXERCISE 3: Dialects for Various Occasions

Educated adult speakers of English have at their command a number of different *styles* of speech. Martin Joos writes of five styles: consultative, casual, intimate, formal, and frozen.[9] The consultative style is chosen for communication between strangers, or for discussion of serious or complicated matters. The speaker supplies background information to the listener, since the listener is not on an insider's casual or intimate basis with the speaker during the conversation. The listener participates continuously in the conversation, if by nothing more than nodding his head to show that he is listening. The following passage is in what Joos calls the consultative style. It was recorded from a phone line in Ann Arbor, Michigan.

[9] Martin Joos, *The Five Clocks* (Bloomington, Ind.: Indiana University Research Center in Anthropology, Folklore, and Linguistics, 1962).

I wanted to tell you one more thing I've been talking with Mr. D—— in the purchasing department about our typewriter (yes) that order went in March seventh however it seems that we are about eighth on the list (I see) we were up about three but it seems that for that type of typewriter we're about eighth that's for a fourteen-inch carriage with pica type (I see) now he told me that R——'s have in stock the fourteen-inch carriage typewriters with elite type (oh) and elite type varies sometimes it's quite small and sometimes it's almost as large as pica (yes I know) he suggested that we go down and get Mrs. R—— and tell her who we are and that he sent us and try the fourteen-inch typewriters and see if our stencils would work with such type (I see) and if we can use them to get them right away because they have those in stock and we won't have to wait (that's right) we're short one typewriter right now as far as having adequate facilities for the staff is concerned (yes) we're short and we want to get rid of those rentals (that's right) but they are expecting within two weeks or so to be receiving—ah—to start receiving their orders on eleven-inch machines with pica type (oh) and of course pica type has always been best for our stencils (yes) but I rather think there might be a chance that we can work with elite type (well you go over and try them and see what they're like and do that as soon as you can so that we'll not miss our chance at these).[10]

The casual style is used among friends and acquaintances in small groups or pairs. Little background is given or necessary. There is much in-group slang and jargon. Formulas are common, such as those of utterance 7 in the passage below. Their function is to signal the casualness of the communication as well as to carry meaning. (The intonation of the exclamations has been marked in the following passage.)

1. [A—— I don't know whether you let B—— go out during the week do you suppose he could come over tonight while we go out to dinner]
2. [Well the difficulty is J—— that he got back in his lessons]
3. [Oh oh]
4. [And in his last report about two weeks ago he was down in two subjects his father hasn't been letting him do anything]
5. [Well that's a good idea]
6. [I'm awfully sorry]
7. [Well that's all right thanks A—— to tell you the truth I don't want awfully badly to go you know what I mean]
8. [M hm]
9. [Well how's the garden]
10. [Oh it's much worse than yours I imagine the only thing that looks decent at all is the strawberries]
11. [Yes I know but you know they're not going to be any good unless they get some sun and dry weather]
12. [No well there's still time for them isn't there]
13. [Yes I know]
14. [I've got strawberries started have you]
15. [What]
16. [Some of the berries have started on my plants][11]

[10] From Charles C. Fries, *The Structure of English* (New York: Harcourt Brace Jovanovich, 1952), pp. 50–51.
[11] *Ibid.*, pp. 24–25.

Joos characterized the intimate style as more expressive than informative. A wife's laconic /tayrd/, said to her husband after a hard day, is not said to inform; he can see she is tired. It draws attention to the fact, though, and can lead to sympathy and a drink. Intimate speech finds certain grammatical details superfluous, and does not require much of the public vocabulary; a married couple or close friends gradually invent a large part of their intimate code.

Formal style is marked by a lack of participation of the audience; it is designed to inform; it is essentially dominating; it expects the listeners to remain silent till the end of the speech.

The sentences of the exercise below cannot show all the characteristics of each style, since they are isolated from context. But there are characteristics of vocabulary and syntax that mark the styles even at the level of sentences.

Translate the utterances below into the other styles. Some of the messages jar the ear when translated into an inappropriate style. For example, the translation of the consultative utterance of number 4 will sound strange when put into formal language. But it is still possible to translate it. The intimate style is not included in this exercise because by nature it is private and most often ambiguous to outsiders. The frozen style has not been included here or discussed previously because it is restricted to printed material and declamation.

1. consultative   *I don't understand this.*

   casual   *Hey prof, that doesn't reach me.*

   formal   *The subject is beyond comprehension.*

2. consultative   _____

   casual   _____

   formal   *We request the honor of your presence for luncheon.*
   Tuesday next at 12:00.

3. consultative   *I would like two hamburgers and one order of french fries.*

   casual   _____

   formal   _____

4. consultative   *Please fill up the gas tank.*

   casual   _____

   formal   _____

5. consultative   *I'm completely exhausted.*

   casual   _____

   formal   _____

VARIATION IN TIME: SOURCES OF VARIATION 12

EXERCISE 1: Speaker's Errors: Confusion of Sound and Sense

Some Changes in Sounds

There are some changes that occur within a language that do not depend on any contact with other languages. These changes are *loss* (**sherf** for **sheriff**), *assimilation* (**grampa** for **grandpa**), *dissimilation* (**purple** for **purpre**), *metathesis* (**revelant** for **relevant**), and *addition* (**ellum** for **elm**). The following is a list of words that illustrate one or more of these changes. Place **L, As, D, M,** or **Ad** beside each word that displays any of these processes.

L 1. *probly* for *probably*

____ 2. *sebm* for *seven*

____ 3. *athalete* for *athlete*

____ 4. *sump'n* for *something*

____ 5. *gimmi* for *give me*

____ 6. *panacake* for *pancake*

____ 7. *ekscape* for *escape*

____ 8. *idear* for *idea*

____ 9. *larnyx* for *larynx*

____ 10. *scant,* historically from *skammt*

____ 11. *ran,* historically from *arn*

____ 12. *Cuber* for *Cuba*

____ 13. *nucular* for *nuclear*

____ 14. *bird* from Old English *bridd*

____ 15. *captol* for *capitol*

____ 16. *acrosst* for *across*

____ 17. *thorol* for *thorough*

____ 18. *final u* in Japanese *wonderfuru* 'wonderful'

____ 19. [fulɨ] from earlier [fullɨ] 'fully'

____ 20. *thimble* from earlier *thymel*

____ 21. child's pronunciation of *bugglegum* for *bubblegum*

____ 22. *eksetra* for *etcetra*

Blends

The words *bash, smash, glimmer, flimmer, clash,* and *flare* are considered blends by the Oxford English Dictionary, which gives the following etymological sources and dates:

$$
\begin{array}{lll}
\text{bat (1205)} & + \text{mash (1000)} & \text{yields bash (1641)} \\
\text{smack (1746)} & + \text{mash (1000)} & \text{yields smash (1778)} \\
\text{gleam (1000)} & + \text{shimmer (1100)} & \text{yields glimmer (1400)} \\
\text{flame (1377)} & + \text{glimmer (1400)} & \text{yields flimmer (1880)} \\
\text{clap (1375)} & + \text{crash (1400)} & \text{yields clash (1500)} \\
\text{flame (1377)} & + \text{glare (1400)} & \text{yields flare (1500)} \\
\end{array}
$$

Consulting your desk dictionary, find the sources of the following blends. In cases where the dictionary does not provide the answer, your own ingenuity will be your guide; for example, knowing *motel,* you should have no difficulty in discovering the blend in *boatel.*

1. alcoholiday _____ *alcohol* _____ + _____ *holiday* _____

2. brunch _____ + _____

3. boatel _____ + _____

4. chortle _____ + _____

5. cinemactress _____ + _____

6. dumbfound _____ + _____

7. fantabulous _____ + _____

8. guesstimate _____ + _____

9. medicare _____ + _____

10. motel _____ + _____

11. sexational _____ + _____

12. simulcast _____ + _____

13. transistor _____ + _____

14. travelogue _____ + _____

15. Stewardess to passengers: "I hope you have a pleasant *flip.*"

_____ + _____

16. Their schoolwork *slagged* all week.

_____ + _____

Neo-suffixation

17. cheeseburger _____ + _____

18. dictaphone   _____ + _____

19. gaseteria   _____ + _____

Phrase Blends

20. long awaited for   _____ + _____

21. keep silent   _____ + _____

22. Feymond's study has shown that Chrétien was **good to his word.**

_____ + _____

23. Newspaper correspondent on TV program: "Peter has **hit it in a nutshell.**"

_____ + _____

24. He didn't say anything **that commits himself.** _____ +

_____

25. Bertrand Russell's **second-hand man.** _____ + __ _____

Spelling Blends   (Consult your dictionary, and guess.)

26. rhyme (historical) _____ + _____

27. compair (contemporary) _____ + _____

A word of caution: not all words that appear to be blends are blends, for example, the word **submerse,** which seems to be a blend of **submerge** and **immerse.** Check the dictionary and you will find that **submerse** comes from the past participle of the Latin **submergere** (**submersus**), which is of course related to **submerge.**

Malapropisms

In the following sentences replace the underlined word with the intended word. The first has been completed as an example.

1. The convict paced within the <u>confounds</u> of his cell. _____ *confines* _____

2. Johnny Logan's "I remember the name, but I can't <u>replace</u> the face."

_____

3. Babe Ruth's "Look at that guy out there in left field. He is in a <u>transom</u>."

_____

4. His antisocial behavior results from lack of attention during his <u>formidable</u> years.

_____

5. When I grow up, I want to be a TV <u>pronouncer</u>. _____

6. Dreyfus' <u>vanishment</u> from France by the French army was unjust.

   _____

7. There was enough <u>leave-way</u> for the readers to interpret the passage as they pleased.

   _____

8. Mozart was a child <u>progeny</u>. _____

9. The <u>flagrance</u> of her perfume filled the room. _____

10. I found the Oriental dishes very <u>palpable</u>. _____

Spelling Pronunciation

The pronunciation of the following words is commonly different from what the spelling would suggest. A non-native speaker's attempt at explicitly pronouncing each morpheme of words of more than one morpheme would lead him to a spelling pronunciation. After looking up the pronunciation of these words in the dictionary, transcribe in phonemic script your own pronunciation and the common spelling pronunciation.

Word	*Your Pronunciation*	*Spelling Pronunciation*
1. ballet	_____	_____
2. bases (pl. of basis)	_____	_____
3. cupboard	_____	_____
4. forehead	_____	_____
5. handkerchief	_____	_____
6. lethe	_____	_____
7. necklace	_____	_____
8. palm	_____	_____
9. perusal	_____	_____
10. subtle	_____	_____
11. toward	_____	_____
12. processes	_____	_____

A news correspondent pronounced the word **instances** as [instənsis]. Comment.

_____

_____

_____

The Oxford English Dictionary gives only the pronunciation [fɔrəd] for *forehead;* other dictionaries list both that and [fɔrhəd]. What do you suppose has happened? _____

EXERCISE 2: Speaker's Errors: Overgeneralization

Determine on what basis a child produces the following erroneous forms:

tooths, foots, gooses _____

drinked, falled, hurted _____

Analogy and Analysis

Suppose the following words come into English usage. Not having heard the plural of the nouns or the past of the verbs, you would probably form the plural and the past in a way that most other speakers of English would. Write the plural or the past beside each of the following words:

Word		Plural	Past
bront	'spider'	_____	
wug	'silver jug'	_____	
laysh	'joy'	_____	
mank	'to hunt'		_____
gade	'to worry'		_____
ludge	'to move'		_____

For the noun plurals, you probably selected an allomorph of the plural morpheme, namely, /s z əz/; for the past, the choice was among the past allomorphs /t d əd/. Survivals such as the historical plural forms in *oxen, brethren, geese, mice,* and *sheep,* or new verbs that change the internal vowel to form the past and the past participle, as in *sink-sank-sunk,* are not prevalent nowadays. What is the most prevalent ending for the past participle? Test the fictitious verbs above. _____

It is interesting that most readers would agree on the pronunciation of the fictitious terms. Why? What process is involved? _____

The plural of *mongoose* is *mongooses.* Are you comfortable with it? If not, what does it illustrate? _____

EXERCISE 3: Reinterpretation: Errors of the Hearer

Folk Etymology

Folk etymology is also called *popular* or *false etymology*. It has existed as long as man has been interested in the etymology of words he has encountered. For example, early Roman grammarians related the Latin **bellum** 'war' to **bellus** 'beautiful' because war is *not* beautiful.[1] At times fictitious etymologies are given to strengthen a notion. Carlyle related the word **king** to 'one who can' associating it with the German word **können** 'to be capable.'[2] Ruskin would remind wives that their place was at home, since **wife** meant 'she who weaves.'[3] In many cases of folk etymology, the spelling of the word changes to accommodate the new sense that it is to bear. Note the change in spelling as you look up the following words. By referring to your dictionary, determine the historically accurate etymology of the words on the left, and underline the correct one on the right.

1. hangnail	aching nail	hanging nail
2. female	a male's companion	little woman
3. shamefaced	bound by shame	face reflecting felt shame
4. crayfish	crawling fish	crab
5. greyhound	a hound	grey-colored hound
6. Jordan almond	imported almond	garden almond
7. Jerusalem artichoke	girasol	imported vegetable
8. acorn	corn	nut
9. chaise longue	lounge chair	long chair
10. couch grass	alive grass	synthetic sofa cover

Fusion

Underline the words or phrases below that demonstrate fusion. Specify the context in the space to the right of each phrase you underline. In making your decision, apply the four criteria mentioned by Bolinger: speed, vowel reduction, regularizing of inflection, and reluctance to separate the words.

1. <u>law and order</u>   *as used in politics* _____

2. law and authority   _____

3. black and white   _____

4. silver and black   _____

---

[1] John T. Waterman, *Perspectives in Linguistics* (Chicago: University of Chicago Press, 1963), p. 10.
[2] Simeon Potter, *Our Language* (Harmondsworth, England: Penguin Books, 1950), p. 106.
[3] *Ibid.*, p. 106.

5. black and blue _____

6. bread and butter _____

7. butter and jam _____

8. life and happiness _____

9. life and death _____

10. assault and battery _____

11. generator and battery _____

12. mother-in-laws _____

13. fathers-in-law _____

14. forecasted _____

15. drug addict _____

16. Yes, indeed _____

17. Yes, truly _____

18. nice and easy _____

19. nice and uncorrupted _____

To which stage in the child's acquisition of language (see Chapter 1) can fusion be compared? _____

Back Formation

According to Bolinger, "back formation is metanalysis combined with overgeneralization." By consulting your desk dictionary, determine the original term from which the following words were back-formed.

1. asset ___*assets*___

2. automate _____

3. burgle _____

4. donate _____

5. enthuse _____

6. escalate _____

7. greed _____

8. homesick _____

9. hush _____

10. peddle _____

11. preempt _____

12. reminisce _____

13. swindle _____

14. televise _____

15. anchors (as in "*Eric Sevareid anchors the news.*") _____

Reinduction

Exaggerated explicit terminology is often accompanied by change in meaning through reinduction.

A. Check the sports section of a newspaper. Find and list a half dozen terms used to express one team's defeating another. Specify the sport they were used for. _____

_____

_____

_____

B. Add at least three examples to the following words, which mean little more than *very:*

awfully, terribly, _____

_____

C. Certain nouns have ready-made adjectives that nearly always occur with them in some people's speech. These adjectives not only do not add any sense; in fact, they usually detract from the full force of the noun. Give some adjectives that are commonly heard with the following nouns:

1. _____*basic*_____ essentials   5. _____ clear

2. _____ necessity   6. _____ circumstances

3. _____ pain   7. _____ shame

4. _____ silence

D. List words that are commonly added before the following:

1. _____ naked   4. _____ new

2. _____ absurd   5. _____ dry

3. _____ wet

EXERCISE 4: Meanings: Basic and Expanded

Connotation

Using a thesaurus or a synonym list (such as *Webster's New Dictionary of Synonyms*), find words that might be applied to the same person by two other individuals, one viewing the person favorably, the other unfavorably. As you complete these, consider whether the words have always had a positive or negative connotation. The etymological information in the dictionary will be helpful in most cases.

	(neutral)	(favorable)	(unfavorable)
1.	liberal	*progressive*	*pinko*
2.	careful		
3.	saves money		
4.	loves his country		
5.	reserved		
6.	independent		
7.	resolute		
8.	levelheaded		
9.	phlegmatic		

Euphemism

With the aid of a dictionary and a thesaurus, determine a few delicate words or expressions that are often used to replace the words below. In some cases the words below are themselves euphemisms. **Bathroom** has a long history of euphemisms, among them **siege-house, bog-house, Sir John, Aunt Jones,** and **throne room.**

1. to be blind _____
2. to be deaf _____
3. to be fired from a job _____
4. defecate _____
5. pregnant _____
6. an old person _____
7. war _____
8. insane _____
9. bathroom _____
10. damn _____
11. copulate _____
12. poor _____

Name a field or activity that does not use euphemisms. _____

EXERCISE 5: Bilingualism

Borrowing

English has borrowed from many languages. By referring to your desk dictionary, identify the immediate etymological source of the following words. (For example, the immediate source of *menage* is French, although the more remote source is Latin.) Specify the dictionary used. _____

Word	Etymological Source	Word	Etymological Source
air	_____	mohair	_____
babel	_____	oil	_____
barbecue	_____	orangutan	_____
buffalo	_____	pajama	_____
bungalow	_____	penguin	_____
cocoa	_____	polo	_____
cola	_____	posse	_____
costume	_____	raccoon	_____
delivery	_____	robot	_____
furlough	_____	slim	_____
guerrilla	_____	slob	_____
gull	_____	sofa	_____
gusto	_____	spy	_____
hallelujah	_____	traffic	_____
halo	_____	tycoon	_____
hustle	_____	veneer	_____
ill	_____	veranda	_____
journey	_____	window	_____
kiosk	_____	yacht	_____
mammoth	_____	yogurt	_____
marimba	_____	zen	_____

Classify the following words as loanwords (LW), loanblends (LB), or loanshifts (LSH):

	Loan Type	Source and Form
1. booby trap	LB	**booby** from Sp. **bobo** 'fool' + **trap**
		from O.E. **treppe**
2. coconut	——	
3. free verse	——	
4. loanword	——	
5. mint ('to coin')	——	
6. monk	——	

English Words of French Origin

Vocabulary accommodates the needs of the times; when the hula hoop was popular, the name was widely known. As objects or concepts lose popularity, the words representing them become archaic and eventually disappear from the language. When a concept or object is borrowed from another culture, its name is often taken as well: the English took the name of *caffe* from the Italians, who had first tasted *qahveh* in Turkey, where the custom of drinking Arabian *qahwah* had been adopted. Such words then become part of the language and literature of the borrowing nation. One language that has strongly affected English is French, although the degree of influence has not been uniform throughout the centuries. It began, logically enough, with the Norman Conquest in 1066, which placed England under French rule for three centuries. But it was, paradoxically, after England became English once again that it acquired the greatest number of French loanwords. These early influences can be seen by taking a modern literary work, selecting those words that are of French origin, and identifying the periods of heaviest borrowing. The types of words borrowed during each period often reflect something of the relationship that existed between the two cultures, as in the case of words like *plaintiff*, *trial*, and *attorney*.

Below is a list of one hundred words of French origin found in J. D. Salinger's short story "Pretty Mouth and Green My Eyes." The date of the earliest occurence of these words in a text may be found in the Oxford English Dictionary (O.E.D.), as well as in the partially completed Middle English Dictionary (M.E.D.). The alphabetical items from **A** to **I** are essentially from the M.E.D. figures. In words of more than one morpheme, the date of borrowing of the elements rather than the date of coining of the specific words has been given.[4]

Word	Earliest Literary Occurrence	Word	Earliest Literary Occurrence	Word	Earliest Literary Occurrence
actual	1315	deference	1647	part	1050
advice	1297	delivery	1350	particular	1386
alert	1598	developed	1656	party	1290
annoyed	1250	difference	1340	passing	1330
apartment	1641	discovered	1380	plaintiff	1278
appeared	1250	distance	1290	policeman	1714
army	1386	exhale	1616	poop	1489
arrangement	1375	extent	1292	quart	1325
attorney	1291	face	1290	reason	1225
average	1500	fault	1290	second	1300
avoid	1382	favor	1340	sign	1225
balanced	1592	foreign	1290	size	1300
barge	1300	gaiety	1634	stayed	1586
bastard	1250	greasy	1514	stew	1386
beautiful	1325	guy	1350	story	1225
blue	1300	helmet	1450	stuff	1330
briefly	1300	honest	1300	support	1421
brush	1377	hotel	1644	sure	1340
case	1225	hour	1225	surface	1611
certainly	1297	humanly	1398	tanked	1660
chambermaid	1230	lampshade	1200	taste	1292
chance	1297	large	1175	train	1330
chiefly	1300	madame	1670	trial	1526
cigarette	1842	maintain	1250	trifle	1225
clear	1297	married	1297	trot	1300
close	1280	matter	1330	try	1292
closet	1370	minor	1297	use	1225
conversation	1340	minute	1370	very	1250
cord	1300	mountain	1205	violet	1330
corner	1292	move	1290	voice	1300
countenance	1250	net	1520	wait	1200
course	1300	nice	1290	war	1154
credit	1542	notice	1483		
damn	1280	page	1300		

[4] We are indebted to William Z. Pentelovitch, from whose paper "A History of French Influence on the English Language" this information is taken.

Date	Number of Words Entered
1051–1100	
1101–1150	
1151–1200	
1201–1250	
1251–1300	
1301–1350	
1351–1400	
1401–1450	
1451–1500	
1501–1550	
1551–1600	
1601–1650	
1651–1700	
1701–1750	
1751–1800	
1801–1850	
1851–1900	

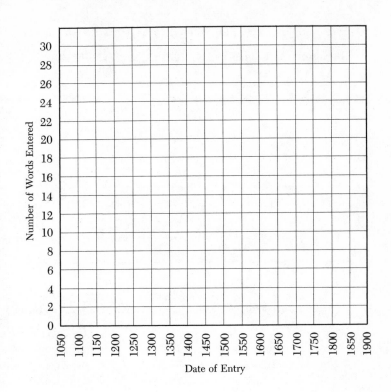

A. Using the chart on the left, determine how many words in the list entered the language during each fifty-year period from 1050 to 1900, and plot them on the graph.

B. When did the period of greatest borrowing occur? _____

C. What events in the history of England account for this extensive borrowing? (For a detailed explanation, see the reading in Chapter 13, "A Brief History of the English Language." _____

_____

_____

_____

D. What are the next two major peaks? How do you account for these in relation to the history of England? _____

_____

_____

E. How might the rise of the printing press have affected the first of these peaks?

_____

_____

_____

_____

F. Jespersen's account of the influx of French words at different periods is as follows:[5]

Before 1050	2	1451–1500	76
1051–1100	2	1501–1550	84
1101–1150	1	1551–1600	91
1151–1200	15	1601–1650	69
1201–1250	64	1651–1700	34
1251–1300	127	1701–1750	24
1301–1350	120	1751–1800	16
1351–1400	180	1801–1850	23
1401–1450	70	1851–1900	2
		Total	1000

Plot these figures on your graph. Since this list is for 1000 words, you will need to divide the figures by ten to make them correspond to the figures on the graph. How do the charts compare with each other? How might you explain the discrepancies?

_____

_____

_____

_____

English Words of Latin Origin

After French, Latin is the language that has affected English vocabulary to the greatest degree. Latin terms have been borrowed throughout the history of English; each period, however, has a characteristic flavor. Aside from household words such as **kitchen, dish,** and

[5] Otto Jespersen, *Growth and Structure of the English Language* (New York: D. Appleton, 1923), p. 94.

cheese, most borrowings during the Old English period were terms connected with the church. Besides religious terms such as *redeemer* and scientific terms such as *medicine,* the Middle English borrowings are generally legal and scholastic terms. The majority of the Modern English borrowings from Latin are generally referred to as *learned terms.* Here are three groups of words; each group contains words from a single period of borrowing. Determine the period of borrowing of each and place **Old English, Middle English,** or **Modern English** in the space provided above each group of words.

Period   _____   _____   _____

abbot	client	data
gospel	subpoena	edition
deacon	scribe	modern
pope	conviction	urban
psalm	index	education
nun	library	delirium

EXERCISE 6: Invention

Metaphor

The Latin words for **egregious, dependent,** and **precocious** are of metaphorical origin, meaning 'outside the herd,' 'hanging from,' and 'unripe' respectively. Explain the metaphors in the following expressions.

1. <u>blanket</u> legislation _____ *covers the whole of an issue as a blanket covers the bed* _____

2. a <u>bright</u> boy _____

3. the <u>head</u> of an army _____

4. a <u>sharp</u> rebuke _____

5. wage <u>ceiling</u> _____

6. <u>cold</u> war _____

7. <u>grasp</u> a meaning _____

8. an aircraft <u>sweeps</u> over enemy territory _____

9. <u>foot</u> of a mountain _____

10. wage <u>freeze</u> _____

11. <u>goose</u> step _____

12. <u>rat</u> race _____

13. road <u>bottleneck</u> _____

VARIATION IN TIME: THE OUTCOME OF VARIATION 13

READING: *A Brief History of the English Language*[1]

Margaret Schlauch

IMPORTANCE OF STUDYING ENGLISH HISTORICALLY

... Our English language is ... such a curious mixture from many sources that a brief sketch of its biography is really essential to an understanding of its structure today. Moreover there is an interesting parallel to be drawn between the development of the language and the vicissitudes of the people speaking it. If we trace the history of English, we shall observe historical relationships which also obtain in the histories of other languages.

THE ROMAN PERIOD

Under the later Roman emperors, as everyone knows, Britain was a Roman province with a flourishing colonial culture. The population was predominantly Celtic, to be sure, and spoke a language akin to modern Welsh. The native dialect no doubt persisted in the countryside, but the cities grew up about former Roman camps and included many Roman families, patrician and plebeian, who used Latin habitually. They did so even when they intermarried with the British or employed them as workers and slaves. All the amenities of Latin culture were enjoyed in the cities of this distant province: baths, forums or market places, comfortable villas with plumbing and tessellated floors, schools of rhetoric, theaters, and libraries. The Roman army was famous for making itself at home and mingling with native populations everywhere, with or without official formalities. It deserves indeed much of the credit for spreading Vulgar Latin as an international language among the common people of the ancient world. Cultured Britons were Roman citizens and used the recognized dominant language of the empire with slight modifications. In due time they were adopting the new religion, Christianity, which was rapidly becoming the chief Roman faith in the fourth century.

THE ANGLO-SAXONS

The ancestor of the English language appeared first in Albion when some tribes from Northern Germany, the Angles, Saxons, and Jutes, began to harry the shores and invade

[1] From *The Gift of Tongues* by Margaret Schlauch. Copyright 1942 by Margaret Schlauch. Reprinted by permission of The Viking Press, Inc. and George Allen & Unwin, Ltd.

the island. This happened in the middle of the fifth century A.D. The raids were part of a larger diffuse movement known to historians as the *Völkerwanderung* or folk migrations. From the shores of the Black Sea to the coasts of Britain, the northern boundaries of the *Imperium Romanum* were harassed by restless Germanic peoples: Ostrogoths, Visigoths, Vandals, Franks, Langobards, Burgundians, and the so-called Anglo-Saxons, who sought foothold within the provinces. Roman resistance was weakened for many reasons, and the Germanic peoples were able to establish themselves in the heart of some of the most fertile sections. The struggle was at its height when the Angles and Saxons began the invasion of Britain. The mother cities, Rome and Constantinople, could give no help. More than that: Rome was obliged to call on the British provincial army to give aid on the continent. So Britain was doubly exposed. By the year 500 the Germanic invaders were established. There was an end of the sophisticated urban culture of the Romans, with their debates and theaters, their laws, government, army, and incipient Christian Church.

The newcomers were pagans, worshipers of Woden and other Teutonic gods. Their organization was tribal rather than urban. They were described by contemporaries as tall, blond, and blue-eyed. In the early days of the "Germanic peril" it had been the fashion for Roman matrons to dye their hair or wear wigs in imitation of barbaric blondness. By this time, however, the threat had become grim earnest; no mere subject for coiffeurs' modes.

The languages spoken by all the Germanic tribes about 450 A.D. were closely alike. They might more properly be called dialects of a General Germanic tongue shared by all, as English now is divided into dialects throughout the English-speaking world. The Germanic dialects had in turn . . . sprung from a fairly unified (lost) ancestor which we call Primitive Germanic.

EARLY OLD ENGLISH

We have no written documents in the Anglo-Saxon or Old English of the first few hundred years. Later, when Christianity was re-established in Britain in the early seventh century, schools, books, and the art of writing followed it. From two sources the newly converted Anglo-Saxons received instruction in these amenities. The missionaries from Rome acted as pedagogues chiefly in the south, in the kingdoms of Kent, Sussex, Wessex, and Mercia. In Northumbria some excellent work was done by Irish Christian missionaries, whose influence was felt in places like Lindisfarne, Yarrow, and Whitby. The alphabet taught here shows clearly its kinship with the Old Irish characters still used in Modern Gaelic. The first blooming of Old English literature occurred in this north country in the latter seventh and the eighth centuries. To the northern English schools of writing belonged Cynewulf, Caedmon, the Venerable Bede (who, like Alcuin, wrote in Latin), and the unknown author of *Beowulf*. Epic poems were written on the native heroic pagan traditions, and Christian themes were also treated in lyrical and heroic style—all in the Northern dialect. Unfortunately this glorious promise was cut short by the violence of the Danish invasions, beginning at the end of the eighth century. Monastic schools were reduced to smoking ruins, the learned writers scattered or killed, and precious manuscripts were destroyed.

WEST SAXON

A revival of letters occurred later, despite the persistent fierce onslaughts of the Danes, in the kingdom of Wessex under King Alfred. The king was acutely aware of the need for education among his followers. According to his own account, even the clergy had sunk into a distressing condition of illiteracy. It was his wish "that all the freeborn youth of England who have sufficient means to devote themselves thereto, be set to learning so long as they are not strong enough for any other occupation, until such time as they can well read English writing. Let those be taught Latin whom it is proposed to educate further, and promote to higher office."

The language spoken by Alfred and his court was the Wessex or West Saxon dialect of Old English. It may be compared to Modern German in many respects. It had similarly inflected nouns with four cases in the singular and plural. There were approximately half a dozen different schemes of declension. In Modern German it is necessary to know what declension a noun "belongs to" in order to give it the proper forms in a sentence (according to use or "construction"); this too was true of Old English. The similarity of pattern is clear if one compares the inflection of two cognate or related words meaning "stone," a masculine noun:

| | SINGULAR | | PLURAL | |
	Old Eng.	*Germ.*	*Old Eng.*	*Germ.*
Nom.	*stān*	*Stein*	*stānas*	*Steine*
Gen.	*stānes*	*Steines*	*stāna*	*Steine*
Dat.	*stāne*	*Steine*	*stānum*	*Steinen*
Acc.	*stān*	*Stein*	*stānas*	*Steine*

There are reasons for the differences to be noted in the plurals. However, the kinship is clear enough. Modern German is a conservative first cousin of Old English.

A Roman missionary trying to learn Anglo-Saxon for purposes of persuasion had to remember which of about six patterns to follow with every new noun acquired. It would have been felt to be a bad blunder if, for instance, he had used the "*-e*" ending of the plural of a feminine noun to make a plural for *stān*. In precisely the same way Americans who learn German are constantly in danger of falling into barbarous error if they choose the wrong pattern in inflecting a newly acquired noun. Since articles and adjectives presented forms for every case, gender, and number, and each form had to be carefully chosen so as to agree with the coming noun, the difficulty was greatly increased.

A Latin-speaking missionary might find all this entirely natural and understandable, since his native speech was also highly inflected, but he would have been puzzled by the existence of two separate and distinct declensions for all adjectives, the "strong" and the "weak." The former was used when the adjective alone preceded a noun, as in "good man"; the latter when an article or demonstrative came before the adjective, as in "the good man." Latin had no such distinction, but German had and still has:

	STRONG SINGULAR DATIVE	WEAK SINGULAR DATIVE
O.E.	*gōdum menn*	*þǣm gōdan menn*
	"[to] good man"	"[to] the good man"
Germ.	*gutem Manne*	*dem guten Manne*

OLD ENGLISH VERBS

In the system of verbs one can see many resemblances between Old English and German. Both languages show a large number of verbs, called "strong," which indicate changes in tense by internal vowel change. The pattern is a very ancient one based on the vowel gradations of the old parent language (Indo-European). Some words still show the basic similarity of pattern:

	INFINITIVE	PAST	PAST PARTICIPLE
O.E.	*rīdan*	*rād, ridon*	*riden*
Germ.	*reiten*	*ritt*	*geritten*
Eng.	ride	rode	ridden
O.E.	*bindan*	*band, bundon*	*bunden*
Germ.	*binden*	*band*	*gebunden*
Eng.	bind	bound	bound
O.E.	*etan*	*æt, ǣton*	*eten*
Germ.	*essen*	*ass*	*gegessen*
Eng.	eat	("et")ate	eaten

In both German and Old English too, there existed a second, larger group of verbs which used a different method for forming tenses. These "weak" verbs used a suffix instead: an added syllable containing a dental consonant. In modern German the suffix is always *-te,* but in Old English it varied. The possible forms were *-de, -ode, -te.* The past tense of Old English *dēman,* "to deem, to judge," was *dēmde,* "deemed"; of *lōcian,* "to look," it was *lōcode;* of *sēcan,* "to seek," it was *sōhte,* "sought."

OLD ENGLISH SOUNDS COMPARED TO MODERN GERMAN

The close relation between Old English and German is further indicated by constant relations in the sound patterns. When you encounter a strange word in the former you can often guess quite accurately what its cognate is in Modern German. Certain consonants have shifted away from the common Germanic position of an earlier day, but the kinship is still clear.*

---

* Bracketed characters refer to sound symbols in the International Phonetic Alphabet.

O.E. *drincan* resembles German *trinken* (drink) d: t
   "   *þencan* [θεŋkʲan] resembles German *denken* (think) þ: d
   "   *twelf* resembles German *zwölf* (twelve) t: z[ts]
   "   *dēop* resembles German *tief* (deep) p: f

By applying a few simple correspondences like these you can use German to help you learn Old English, or Old English to help you learn German. Moreover, even the vowels show fairly consistent parallelism. The Old English *ā* [ɑ:] parallels Modern German *ei*, pronounced [ai], in a multitude of words: *stān, Stein* (stone); *bān, Bein* (bone); *ān, ein* (one), etc. So with the Old English diphthong *ēa* [ε:a] and Modern German *au* [aʊ]: *hēap, Haufen* (heap); *lēapan, laufen* (run, leap); *ēac, auch* (also, eke). It is useful to compile your own list as you proceed.

To be sure, minor changes in both languages have by now obscured some of the neat correspondences. Old English was particularly prone to assimilations of various sorts: palatalizations which changed [k] into [tʃ]—as you will note in the pair of words "church," *Kirche*—and subtle changes in vowels, also of an assimilatory character. The causes of these changes become apparent, usually, when the Old English forms are compared with others in the related Germanic dialects. For practical purposes Modern Dutch is even more useful than Modern German in showing family similarities.

A few lines of Old English, from a Biblical translation, will illustrate some of the characteristics of the language:°

Ond Pharāōnes dohter cwæð tō hire: "Underfōh þis cild ond fēd hit mē, ond ic sylle þē þīne mēde." þæt wīf underfēng þone cnapan, ond hine fēdde ond sealde Pharāōnes dehter.

Ond hēo hine lufode ond hæfde for sunu hyre, ond nemde his naman Moises, ond cwæð: "Forþāmþe ic hine of wætere genam."

Exodus 2:9-10

And Pharaoh's daughter quoth to her: "Receive this child and feed it (for) me, and I (shall) give thee thy meed." The woman took the boy and fed him and gave (him) to Pharaoh's daughter.

And she loved him and had (him) as her son, and named his name Moses, and quoth: "Because I took him (out) of water."

(Literal translation)

CONNECTIONS WITH INDO-EUROPEAN

Even in this short passage there are a few words which show the more remote kinship of Old English with languages outside the closely knit Germanic family. No specialized knowledge is required in order to see these similarities:

O.E. *sunu* (son) corresponds to Russian *syn*, Sanskrit *sūnú*.
   "   *nama* (name) corresponds to Latin *nōmen*, Greek *onoma*.
   "   *dohtor* (daughter) corresponds to Greek *thugátēr*, Sanskrit *duhitá*.
   "   *mē* (me) corresponds to Latin *mē*, Russian *me'nʲa*.

° Note that þ, ð stand for [θ] and [ð] indiscriminately. The letter *h* stood for a rougher sound than ours today, something like [χ].

It is by resemblances such as these that the wider relationships are established among the various families called Indo-European.

Once the language of the Anglo-Saxons began to be written and to be studied along with Latin, it was brought into contact with the wide currents of world culture still pulsing strongly from the great center of Rome. The influence was felt in several ways. First of all, the study of classical Roman writers, which was more enthusiastic and intense than many readers may suppose, made Old English authors conscious of style and sentence structure in their own language. They began to cultivate certain effects they had admired in writers like Virgil, Ovid, and the prose historians. That is why the great prose translations and even the original works fostered in Old English by King Alfred have the air of being done by cultured, sophisticated writers, who knew very well what effect they were striving for. At times their admiration of Roman prose style led to unfelicitous imitation. When the translator of *Apollonius of Tyre* writes "all these things thus being done" (*ðisum eallum ðus gedōnum*) in the dative case, he is trying slavishly to follow a famous Latin construction in the ablative case: something like *hīs omnibus ita factīs*. It just doesn't fit. The effect remains foreign and awkward. But other writers combined planned intricacy and simplicity with more success. There are passages in the Alfredian translations of Bede, St. Gregory, Boethius, and Orosius which represent a happy marriage of Roman rhetoric with native English usage in sentence structure. In describing the death of Cædmon, the Old English version of Bede's history shifts from elaborate description to the direct recording of Cædmon's simple request: *"Beraþ mē hūsl tō"* (Bring me last sacrament). Nothing could be more English, including the ancient and entirely legitimate ending of a sentence with a preposition or adverb-particle. Thus while vigor of native idiom was retained, the very architecture of English was somewhat modified, at least among the cultured few at the courts and churches and schools, by association with the Roman literary heritage.

In the second place, the Old English vocabulary was enriched by a number of direct loans from Latin. The implanting of Christianity brought a number of direct transfers from one language to the other. Most have survived to this day. The list includes:

abbot	hymn	organ	shrive
altar	martyr	pope	synod
angel	mass	priest	relic
candle	noon	psalm	temple
deacon	nun	shrine	

Flourishing trade with Roman merchants continued the borrowings which had begun long ago on the continent when Germanic tribes first encountered salesmen from the Mediterranean. To the list above belong words like *cycene* (kitchen) from *coquīna; disc* (dish) from *discus; cīese* (cheese) from *cāseus; pund* (pound) from *pondus; mynet* ("mint" of money), from *moneta; copor* (copper) from *cuprum; tigele* (tile) from *tegula; strǣt* (street) from *strāta via;* and *ynce* (inch) from *unica.*

The debt to Roman word material was increased in another less obvious manner. For abstract learned concepts the Anglo-Saxon writers frequently coined words out of simple forms already existent in their own language. But they did this by translating literally the elements of the Latin words. . . . Thus the Old English vocabulary was increased under Roman inspiration without sacrifice of native ingredients. German has often followed the same method of constructing new learned words out of native elements, with an eye to the Latin model. The similar method of compounding appears in these typical examples:

O.E.	German	English
efen-sārgian	mit-leiden	com-miserate
fore-sprǣc	Vor-wort	pre-face
mid-wyrhta	Mit-arbeiter	col-laborator
ofer-ferian	über-führen	trans-fer
wið-standan	wider-stehen	op-pose
ūt-drǣfan	aus-treiben	ex-pel

Old English writers were thus exploring the possibilities of elaborate compounding in order to express new ideas. They never went very far in this direction—not so far, say, as some modern German writers—but it is possible that the tendency might have led to unwieldy polysyllables if Old English had developed into Modern with no disturbances from without.

INFLUENCE OF DANISH

There was one other foreign language besides Latin which exercised a measurable influence on Old English. The long-continued attacks by Danes and other Scandinavians on the English coasts were attended by some measure of success. At one time a Danish king, Knut or Canute, actually ruled the country. Large settlements were established, especially in the northern districts. They eventually remained on a peaceful footing, and the settlers merged with the English population. Before losing their identity entirely, however, they contributed a list of loan words to the English vocabulary. Most of them are so homely and practical that we may be sure that the immigrants rapidly attained neighborly status with the people they had but recently been harrying. Words borrowed at this period include "husband," "fellow," "law," "take," "store," "gate," "skill," "sky," "ransack," "call," "thrive," "skull." A personal pronoun was taken over bodily. We owe our plural forms, "they, their, them" to the Scandinavian þeir, þeira, þeim which gradually displaced Old English hīe, hīera, hem (confusingly like the singular masculine pronoun). The loans show the intimacy finally achieved by northern settlers who must have been at first bitterly resented.

LATE OLD ENGLISH

By the end of the Old English period, then, England had what might be called a recognized literary language, already used for several hundreds of years for important creative and translated writings. By the year 1000, however, certain changes were beginning to affect the literary language. The multiplicity of endings was gradually being reduced. Cases originally kept distinct were beginning to fall together with identical terminations. You could no longer be sure, without relying more and more on context, whether a given form meant a dative singular or a dative plural. If the confusion was appearing in formal documents written by men at least semi-learned, it was no doubt far more wide-spread among the unlearned. And very soon the process of confusion or leveling was speeded up by an important political event.

THE NORMAN CONQUEST

In 1066, as every school child knows, England was invaded and conquered by William, Duke of Normandy, commonly called "the Bastard." He used as pretext a doubtful claim to the English crown after the death of Edward the Confessor, "last of the Saxon Kings." The army attendant upon William was chiefly composed of Normans, men speaking a provincial dialect of French but related by blood to the Danes. Their forefathers, most of them, had migrated from Scandinavia and conquered the land of Normandy even as they themselves were now proposing to conquer England. Their success meant more than a mere change in dynastic rule for the inhabitants of Britain. The old local kingdoms and tribal organizations were swept away— such as had survived the period of unified Danish rule. In their stead the whole of England, excluding Scotland and Wales, was placed under a single complex feudal system of administration.

FEUDALISM IN ENGLAND

Feudalism of course was a highly stratified organization of society. In France there were already many ranks or orders of men, from the lowly unfree serf, up through free traders and workers, landless knights, land-owning knights, little barons, big barons, and recognized kings. Military service and other obligations were the basis of land ownership. Rights and prerogatives were at times vague or conflicting, and hence gave rise to fierce combats. Feudal France was divided into great duchies, each with a hereditary overlord at his head. Roughly speaking the dialects of medieval French corresponded to these feudal divisions. Within the confines of each duchy there was not a great deal of difference between the language of the lower and the higher orders, except insofar as differences of interest and preoccupation tended to mark off the stores of words used. The husbandman talked about agricultural matters, using more or less simple sentences studded with the technical terms of his job; the knight employed a more aristocratic vocabulary referring to tournaments, etiquette, literature, and art (within limits!), terms of inheritance, and the techniques of warfare; but in general they spoke the same dialect within the same region. The regional dialect divisions were probably much more noticeable than class divisions, apart from limited items of specialized vocabulary.

BILINGUAL ENGLAND

When William of Normandy transferred this feudal organization to England, the linguistic situation became more complex. At once the lowest orders were doubly marked, not only by inferior economic position but also by the use of a separate, despised tongue.

Since the Church, which conducted most of the schooling of the time, was also taken over by Norman-French bishops, abbots, and other prelates, instruction in English practically ceased. Most of the native speakers became necessarily illiterate and remained so for several generations. The recording of English came to an abrupt stop almost everywhere. While English thus remained unrecorded in writing and uncorrected by formal teaching, it tended to change more rapidly than it had been doing before 1066. The leveling of forms, now accelerated, produced a greatly simplified grammar. Many of the distinctions of Old English were lost in the process. Earlier writers like Sir Walter Scott have probably exaggerated the cleavage between Norman French and English, and the length of time it endured. But it was sufficiently marked at least to intensify the drive towards simplicity, already noticeable in Old English.

EARLY MIDDLE ENGLISH

English re-emerged as a literary language in the hands of churchly writers in the latter twelfth century. These men, schooled primarily in Latin and Norman French, merely adapted the classroom spelling of these upper-class languages to the native idiom. Some few may have known a little about the Old English written before 1066, especially in places where efforts had been made to keep the old *Anglo-Saxon Chronicle* up to date under the Normans. In all cases they tried to write what they actually heard, phonetically. Where inconsistencies arose they were due to regional dialects in English itself, or to a conflict between French and traditional English orthography. In Old English, for instance, the word *hūs* for "house" was pronounced with a single long vowel [hu:s], and was so written. In the so-called Middle English period, from 1100 to 1400, it was still being pronounced as before, but under French influence the spelling became *hous* for [hu:s]. We can be fairly certain of the pronunciation because of the general consistency. Some writers, moreover, were interested enough in the problem to indicate the reasons for their spelling, and what it was supposed to represent.

CHANGES IN GRAMMAR

With the reduction of Old English declensions the English sentence fell increasingly into the word order habitual with us today: subject, predicate, complement. Otherwise it would have been impossible, eventually, to distinguish one part from the other. (Old English sentences had used the inverted order and delayed clausal verbs to be found in Modern German.) Almost all the nouns were attracted into the declension represented by *stān*, with a plural in *-as* later weakened into *-es*. Only a few survived in the other declensions. The vowels of unaccented endings were reduced to the obscure sound [ə], written *-e-*. The verbs retained endings not unlike those current in the time of King Alfred:

Ī singe	*we singen*°
þū singest	*yē singen*
hē singeth	*þei singen*

° This is the Midland form of the plural. In the South it was *singeth*, in the North *singes*. The distinction is typical of many others which demarked the dialects from one another.

The adjectives retained vestiges of inflection, even slightly differentiating strong forms from weak; but the elaborate declensions of Old English adjectives were forgotten. The reduction of endings to short, unstressed syllables gave the language a trochaic and dactylic effect.

CHANGES IN SOUNDS

Although the consonants survived with little change, there was some shifting in the quality of the vowels. Old diphthongs were simplified and new ones arose. Old long vowels were shortened and short ones were lengthened under special conditions and for special reasons which need not be rehearsed here. In general the resulting new vowels were pronounced as in Modern Italian, Spanish, or German: in short, with the so-called "continental" values. Thus:

> ā was [ɑ:] as in "father";
> ē was [e:] or [ɛ:] as in "they" or "there," respectively;
> ī was [i:] as in "machine";
> ō was [o:] (not [ou]) as in "lone";
> ū was [u:], sometimes written "ou," as in "rouge";
> ȳ was identical with ī in pronunciation.

All vowels were intended to be spoken, except when two coming together in a sentence were elided (*thē intente* became *th' intente,* with three syllables to the second word). Diphthongs were pronounced by giving the above values to the separate parts: thus *"au"* represented [ɑ] plus [u] in one syllable. When you have grasped these few principles you can read Middle English aloud and enjoy the music of it along with the sense.

PERSISTENCE OF OLD ENGLISH WORDS

The earliest Middle English texts were still composed with an almost pure English vocabulary. The spelling, too, was conservative for a time, especially in the South, so that a casual glance at some of the early texts (ca. 1200) leaves the impression that Old English was still being written. A closer examination, however, shows that the simplification of forms was already far advanced at this time. Here is a short passage from a poem written in the South about 1170. It deals in a quaint medieval manner with the transitoriness of earthly happiness, yet there is a perennial appeal about its grave simplicity:

> Ich æm elder þen ich wes a wintre and a lore;
> Ic wælde more þanne ic dude; mi wit ah to ben more.
> Wel lange ic habbe child i-beon a weorde and ech a dede;
> þeh ic beo a wintre eald, to ying I eom a rede. . . .
> Ylde me is bestolen on ær ic hit awyste;
> Ne mihte ic iseon before me for smeche ne for miste.

(I am older than I was in winters and in lore; I have more strength than I did; my wit ought to be more. For a long time I have been a child in word and eke in deed; though

I be in winters old, too young I am in rede. Old age has stolen on me before I ever wist it; I could not see before me for the smoke and for the mist.)

Some of the lyrics retain pure English vocabulary at an even later date, because they deal with warm intimate things which we still prefer to express with the "Anglo-Saxon" part of our language.

> Wynter wakeneth al my care,
> Nou thise leves waxeth bare;
> Oft I sike and mourne sore   [sigh and mourn sorely]
>   When hit cometh in my thoht
>   Of this worldes joie, hou hit geth al to noht.
>
> Nou hit is, an nou hit nys,
> Al so hit ner were, ywys;
> That moni mon seith, soth hit ys:
>   Al goth bote Godes wille:
>   Alle we shule deye, thoh us like ylle. [though it displeases us]

FRENCH LOAN WORDS

Meanwhile, however, French was still the language of court, school, diplomacy, and Parliament. Even as late as the fourteenth century some outstanding English men of letters wrote exclusively in French. The English vocabulary could not long remain unaffected by this environment. What had at first been a mere infiltration of French words into English increased until by 1300 it was flood-tide. The new terms came from many occupations: from law, philosophy, theology, and military science; cookery, weaving, architecture, book-making; and the trade in wool, wine, and other commodities. Many of the more learned importations were long words which must have seemed by their vagueness imposing and slightly awesome to English ears. French words like *contritioún, transubstantioún, reverénce, penaúnce, obligacioún, dominacioún* must have arrived with double impressiveness: first because they referred to lofty matters of religion and government which the common man uneasily shies away from; and second because they simply sounded different from the native vocabulary. During the years when it was chiefly the language of illiterates, English had naturally veered away from the tendency to form lengthy compound abstractions out of native elements. Only a few like *rihtwysnesse* ("righteousness") and *agenbit* ("remorse") had survived. On the whole the native vocabulary had conserved best the basic non-abstract terms and hence turned now to an alien treasury for the needed terminology of learning.

The loans were conspicuous for another reason besides their length. They still preserved the French accentuation on the last syllable, in direct opposition to the English tendency to throw accents forward. Even when this English tendency began to affect the French importations, a strong secondary stress was retained on the last syllable: *con-trí-ci-oùn, ré-ve-rèn-ce, dó-mi-ná-ci-oùn*. The struggle between French and English tendencies in accentuation produced a wave-like rise and fall of stress which added even more dignity, it may well be, to the physical impressiveness of the words. The alternation of strongly stressed root syllables in native English, followed by the shrinking unstressed endings, was already contributing to the same effect. Out of these divergent sources came the iambic-trochaic movements of English which Chaucer used so brilliantly in his narrative verse.

THE COMBINED VOCABULARY IN CHAUCER

And Chaucer illustrates, too, the aesthetic uses to be made of the new polyglot vocabulary. No one knew better than he how to juxtapose, contrast, or temporarily isolate the dual elements of fourteenth-century English. In this respect he may be compared to his own advantage with many modern poets. At one time Chaucer permits the full grandeur of the French polysyllables to roll out:

> For of *fortúnes* sharpe *adversité*
> The worste kynde of *infortúne* is this:
> A man to han been in *prospérité*,
> And it remembren when it passed is.
>
> *(Troilus and Cressida,* III, 1. 1625 ff.)

This poignant comment on human felicity, paraphrased from Dante, gains in dignity from the use of the italicized Romance words. At the same time, the last line has a simplicity of everyday speech, the more effective by contrast; and the delayed verb in the archaic Old English style gives it a falling cadence which heightens the wistfulness. The same artful contrast of polysyllabic dignity and native simplicity is found in many other Chaucerian passages. In the ballade called "Fortune" he begins:

> This wrecched worldes *trānsmutácioùn*
> As wele or wo, now povre and now *honoúr*
> Withouten ordre or wys *discrécioùn*
> *Govérned* is by *Fórtunès erroúr.*

He laments the passing of a happier day when people told the truth and their word was as good as their bond:

> Sometyme this world was so stedfast and stable
> That mannes word was *obligácioùn.* . . .
>
> ("Lak of Stedfastnesse")

You will notice that the melody of Chaucer's lines depends on a correct rendering of the unaccented syllables. Unless the vowels are pronounced in these, the verse is harsh and unmetrical. Give due value to the unstressed vowels (including final *-e's*), however, and retain strong secondary stress at the end of French loan words, and you will have verse as musical and diversified as any in English.

In less exalted moods Chaucer often undertook to describe the lives and persons and small adventures of common folk. Here his brilliant realism was re-enforced by an appropriate vocabulary and a sentence structure echoing the cadences of ordinary speech. In drawing the picture of an elderly carpenter's young wife, with her gay amorous ways, her "likerous eye" and her "middle gent and smal" as any weasel's, he concludes gustily:

> Hir mouth was sweete as bragot or the meeth, [ale or mead]
> Or hoord of apples leyd in hey or heeth. [hay or heath]
> Wynsynge she was, as is a joly colt,
> Long as a mast, and upright as a bolt. . . .
> Hir shoes were laced on hir legges hye.
> She was a prymerole, a piggesnye [primrose or "pig's-
> For any lord to leggen in his bedde, eye" (a flower)]
> Or yet for any good yeman to wedde.

The homely details and comparisons expressed in everyday language—"sweet as apples laid in heath or hay"—are enough to make the reader's mouth water, as indeed they were intended to do. And the simple vocabulary of ordinary life is beautifully used when the same fair Alison rebuffs (but not permanently!) an amorous overture by her boarder, a handsome young student:

> [She] seyde, "I wol nat kisse thee, by my fey!
> Why, lat be," quod she, "lat be, Nicholas,
> Or I wol crie 'out, harrow' and 'allas'!
> *Do wey youre handes*, for youre curteisye!"
> ("Miller's Tale," *CT*, A3261 ff.)

With the English vernacular being handled in so masterful a manner, it had surely reached legal majority and could no longer be regarded as a subject dialect. Conversely, it was because English had already won recognition that Chaucer devoted his genius to it rather than French or Latin. Significantly enough, Parliament was first opened in English in 1362, and the chronicler Trevisa tells us the native language was used in the schools in 1385. Both events fell in Chaucer's lifetime.

THE FIFTEENTH CENTURY

Soon after Chaucer's death, in the fifteenth century, there was a renewed drift towards simplification in English. Final unaccented vowels, by 1400 already reduced to a very slight murmur, were entirely lost. Still more nouns were shifted to the majority declension (with plurals in -*s*) out of the small group left in the minority declensions. More and more verbs were shifted to the weak conjugation from those still retaining the internal vowel change. For a time, of course, there was a choice of forms: Malory could decide between either "he clave" or "he clefte" in telling how one knight smote another asunder, as they were so frequently engaged in doing in the *Morte d'Arthur*. Similar fluctuations arose between "he clomb" and "he climbed"; "he halp" and "he helped." Some of the quaint surviving constructions out of Old English, such as impersonal verbs with the dative, the inflected genitive case for nouns denoting things, and the double negative, began to fall into disuse.

They persist in the fifteenth century, indeed even into the sixteenth, but they are felt increasingly to be archaic survivals.

Where Chaucer said:	Later English has:
He *nevere* yet *no* vileynye *ne* sayde In al his lif unto *no* manner wight.	He never said *any*thing villainous about *any*body
Me [to me] were levere a thousand fold to dye.	In all his life to *any* person. *I'd* liefer [rather] die a thousand times over.
Me thynketh *it* acordaunt to resoun.	*It* seems reasonable *to me*.
Our present *worldes lyves* space. . . .	The space *of* our present life *of* [in] this world.
In hope to stonden in his *lady* [gen. sing. fem.] grace. . . .	In hope to stand in his *lady's* grace.

Another important usage became increasingly prevalent in the fifteenth and early sixteenth century: the bolstering of verbs with a number of auxiliaries derived from "do" and "be." In Middle English a question was asked with the simple form of the verb in inverted position: "What say you? What think you?" For a couple of centuries after 1400 this was still done habitually, but more and more people fell into the habit of saying "What do you say? What do you think?" The "do" was colorless and merely brought about a deferment of the main verb. In effect it makes our English usage somewhat like Russian, which says "What you say? What you think?" without any inversion of the verb before the subject. In simple statements the "do" forms were used for situations where we no longer feel the need for them. An Elizabethan would say "I do greatly fear it" (an unrestricted statement). We should use the less emphatic "I fear it greatly." Compare Shakespeare's

> I *do prophesy* the election lights
> On Fortinbras; he has my dying voice—

and many other instances.

During the same period there began the gradual spread of the so-called progressive conjugation, with forms of "to be": I *am coming; he is sitting* down." These two special forms of English conjugation have developed an intricate etiquette, with many modifications of usage, which cause great trouble to the foreign student. One of the last distinctions he masters is the one between "I eat breakfast every morning" and "I am eating breakfast now"; between "I believe that" and "I do indeed believe that."

One of the most fateful innovations in English culture, the use of the printing press, had its effects on the language in many ways. The dialect of London, which had for over a century been gaining in currency and prestige, took an enormous spurt when it was more or less codified as the language of the press. As Caxton and his successors normalized it, roughly speaking, it became the language of officialdom, of polite letters, of the spreading commerce centered at the capital. The local dialects competed with it even less successfully than formerly. The art of reading, though still a privilege of the favored few, was extended lower into the ranks of the middle classes. With the secularizing of education later on, the mastery of the printed page was extended to still humbler folk. Boys who, like William Shakespeare, were sons of small-town merchants and craftsmen, could learn to read their Virgil and Ovid and Holy Writ even if they had no intention of entering the Church. Times had distinctly changed since the thirteenth century. It may be added that changes in society—the gradual emergence of a mercantile civilization out of feudalism— gave scope to printing which it would never have had in the earlier Middle Ages. The invention was timely in more than one sense.

All this may have been anticipated by the early printers. Their technological innovations may have been expected to facilitate the spread of culture. But they could not have foreseen that the spelling which they standardized, more or less, as the record of contemporary pronunciation, would have been perpetuated for centuries afterwards. Today, when our pronunciation has become quite different, we are still teaching our unhappy children to spell as Caxton did. Respect for the printed page has become something like fetish-worship. A few idiosyncrasies have been carefully preserved although the reason for them is no longer understood. When Caxton first set up the new business in London he brought with him Flemish workers from the Low Countries, where he himself had learned it. Now the Flemish used the spelling "gh" to represent their own voiced guttural continuant, a long-rolled-out sound [γ] unlike our English [g]. English had no such sound at the time, but the employees in Caxton's shop were accustomed to combining the two letters, and continued to do so in setting up certain English words. In words like "ghost" and "ghastly" it has persisted, one of the many mute witnesses to orthographical conservatism.

HUMANISM AND CLASSICAL INFLUENCES

English vocabulary continued to be diversified as printing and increased communication with the continent diversified its cultural needs and interests. The Renaissance (a term we shall not attempt to define here) brought with it widened interest in pagan classical learning. It was not so much an innovation as an extension of the already lively medieval interest in the same heritage. But linguistically the debt was expressed in a new manner. Whereas Roman words had formerly been taken over in French form, with all the modifications due to centuries of use, now the Latin vocabulary was plundered direct, at least to a much greater extent than before. Writers who knew some classical philology did not hesitate to adopt into English a number of forms unmodified except for a slightly Anglicized ending. Words like "armipotent," "obtestate," "maturity," "splendidous," "matutine," and "adjuvate" had not been in French popular use for centuries before reaching English; they were lifted directly out of classical texts with little change. Browne's *Religio Medici* furnishes many examples. Some writers went to such lengths that their language was crusted over with Latinisms.

The tendency had begun in the fifteenth century and went to absurd lengths in the sixteenth. Ben Jonson satirized it in his *Poetaster*, a play in which a character guilty of pretentious verbal concoctions is made to vomit them forth in a basin, in sight of all. The victim, named Crispinus, is supposed to stand for the playwright Marston who actually committed verbal atrocities of the sort. When the pill is administered Crispinus cries out:

CRISPINUS.	Oh, I am sick—
HORACE.	A basin, a basin quickly, our physic works. Faint not, man.
CRISPINUS.	Oh—*retrograde—reciprocal—incubus.*
CAESAR.	What's that, Horace?
HORACE.	*Retrograde,* and *reciprocal, incubus* are come up.
GALLUS.	Thanks be to Jupiter.
CRISPINUS.	Oh—*glibbery—lubrical—defunct;* oh! . . .
TIBULLUS.	What's that?
HORACE.	Nothing, yet.
CRISPINUS.	*Magnificate.*
MAECENAS.	*Magnificate?* That came up somewhat hard.

Among other words thus "brought up" are "inflate," "turgidous," "oblatrant," "furibund," "fatuate," "prorumped," and "obstupefact." The ungentle satire concludes with admonitions by Virgil to the exhausted Crispinus: among other things

> You must not hunt for wild, outlandish terms,
> To stuff out a peculiar dialect;
> But let your *matter* run before your *words;*
> And if, at any time, you chance to meet
> Some Gallo-Belgic phrase, you shall not straight
> Rack your poor verse to give it entertainment,
> But let it pass. . . .

The critical attitude represented by Jonson was exaggerated in some cases into a fanatical purism. There were some who leaned over backwards in their attempts to avoid English neologisms out of Latin or Greek. If they went too far it was because the "ink-horn" terms of "aureate" or gilded English had become a kind of stylistic rash on the literary language. Still, many of the conscious creations of this period filled a real need, and were permanently adopted into standard speech.

Another consequence of the renewed, if not at all new, devotion to Latin was the freshened awareness of the component parts of Latin words in English. In the hands of gifted poets this resulted in a semantic rejuvenation of words. . . . Even spelling was affected by this awareness. Words pronounced still in a French manner were given a Latinized orthography which did not correspond to usage: thus "victuals" for ['vitlz] from French *vitaille.*

LATIN SYNTAX IN ENGLISH

Not only the English vocabulary was affected by the intensified devotion to Latin. Many attempts were made to have syntax and sentence structure conform too. There were attempts to implant long absolute constructions as an imitation of the Latin ablative absolute, and to make the sentence a tissue of intricately related clauses. The results were at times monstrous. This is one sentence committed by Sir Philip Sidney in the *Arcadia:*

> But then, Demagoras assuring himself, that now Parthenia was her own, she would never be his, and receiving as much by her own determinate answere, not more desiring his own happiness, envying Argalus, whom he saw with narrow eyes, even ready to enjoy the perfection of his desires;

strengthening his conceite with all the mischievous counsels which disdained love, and envious pride could give unto him; the wicked wretch (taking a time that Argalus was gone to his country, to fetch some of his principal friends to honor the marriage, which Parthenia had most joyfully consented unto), the wicked Demagoras (I say) desiring to speak with her, with unmerciful force (her weak arms in vain resisting), rubbed all over her face a most horrible poison: the effect whereof was such that never leper looked more ugly than she did: which done, having his men and horses ready, departed away in spite of her servants, as ready to revenge as they could be, in such an unexpected mischief.

You can amuse yourself by counting up the numbers of times you are delayed in this sentence by participial constructions in -ing ("assuring," "desiring," "strengthening") just when you are waiting breathlessly for the main verb. The end of the sentence (after the last colon) starts with "which done," something as close as we can get to a passive absolute construction on Latin lines; and it omits a necessary pronoun subject to "departed," since Latin verbs do not normally need to express "he" or "she" or "it" as subjects. Moreover, a number of words are used by Sidney in their original Latin sense rather than the familiar English one: "perfection" means "accomplishment, completion" as *perficere, perfectus* had meant "to complete."

LATIN STYLE IN ENGLISH

Even those authors who tried to eschew an excessive Latin vocabulary sometimes followed Latin sentence structure and idiom very closely. Reginald Pecock begins one of his sentences thus:

Even as grammar and divinity are 2 diverse faculties and cunnings, and therefore are unmeddled [distinct from each other], and each of them hath his proper to him bounds and marks, how far and no farther he shall stretch himself upon matters, truths, and conclusions. . . .

Every reader will notice how foreign-sounding is the expression "his proper-to-him bounds." Today we should consider it impossible to thrust a modifying phrase between "his" and the word it limits. But the phrase was so handled by Pecock, no doubt, because he was thinking of the Latin *fines sibi proprias*. The "how far" clause modifying "marks" has a Latin flavor also, recalling *quousque* clauses.

Notice too how Pecock creates new English idioms by translating literally certain Latin compounds. By "stretch himself upon," used in the non-physical sense, our author means "extend," from Latin *ex-tendere* "stretch out." In all self-conscious writers of the time there was a strong inclination to build elaborately balanced sentences, with clause counterweighing clause, in the manner of Roman rhetoricians. Pecock did this too. In formal exposition there was great use of constructions to contrast ideas "on the one hand"—"and on the other hand. . . ." In belles-lettres these elaborate balancings, both great and small, were often underscored by alliteration, making an intricate pattern of sound to correspond to the pattern of sense:

It happened this young imp to arrive at Naples, a place of more pleasure than profit, and yet of more profit than piety, the very walls and windows whereof showed it rather to be the tabernacle of Venus than the temple of Vesta.

Thus John Lyly starts his hero Euphues on the artfully worded chronicle of his adventures. The italicized letters show how alliteration calls attention to the ideas put in antithesis. And once again we find illustration of Latin sentence structure used contrary to English idiom. It is not natural for us to say "It happened this young imp to arrive"—with "imp" presumably in an oblique (inflected) case as subject of the infinitive; nor was it probably a natural way of talking in Lyly's day. It is, however, a literal rendering of the Latin accusative with infinitive—*contigit iuvenem pervenīre.*

One more instance of non-English structure has persisted in limited scope into our day. It is the placement of adjectives after nouns on the model of both French and Latin—more particularly the former. Phrases like "lords appellants," "blood royal," "siege apostolic" are paralleled in contemporary use by surviving legal inversions: "notary public," "estates general," "body politic." Only the stereotyped inversions live on in ordinary speech, but poets avail themselves of the ability to create new ones when they are trying for an exalted effect. Thus Hart Crane, writing "wings imperious" and "junctions elegiac" is carrying on a minor Latin-Romance heritage of word order. In a phrase like "court martial" the unaccustomed inversion adds to the sense of ominous strangeness. Poets use this atmosphere to heighten desired effects deliberately.

UNSTANDARDIZED ELIZABETHAN GRAMMAR

Attempts to stretch English on the Procrustes bed of Latin grammar delayed the achievement of a generally accepted style of vigor and simplicity. (Francis Bacon represented simplicity of a sort, but it was highly mannered.) Besides, English grammar was in a fairly unstable condition. There were conflicts of usage due to the heritage of archaisms from the Middle English period, and the competition of dialect forms from the regions outside of London, which persisted into the Elizabethan era.

The third singular present of the verb is a good example of this fluctuation. If Shakespeare, writing in London, had followed the London tradition in this he would have used the *-eth* ending always, and consistently set down "singeth, loveth, creepeth." But another ending, *-(e)s*, had been gaining popularity at the expense of *-eth*. Originally *-es* developed in the North country, but it spread southwards until in the sixteenth century it was becoming as acceptable as the native southern form. Shakespeare was able to use the two indifferently: "the bird of dawning *singeth* all night long" but "Tomorrow and tomorrow and tomorrow *Creeps* in this petty pace from day to day."

Other matters of grammar were less rigidly established in Shakespeare's day than ours. There were still strong traces of grammatical gender in the use of "he" and "she" for inanimate objects where we should say "it." Pecock, it will be noticed, spoke of each faculty having "his" proper bounds, instead of "its." Shakespeare wrote, "The corn hath rotted ere *his* youth attained a beard," and spoke of the soul as "she," as when Hamlet says to Horatio:

> Since my dear soul was mistress of *her* choice
> And could of men distinguish, *her* election
> Hath seal'd thee for *herself.* . . .

(Hamlet, III, ii)

The leveling of forms having proceeded with uneven tempo, there was considerable latitude of usage in inflected forms. Nominative and oblique cases of pronouns became somewhat confused; the newer usages have in many cases been approved by custom. The plays give us such forms as "My father hath no child *but I*," "When *him* we serve's away," "And damned be *him* that first cries 'Hold, enough!'" and "*Who* does he accuse?" There are also examples of compound subjects and even straight plural subjects with singular verbs, singular verbs with plural subjects, plural pronouns like "they" referring to singular indefinites like "everyone," double comparatives like "more braver"—in short, most of the hair-raising mistakes which cost students bad marks today. In formal prose there was more rigid usage than this, but the drama, closer to current speech, reflects a wider tolerance. In addition there were commonly accepted formulas which we now feel to be quaint rather than wrong. We are accustomed to think of abstract qualities such as "honor," "truth," and "courtesy" as single indivisible units: an Elizabethan, however, often made plural forms to indicate distributive use. His "Commend me to their loves," a very fair way of expressing things, simply appears odd to us, like the numerous words and phrases that have fallen into disuse: "I fain would know it," and so on.

THE AGE OF CLASSICISM AND FORMAL RULES

In the seventeenth and eighteenth centuries there was a strong reaction away from Elizabethan laxity and in favor of formal regularity of grammatical usage. Once more Latin exerted an influence, this time for the legislation of "rules": the intricate "do's" and "dont's" to be observed if, as simple people often express it, one is to "talk grammar." The drive toward regularity and conformity in speech may be considered part and parcel of the general cultural manifestation known as "classicism," another term which we shall not attempt to define here. At least there is a certain appropriateness in the fact that grammatical relations were treated with a free and easy tolerance during an age of exploration, conquest, and colonization when plain piracy and robbery of land were being idealized; and that decorum and strict congruence were demanded as matters of taste (not only in grammar) when conquest had been organized into accepted, consolidated, and hence respectable empire. The parallelism may be worked out by students of culture in the large.

What we do know is that grammarians of the classical period set down fixed rules for the behavior of pronouns and verbs with a definiteness new in the history of English. A "good" writer could no longer put down "Between who?" even for the stage, if he intended it to be spoken by a prince like Hamlet. Such a locution was limited to low-class characters on the rare occasions when they were permitted to appear (for relief) in polite literature. When in doubt, the legislators of grammar appealed to Latin for authority. Was there some doubt about expressions such as "It is I," "It is me" or even "It am I"? The Latin rule about nominative cases as predicates after a finite form of "to be" decided the matter, and "It is I" was decreed despite a strong native tendency to say "It's me." In this period too, the fluctuating uses of "shall" and "will" were subjected to rules with complicated minor ramifications. Significantly enough, it was not a native Englishman but a French grammarian (George Mason) writing in 1622 for foreigners, who first tried to lay down the rules. In France as well as in England the dominant cultural tendencies favored regularity, probably for the same reasons. A Frenchman learning English would have been shocked at anything so chaotic as the "shall-will" conjugation, and it was natural for him, at that particular period, to try to give it a formal (if intricate) pattern.

Such an attitude affected the conservation of grammatical distinctions, too. While it regularized it also arrested leveling. For instance, the subjunctive in forms like "If I *were* you" or "If it *be* possible" had been giving way to the indicative, but a clear distinction was now reaffirmed in the precepts of eighteenth-century grammar. That codification has remained in force until our own times. Teaching has as usual had a conservative effect. If it were not for the careful preservation of these dying forms in school books, I should have begun this sentence with the words "If it was not. . . ." As it is, we tend to limit the few surviving subjunctives to formal discourse, printed or spoken.

In France an Academy had been established in order to give final, authoritative judgment on disputed questions of grammar and usage. Some writers in England advocated the establishment of a similar British Academy to legislate for the English language. It was felt in some quarters that refinement and formality should be made official. However, the project was never realized. Historians of English explain the resistance to it by citing the rugged independence of English character. This is no doubt true as far as it goes, but it is not a basic explanation. The rugged independence paradoxically manifested even in an age of conformity must itself be explained: perhaps by reference to the political interlude of the English Commonwealth, which effectively and permanently checked absolutism in government in the seventeenth century. It could not be successfully tried for any length of time after 1649. Any tendency towards absolutism in language was to some extent, therefore, checked by the changed political atmosphere resulting from the Commonwealth. Voltaire found this atmosphere to be very libertarian as compared with the French. Despite great similarities between French and English taste, there were great differences. France, lacking such a check as the experience of a republican government in the seventeenth century, showed the exaggerated effects of absolutism in both linguistic and cultural matters, down to 1789. The readjustment was the more drastic because it was so long delayed. The French Revolution, too, had its effect on the style and vocabulary of accepted speech—not only in France, but in England to a certain extent. The vogue of "simple" speech and rural dialects (one of the aspects of "romanticism") is connected with shifts in taste which heralded and accompanied the French Revolution.

IMPERIAL EXPANSION

Meanwhile the English language had been spread far and wide over the globe, following the course of imperial expansion. India, at first settled and claimed by the French as rival colonists, fell under exclusively English sway in the eighteenth century. In North America also French claims were forced to yield throughout the entire territory represented by Canada and the Thirteen Colonies. French survived as a language only in the Quebec region of Canada. English discoveries and settlements led to the claim over Australia and New Zealand. In the nineteenth century the greater part of the continent of Africa fell under English sway, both direct and indirect. The Dutch Colony of South Africa was taken over after the Boer War; large territories like the English Sudan became British dependencies in the form of colonies of "backward" peoples; and some countries like Egypt were in practice directed by British commercial and administrative interests while maintaining formal independent statehood. Not everywhere in this far-flung territory has English been adopted as the prevalent speech. The dominions use it, of course; but in some of the colonies there has been little attempt to disseminate it beyond the circle of resident administrators, and in certain quarters (in India, for instance) it has met with conscious opposition.

The linguistic results of imperial expansion were manifold. We have already noticed the influx of foreign loan words into English from all quarters of the globe. In addition, each colonial dialect separated from the mother country has developed its own special idiosyncrasies, so that English-speaking visitors to England can be labeled, by their pronunciation, as emanating from Canada, Australia, South Africa, or "the States."

The settlement of Englishmen in India was particularly momentous for the history of linguistic science. When the dust of battle died down somewhat and peaceful contacts became possible, administrators with the gift of intellectual curiosity began to be impressed with the character of the various Indian languages belonging to the Indo-European family. When some of the bolder spirits extended their inquiry so far as to undertake the study of ancient Sanskrit, the classical literary language, they were further impressed by its affinities with the known classical languages of Europe. Sir William Jones was able to draw the proper conclusion as early as 1786: he wrote that Sanskrit, when compared to Greek and Latin,

> bears a stronger affinity, both in the roots of verbs and in the forms of grammar, than could possibly have been produced by accident; so strong, indeed, that no philologer could examine them all three without believing them to have sprung from some common source, which, perhaps, no longer exists: there is a similar reason, though not quite so forcible, for supposing that both the Gothick and the Celtick, though blended with a very different idiom, had the same origin with the Sanskrit.

Sir William was quite right. His studies may be said to have opened the door on comparative philology, encouraged the work of Rask, Bopp, Grimm, Leskien, and the other pioneers who established family relations among languages in the nineteenth century.

CONTEMPORARY ENGLISH

In the recent past our language has shown no new tendencies of major importance. A great vowel shift has occurred since 1500, producing the modern sounds we associate with the printed symbols. The host of borrowed words is increasing daily, from all parts of the world. A supplementary list is being created from Latin and Greek roots to serve the purposes of scientific research. There is a revolt—within limits—against the rigid rules of classical grammarians. "Good" writers are again permitting themselves forms like these:

> Those two, no matter who spoke, or whom was addressed, looked at each other. (Dickens, *Our Mutual Friend*.)
> It depends altogether on who I get. (May Sinclair, *Mr. Waddington of Wyck*.)
> If I were her. . . . (Middleton Murry, *The Things We Are*.)
> Kitty and me were to spend the day there . . . (by the bye, Mrs. Forster and me are such friends!) (Jane Austen, *Pride and Prejudice*.)
> Her towards whom it made/Soonest had to go. (Thomas Hardy, "In the Garden.")

Until very recently, histories of the English language usually ended with cheerful specu- lation on the outlook for it as a world language. There were several cogent arguments in favor of it. First, it was pointed out that it is a living language already spoken by a great number of persons all over the globe. Second, it has a comparatively simple grammar. It boasts of a rich and glorious literature which offers a strong inducement for any student to acquire mastery of it. It offers pleasure, in other words, as well as profit. And within the last few years a simplified form of it, Basic English, has been offered to beginners as a means of expediting communication through a vocabulary of 850 words, adequate for all practical purposes. By means of this list a student is able to express any ideas, and even achieve cer- tain aesthetic values of simple poignancy, within a very short time. He learns to say "go in" for "penetrate" and "flow out" for "exude," and is thus able to meet any situation with an adequate periphrasis. (Whether he can understand the fluent replies of a native ignorant of Basic is a different question!) These are surely inducements towards the adoption of English. Mr. Ogden claimed too much when he stated that absence of an international language like Basic English is "the chief obstacle to international understanding, and con- sequently the chief underlying cause of war." Unhappily, much more will be needed than a single speech to end wars. Nevertheless, Basic has many supports from the point of view of pure reason. At a later date they may be discussed for practical application.

But in the present shock and roar of clashing empires, it would appear foolhardy to make any arguments or prophecies. The advantages of English, aside from its archaic spelling, still stand. But it may be some considerable time, longer than many of us had hoped, before these matters are decided by such mild individuals as professional philologists. The appeal to reason, the argument from simple practicality for all mankind, may have to wait upon history for a long time. And by then it may be that another candidate among the languages of the world may have achieved the position of outstanding advantage. We can only wait and see.

EXERCISE 1: Periods of English

Identify the following English writings as Old English (OE), Middle English (ME), Early Modern English (EME), and Modern English (MnE) by comparing them to the samples in the text. In each case give some reason for your decision, for example, spelling, inflections, word origin, syntax, or content. The first has been completed for you.

Modern English 1. Now, you ask what rule you anchoresses should hold. You should always, with all your might and with all your strength, keep the inner and the outer rule well for its sake. _____ _No archaic spellings or inflections_ _____

_____ 2. Nu aski ʒe hwat riwle ʒe ancren schullen holden. ʒe schullen allesweis mid alle mihte & mid alle strencðe wel witen þe inre, & te vttre vor hire sake.

_____ 3. Ælfred kyning hate gretan Wærferð biscep his wordum luflice & freondlice; & ðe cyðan hate ðæt me com swiðe oft on gemynd, hwelce wiotan iu wæron giond Angelcynn, ægðer ge godcundra hada ge worul(d) cundra. _____

_____ 4. King Alfred greets Bishop Warferth with his loving and friendly words; please know that it has often come to my mind what wise men, either of the religious or secular orders, have formerly been throughout England. _____

_____ 5. Whan that Aprille with his shoures soote/ The droghte of March hath perced to the roote,/ And bathed every veyne in swich licour/ Of which vertu engendred is the flour. _____

_____ 6. Wæs sē grimma gǣst Grendel hāten,/ mǣre mearcstapa, sē þe mōras hēold,/ fen ond fæsten; fīfelcynnes eard/ wonsǣlī wer weardode hwīle.

_____ 7. I do beseech yee, if you beare me hard,/ Now whil'st your purpled hands do reeke and smoake,/ Fulfill your pleasure. _____

_____ 8. All this should not be taken as a sign that our lords are lazy or unenterprising. The point is that, in their view, effort is unrelated to money.

_____ 9. Of which spede and welfare, and al your oþer kyngly lustes and pleasaunces, we desire highly be the sayd berers of these lettres, or oþerwhom your soueraign highnesse shal like, fully to be lerned and enfourmed. _____

_____ 10. Our father which art in heauen, hallowed be thy name. Thy kingdome come. Thy will be done in earth, as it is in heauen. Give vs this day our dayly bread. _____

EXERCISE 2: Times of Borrowing

On the basis of the understanding you have gained about word borrowings of different periods, estimate the period of borrowing of the following words and check them with the table of the earliest literary occurrence of these words in Chapter 12. Place the letters ME (1100–1450), EME (1450–1650), or MnE (1650–present) beside each word.

1. _____ alert
2. _____ apartment
3. _____ army
4. _____ attorney
5. _____ bastard
6. _____ chambermaid
7. _____ cigarette
8. _____ countenance

9. _____ course
10. _____ credit
11. _____ damn
12. _____ foreign
13. _____ hotel
14. _____ humanly
15. _____ madame
16. _____ net

17. _____ notice
18. _____ party
19. _____ plaintiff
20. _____ policeman
21. _____ reason
22. _____ sure
23. _____ train
24. _____ war

EXERCISE 3: Etymological Composition of English

Many people are surprised to learn that English is a Germanic language. The Italic branch, particularly French and Latin, has had such a great influence on the vocabulary of English that the surprise is understandable. If we consider the etymological make-up of English on the basis of frequency of words used, we find that in the first decile (the 10 percent most frequently occurring words), 83 percent are of Anglo-Saxon (OE) origin.[2] Look at the graph and answer the questions that follow.

1. What is the most striking difference between the first and the second deciles?

_____

2. In the first decile, the greatest percentage of words are of Anglo-Saxon origin. Which language leads in the other deciles? _____

3. Which language contributes to English fairly equally in all deciles? _____

4. How would you explain the low frequency of Latin in the first decile, but its increase in later deciles? _____

_____

_____

[2] A. Hood Roberts, *A Statistical Linguistic Analysis of American English* (The Hague: Mouton & Co., 1965), p. 36.

Etymological composition of English by relative frequency and by decile[3]

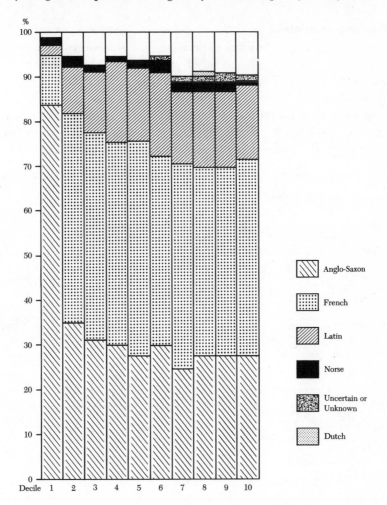

5. Estimate the overall percentage of words from Anglo-Saxon, French, Latin, and Norse. (The first decile is the most crucial in determining such an answer; each following decile plays an increasingly smaller role.) Anglo-Saxon _____ percent, French _____ percent, Latin _____ percent, Norse _____ percent. After estimating, check your figures below.[4]

[3] *Ibid.*, p. 37.

[4] Roberts (*ibid.*, p. 38) gives the following figures: Anglo-Saxon 78.1 percent, French 15.2 percent, Latin 3.1 percent, Norse 2.4 percent, others 1.2 percent. Another analysis, quoted by Robertson and Cassidy in *The Development of Modern English* (Englewood Cliffs, N.J.: Prentice-Hall, 1954), p. 155, gives a strikingly different proportion: Anglo-Saxon 61.7 percent, French 30.9 percent, Latin 2.9 percent, Norse 1.7 percent, others 2.9 percent.

EXERCISE 4: Resistance

Expansion and Restriction

Expansion, the widening of the scope of meaning, is also called *generalization. Restriction,* a narrowing of scope of meaning, is also called *specialization.* The word **dog** (Middle English **dogge**) once referred only to dogs of native breed, whereas **hound** (Old English **hund,** akin to German **Hund**) was the general term for all dogs. The word **dog** has generalized while **hound** has specialized. With the aid of your desk dictionary, determine which of the two processes each of the following words has undergone. Place an *E* or an *R* before each of the words to denote the process. In the space on the right, specify the earlier meaning.

Earlier Meaning

1. __R__ meat   *all foods* _____

2. _____ layman _____

3. _____ deer _____

4. _____ assassin _____

5. _____ cattle _____

6. _____ diaper _____

7. _____ zest _____

8. _____ fee _____

9. _____ wealth _____

10. _____ meander _____

11. _____ doctor _____

12. _____ affection _____

13. _____ bonfire _____

14. _____ mansion _____

15. _____ thing _____

16. _____ fable _____

A western city has special lanes along the sides of its streets marked "Bicycles Only." A young man on a two-wheeled motorcycle attempts to use them and receives a traffic citation. A middle-aged woman on a tricycle rides in the middle of the street in order to avoid the lanes and is ticketed for obstructing traffic. What exactly is the problem?

_____

_____

Conflict of Homonyms[5]

1. When two semantically related words are so similar phonetically that they may be confused, one or both of the words may be dropped in favor of a competing term. Consider the Middle English words for *ear* and *kidney: ere* and *nere.* In Modern Scottish dialect of English they are *lug* and *neer* respectively. Compare the modern English and Scottish dialects:

Middle English	ere	nere
Scottish dialect	*lug*	neer
Standard English	ear	*kidney*

What phonetic fact might have served to intensify the need for a change? (Consider *a napron-an apron,* discussed earlier.) _____

_____

_____

2. A case in which both conflicting terms were dropped is that of the Old English *lǣn* 'a loan' and *lēan* 'reward'. As the two words came to be pronounced alike in the Middle English period, both were dropped; the first was replaced by the Old Norse cognate *lān,* which developed into Modern English *loan,* and the second was replaced by the words *reward* or *recompense.* What factor besides homonymy probably enhanced this change? (Consider the meanings of the words.) _____

_____

Conflict of Synonyms

The present meaning of the first word in each set below was shared by other members of the group at one time. But when there is a distinction in form, language makes use of it with a distinction in meaning. Specify what has happened to the meaning of each word.

1. animal, deer (German *Tier*), beast _____

_____

2. chair, stool (German *Stuhl*) _____

_____

3. girl, maid _____

_____

4. bird, fowl (German *Vogel*) _____

_____

[5] All examples in this section are from Edna Rees Williams, *The Conflict of Homonyms in English* (New Haven, Conn.: Yale University Press, 1944), pp. 47–55, 72.

5. boy, knave _____

_____

EXERCISE 5: Acceptance

Bifurcation

A. Group I contains a list of words that are related to the words in II. They not only look alike but also are of the same origin. Place each word in I beside the etymologically related word in II, and in the space on the right give their common form of origin.

    I. glamour   leal   real
       hospitality   legal   royal
       host   major shatter
       hostel   pauper skirt
       hotel   poison

    II. 1. poor _____ *pauper, both from Latin* **pauper** _____

         2. shirt _____

         3. scatter _____

         4. regal _____

         5. mayor _____

         6. guest _____

         7. grammar _____

         8. loyal _____

         9. potion _____

        10. hospital _____

B. The adjectives *swollen* and *swelled* are variations of the past participle of the verb *to swell*, but they have developed independent meanings.

swollen–swelled _A swollen head is an injured head. A swelled head refers to one who overestimates his own worth._

Other pairs are **struck–stricken, broke–broken.**

Give another pair of adjectives that displays the same process. Describe the difference in meaning. _____

_____

EXERCISE 6: Cumulative Change

A Sixteenth-Century Text

Read the following passage from *The French Schoolemaister*, written in the sixteenth century by Claudius Desainliens (alias Claude Hollyband), and answer the questions that follow. The conversation is between Fraunces (Francis), a schoolboy, and Margerite (Margaret), the maid, and later between Fraunces and his father. You should be able to read this Early Modern English text without much difficulty. A brief lexicon is provided at the end of the selection.

Margaret: Ho Fraunces rise, and get you to schoole: you shalbe beaten, for it is past seven: make yourself readie quickly, say your prayers, then you shall have your breakfast.

[*F.*] Margerite, geeue mee my hosen: dispatche I pray you: where is my doublet? bryng my garters, and my shooes: geeue mee that shooyng horne.

[*M.*] Take first a cleane shirte, for yours is fowle.

[*F.*] Make hast then, for I doo tarie too long.

[*M.*] It is moyst yet, tary a little that I may drie it by the fier.

[*F.*] I cannot tarye so longe: go your way, I will none of it.

[*M.*] Your mother will chide mee if you go to schoole without your cleane shirt.

[*F.*] I had rather thou shouldst be shent, than I should be either chid or beaten: Where haue you layde my girdle and my inckhorne? Where is my gyrkin of Spanish leather? Where be my sockes of linnen, of wollen, of clothe. Where is my cap, my hat, my coate, my cloake, my kaape, my gowne, my gloves, my mythayns, my pumpes, my mayles, my slippers, my handkarchief, my poyntes, my sachell, my penknife, and my bookes. Where is all my geare? I haue nothyng ready: I will tell my father: I will cause you to be beaten: Peter, bring me some water to wash my hands and my face. I will have no river water, for it is troubled: geue me well, or Fountayne water: take the ewre, and powre uppon my handes: powre high.

[*M.*] Can you not wash in the baason? Shall you haue alwayes a seruaunt at your tayle? You are to wanton.

[*F.*] Wilt thou that I wash my mouthe and my face where I haue washed my handes, as they doo in many houses in England? Geue mee a towell: mayden. Now geue me my breakefast, for I am readie: make haste.

[*M.*] Haue you saluted your Father and your Mother? Have you forgotten that?

[*F.*] Where is he?

[*M.*] He is in the shoppe.

[*F.*] God geeue you good morow my father, and all your companie: father geeue mee your blessyng if it please you.

[*Father.*] Are you up? is it time to rise at eight of the clock? You shall be whipt: go, and kneele downe, and say your prayers: God blesse thee. . . . Now goe, and haue mee

recommended vnto your maister and maistress, and tell them that I pray them to come tomorow to dinner with mee: that will keepe you from beating. . . . learne well, to the end that you may render vnto mee your lesson when you are come againe from schoole.
[F.] Well father.[6]

Lexicon

hosen	close-fitting leg covering or tights fastened to the doublet
doublet	man's close-fitting garment, with or without sleeves, covering the body from the neck to the waist or a little below
tary	to linger
shent	harmed or disgraced
girdle	belt or sash
pumpes	low-heeled, slipperlike shoes
mayles	bag
inckhorne	ink container
gyrkin	jerkin, a close-fitting waistcoat
kaape	cape
poyntes	strings or ribbons fastening the hosen to the doublet
geare	apparel
ewre	ewer, wide-mouthed pitcher or jar
baason	basin

A. List five words from the passage that are spelled differently today. _____

_____

B. At first reading you might believe Fraunces is a woman for asking for **hosen, garters, girdle,** and **gowne.** List three other words that have undergone change in usage. Describe the difference in each case.

   1. _____

   2. _____

   3. _____

C. Find three archaic sentences or phrases (for example, "Can you not wash in the baason?").

   1. _____

   2. _____

   3. _____

D. Write in contemporary English the passage in the last paragraph that starts with "Now goe . . . ," and continue to the end of the paragraph.

[6] A. W. Pollard, "Claudius Hollyband and his *French Schoolmaster* and *French Littleton*," *Bibliographical Society Transactions* XIII (1915), pp. 226–28.

_____

_____

_____

_____

_____

_____

_____

_____

_____

_____

_____

EXERCISE 7: The Comparative Method

Related Languages

By comparing the sounds, words, and syntax of different languages or dialects, we arrive at clues to their relationship to each other; in addition, we learn something about the earlier forms of the languages. A form that is shared by most of the languages under consideration, particularly those that are geographically separated, is very likely an early form. An innovative, or later, form is regularly dissimilar to others. Consider the following words in three geographically and temporally separated Germanic languages, and answer the questions that follow.

	Old English	*Gothic*	*Old High German*
'pound'	pund	pund	pfund
'ten'	tīen	taihun	zehan
'known'	cūþ	kunþs	chund

$$c = [k], \quad z = [ts], \quad ch = [kx] \text{ or } [x]$$

A. What are the words with the innovative forms? (Consider the pronunciation of the initial consonant in each case.) _____, _____, and _____.

They are all in the _____ language.

B. What are the earlier, or "proto," forms of the initial consonants in this limited amount of data? _____, _____, and _____.

Innovations in Dialects

A list of words from four old Germanic dialects is given below. Assume that the innovation is a change from stops to fricatives, and arrange these in the order of increasing change from the oldest form. (The spelling **ch** represents a voiceless dorsovelar fricative [x].)[7]

(English)	1	2	3	4
'I'	ich	ich	ich	ik
'make'	machen	machen	machen	maken
'village'	dorf	dorp	dorf	dorp
'that'	das	dat	das	dat
'apple'	appel	appel	apfel	appel
'pound'	pund	(p)fund	pfund	pund

Not affected by the innovation ___4___, _____, _____, _____ Most affected by the innovation

EXERCISE 8: Internal Reconstruction

"A linguistic state is to a large degree a partial summary of the history of the language."[8]

One of the changes that took place from the Primitive Germanic period to Old English was the loss of the nasal and lengthening of the vowel in the following combination:

short vowel	+	nasal	+	voiceless spirant
[ɪ ʊ a ɛ]		[m n]		[s f], þ (= [θ]), h (= [x] and written **gh** in modern forms)

It partially accounts for the existence of the word **tooth,** which is from the same etymological source as **dental.**

A. For the words that follow, guess the modern English forms. Gothic [ū] has become Modern English [aw], Gothic [ī] has become Modern English [ay], and Old High German [ā] has become Modern English [u].

1. Gothic **Munþs** = Modern English _____

2. Gothic **fimf** = Modern English _____

3. Old High German **Gans** = Modern English _____

B. The same change can be found in the pairs **think–thought, bring–brought.** Why has **n** not been lost in the past form of the following pairs?

drink–drank	cling–clang	sing–sang	grind–ground
find–found	bind–bound	sink–sank	sting–stung

---

[7] We are indebted to Professor Stephen Schwartz of the University of California at Los Angeles for these examples.

[8] Raimo Anttila, *An Introduction to Historical and Comparative Linguistics* (New York: Macmillan, 1972), p. 84.

_____

_____

_____

EXERCISE 9: Indo-European Languages

The names of the languages listed below are found in your desk dictionary (*Standard College Dictionary, Webster's Seventh New Collegiate Dictionary*, and others). Not all these languages are of Indo-European origin, nor are they all spoken today. Consult your dictionary and give the subfamily of those languages that are of Indo-European origin. Place an X before the names of languages no longer spoken. The ten commonly recognized subfamilies of Indo-European are Albanian; Armenian; Balto-Slavic; Celtic; Germanic; Hellenic, or Greek; Hittite, or Anatolian; Indo-Iranian; Italic, or Romance; and Tocharian.

____ Albanian	*Albanian*		____ Hungarian	_____
_X_ Aramaic	_____		____ Italian	_____
____ Armenian	_____		____ Latin	_____
____ Basque	_____		____ Norwegian	_____
____ Bengali	_____		____ Pahlavi, or Pahlevi	_____
____ Bulgarian	_____		____ Persian	_____
____ Czech	_____		____ Polish	_____
____ Dutch	_____		____ Portuguese	_____
____ English	_____		____ Prussian	_____
____ Estonian	_____		____ Russian	_____
____ Finnish	_____		____ Sanskrit	_____
____ Flemish	_____		____ Slovak	_____
____ French	_____		____ Spanish	_____
____ Gothic	_____		____ Tocharian	_____
____ Greek	_____		____ Turkish	_____
____ Hindi	_____		____ Urdu	_____
____ Hindustani	_____		____ Walloon	_____
____ Hittite	_____		____ Welsh	_____
____ Hottentot	_____			

Write the names of the Indo-European languages in the preceding exercise under the proper subfamilies below. (You might check your answers against the chart found with the listing of Indo-European languages in *Webster's Seventh New Collegiate Dictionary*.)

Albanian	Armenian	Balto-Slavic	Celtic	Germanic
___	___	___	___	___
___	___	___	___	___
___	___	___	___	___
___	___	___	___	___
___	___	___	___	___

Greek	Hittite	Indo-Iranian	Italic	Tocharian
___	___	___	___	___
___	___	___	___	___
___	___	___	___	___
___	___	___	___	___
___	___	___	___	___

EXERCISE 10: Language Adjusts

Compensatory Change

If the Old English sentences given below were to be translated into Modern English following the Old English word order, most would be ungrammatical, and one would be misleading. If we were to disregard the endings and translate *glædne giefend lufað God* as 'A cheerful giver loves God,' the sense would be changed. Endings such as *-ne* of *glædne*, the *-e* of *Gode*, the *-es* of *Godes*, and the lack of ending in *God*, as well as the variations of the Modern English 'the' (*sē* and *þām*), signaled the relation of words to each other in Old English. Such relationships in Modern English are usually shown by position; that is, the common sentence pattern is subject, verb, object, as, for example, *God loves a cheerful giver.* Relationships among words are also shown by the use of prepositions, as in *He gave me it* vs. *He gave it to me.* Some personal pronouns in English (*he, his, him*) preserve the earlier means of showing relation by inflection. The possessive *s* inflection still remains in nouns (*God's*). Note also that sentence 8 has three negatives; having that many only serves to intensify the negation. Study the structures of the following ten sentences with the aid of the glosses below each word.

Old English	Modern English
	God loves a cheerful giver.

1. *glædne giefend lufað God.*
cheerful giver   loves God
(object)   (subject)

2. *ealle his þing gegaderude.*
all his things gathered
sē gingra sunu.
the younger son

3. *hē him   lēof wæs.*
he to them dear was

4. *ich bēo   mid ēow ealle*
I (shall) be with you all
dagas oþ worulde   geendunge.
days up to of the world end

5. *mē   þæt riht ne þinceð.*
to me that right not seems

6. *Godes yrre bær.*
God's anger he bore

7. *hwī wepest þū Paul?*
why weep you Paul

8. *ne ēow nan man ne nemne*
nor you no one not (shall) call
lāreowas.
masters

9. *hē Gode þancode.*
he to God thanked

10. *ic forgiefe þām þēowum.*
I forgive to the servants

A. In the space provided above translate each Old English sentence into Modern English.
B. Is the word order of any of the Old English sentences acceptable in Modern English?

    Specify. _____

C. If the sentences *I saw the boy* and *George tore the boy's book* are combined into *I saw the boy whose book George tore,* the subject-verb-object order of the second sentence is reflected in the combined sentence as object-subject-verb. Give two other examples of such inverted order. _____

_____

_____

D. Some evidence that Modern English speakers think of the first position as the subject position and the third position as the object position can be seen in the following sentences: *He was given a gift* and *That is him.*[9] The first is the passive of *Somebody gave him a gift,* which might be rephrased as *A gift was given (to) him,* but not as *°Him was given a gift.*[10] The sentence *That is him,* although common, is not accepted by the purist, who would demand *That is he* or the less jarring *He is the one.* Note that *He* is in the first position and *him* in the third position. How would you explain the anomalous *Me and him went* and *between you and I?* Does it mean that these speakers do not have the first-position-as-subject and third-position-as-object in their grammar?

_____

_____

_____

Compensatory Change in Spelling

When the accent sign ^ occurs over a French vowel, it often signifies the loss of a following *s* from an older form. Give the English cognate that has preserved the following *s.*

1. fête   *fest, feast* _____   5. bête _____

2. île (in spelling) _____   6. hôtel _____

3. forêt _____   7. hôte _____

4. conquête _____   8. côte _____

[9] For a more detailed explanation, see S. Robertson and F. G. Cassidy, *The Development of Modern English* (Englewood Cliffs, N.J.: Prentice-Hall, 1954), pp. 285–91.

[10] In syntax the asterisk marks utterances regarded as ungrammatical.

WRITING AND READING 14

EXERCISE 1: Pictograms

Communication through pictures was a preliminary stage in the evolution of the symbolic representation of language. These pictures, called pictograms, convey only concepts, not speech. Some pictograms are merely records of a name or event.

The example given below was obtained in 1888 from the Passamaquoddy Indians in Maine. They kept records of their trade with the white man; this is a record of one such transaction.[1] Fill in the parentheses in the interpretation with the proper letters from the picture.

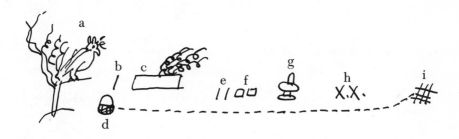

Interpretation: A woman called "Owl" ( ) bought one ( ) plug of smoking tobacco ( ), two ( ) quarts ( ) of kerosene for her lantern ( ), and all this is worth twenty cents ( ). To barter for this, she brings in a basket ( ) and the basket cancels the debt ( ).

EXERCISE 2: Word Symbols

Pictograms are not *writing* symbols, since they do not symbolize speech. They symbolize the information directly; speech never enters the picture. One method of writing is to use different symbols for each word. Pictograms bypass speech; word symbols make it possible for the exact wording of a message to be preserved. In modern English **2**, *&*, and *$* are examples of word symbols.

[1] Adapted from Garrick Mallery, *Picture Writing of the American Indians,* Tenth Annual Report of the Bureau of Ethnology, 1888–89 (Washington, D.C.: Government Printing Office, 1893), pp. 259–61.

A. Give a conventional word symbol for each of the following.

half _____   percent _____   equals _____

at . . . a piece _____   divided by _____   male _____

female _____   star _____   cent _____

B. Some of the word symbols in modern English writing can stand for syllables within words as well as for words. For example, the terms *quarto, octavo,* and *duodecimo* (also called *twelvemo*) may be abbreviated *4to, 8vo,* and *12mo.* Most word symbols have traditionally not been arbitrary in origin: the Roman numeral *III* is not arbitrary because the symbol itself carries a hint of its meaning.

C. Devise a set of symbols to represent the words used in the following sentences and try to duplicate the sentences with them. You may find it convenient to picture some words with two symbols.

1. A horse walks to a tree.

2. Two horses run through a forest.

3. A big horse gallops to the house in the forest.

4. A little red horse ran to the big house.

D. What would a foreigner be able to learn about the structure of English from messages such as this if it were all the information available?

About morphology? _____

_____

Phonology? _____

_____

English syntax? _____

_____

EXERCISE 3: Rebus Writing

Most of the words in the previous exercise can be symbolized by drawings, but the system is cumbersome and inadequate. What could be done with such relatively abstract words as *good, hot,* or ***would?*** How could you handle the old political slogan "Tippecanoe and Tyler too"? A picture of a canoe tipping over might communicate the first word. Or the reader might puzzle through pictures of a tepee and a canoe, a plus sign, a picture of a tie, and a **2,** in that order. This leaves out the last syllable of ***Tyler,*** but a person with some knowledge of American history would most likely be able to read it anyway. This method of symbolizing is called *rebus writing:* word symbols are used to symbolize, not a particular word, combining sound and meaning, but only the *sounds* of the word. The sounds of the word that is meant are the sounds of the word actually signified, or nearly so. At this point in the evolution of writing, phonetization begins; a sign stands for a complex of sounds. The ability to symbolize the sounds of words as well as their meanings makes writing easier; fewer symbols are needed, and more words can be successfully symbolized. Try to invent rebus symbols or word symbols for the following words and phrases.

would be   loggerhead

mumble   fancy

EXERCISE 4: A Combination of Rebus and Word-Symbol Writing

Men of past ages devised several methods of getting around the cumbrous word-symbol writing. You have seen one, the rebus. Another system, presented in this exercise, is used in Chinese writing.

How would you write *binge?* Word symbols could get the idea across, but not, perhaps, the exact word. The following process, however, might succeed in catching the exact word: draw two symbols, one of a door hinge, and another of a bottle of liquor. If the reader knows by convention that the word he is trying to guess sounds like a word symbolized by the first symbol and has to do with the general semantic area of the second symbol, then he might be successful.

The Chinese use this method by combining two of their symbols into one. The symbol 工 is pronounced *kung*[1] and means 'work'. (The number refers to the pitch phoneme of the word.) The Chinese symbol 水 means 'water'. The symbol 汞 asks the reader to determine a word that sounds like *kung*[1] and in some way has to do with water or has some quality of water. The desired word is *hung*[3] 'quicksilver,' or 'mercury,' which is a liquid, like water.[2]

For the following words, devise symbols based on the method explained above. First give the symbol for the word that the desired word sounds like and then the symbol for the general area of meaning.

cook   _____   _____

rook (to gyp)   _____   _____

look   _____   _____

dead   _____   _____

red   _____   _____

lead (metal)   _____   _____

[2]Holger Pederson, *The Discovery of Language* (Bloomington, Ind.: Indiana University Press, 1959), p. 144.

EXERCISE 5: The Cherokee Syllabary

Writing systems using word symbols usually had symbols for syllables as well. The last two exercises showed how making the word symbols stand for sounds extended their usefulness. This phonetizing often led to a syllabary, a list of symbols for the syllables of a language. In the preceding exercises, you probably have already devised over twenty symbols used to stand for the sounds of words or syllables. In 1821 the Cherokee Indian Sequoya devised a syllabary of his language with eighty-five signs. His symbols are arbitrary, while most of yours are not. He attempted completeness, while your list covers only a few syllables, and you would find it difficult to complete the job for English.

Transliterate the following words written in the Cherokee syllabary.[3] The syllabary is on page 487 in *Aspects of Language*.

Cherokee	Transliteration	Translation
ᏣᏯᏥ	————————	Cherokee
ᏍᏆᏖ	————————	Sequoya
ᏍᎯᏃᏗ	————————	October, harvest month
ᏆᏏᏗᏛ	————————	instantly
ᏓᏬᏋ	————————	war club

Now go through the syllabary and its transliteration in *Aspects of Language*, and find the list of symbols Sequoya would have had to use if he had devised one symbol for each phoneme. (You must assume that the transliteration is correct.) Write the list of phonemes below.

———— ———— ———— ————

———— ———— ———— ————

———— ———— ———— ————

———— ———— ———— ————

———— ———— ————

---

[3]The Cherokee words and translations are from John Algeo and Thomas Pyles, *Problems in the Origin and Development of the English Language* (New York: Harcourt Brace Jovanovich, 1966), p. 32.

EXERCISE 6: The Hebrew Writing System

English words have a variety of morpheme endings for inflections and derivations, such as the /z/ of /dɔgz/ or the /šən/ of /ǽkšən/. Words in Semitic languages are for the most part forms with three consonants; vowels come before and after the consonants, with the function that affixes have in English. For example, Arabic **KTB** is a root whose basic meaning refers to writing. **KaTaBa** means 'he wrote,' **aKTuBu** 'I write,' **yuKTaBu** 'it is written,' **KiTāB** 'book,' **KuTuB** 'books,' **KāTiB** 'writer'. The classical writing system reflected the root importance of the consonants; the reader was expected to figure out the vowels from the context. We do much the same thing when we guess at poor handwriting.

A. The consonants of the Hebrew writing system are given below. Find out their values by studying the list of Hebrew words with their transliterations. The Hebrew writing is read from right to left. Ignore the vowels of the transliterations.

צ	___	ם	___	ח	___	א	___
ץ	___	נ	___	ט	___	ב	___
ק	___	ן	___	י	___	ב	___
ר	___	ס	___	פ	___	ג	___
שׁ	___	ע	___	כ	___	ד	___
שׂ	___	פ	___	ך	___	ה	___
ת	___	פ	___	ל	___	ו	___
ת	___	ף	___	מ	___	ז	___

'father'	['av]	אב
'clothing'	[bégɛd]	בגד
'Eve'	[xáva][4]	חוה
'purity'	[tóhar]	טהר
'armor'	[záyin]	זין
'all of them'	[kulám]	כלם
'go'	[lɛx]	לך
'he entered'	[nɪxnás]	נכנס
'experienced'	[mnusá][4]	מנסה
'he, it flew'	['af]	עף
'he, it exploded'	[patsáts]	פצץ
'beauty'	[šefɛr]	שפר
'sack'	[sak]	שק
'sub-'	[tat]	תת

[4] The final -[h] in the Hebrew in these two words is a survival of a *mater lectionis,* a consonant symbol used to indicate a vowel.

How many symbols are there for [v]? ____ For [t]? ____ For [k]? ____ For [s]? ____
Some Hebrew letters are positional variants of the same sound. Give the positional

variations of [x] ____ ____, [m] ____ ____, [n] ____ ____, [f] ____

____, [ts] ____ ____. The symbol [x] indicates an unvoiced velar fricative.

B. There is a limit to guessing, and at times it was desirable to be able to indicate a vowel
exactly. From about the ninth century B.C., three of the Hebrew letters were sometimes
used as vowels. The three letters ה,ו, and י kept their customary consonant values when
they were not being used as vowels.

[bíra]	ב י ר ה	'beer'
[ben]	ב י ן	'between'
[bɔr]	ב ו ר	'well'
[bul]	ב ו ל	'stamp'
[buba]	ב ו ב ה	'doll'

What vowels can each of these three letters represent? _____

C. In the eighth century A.D., other marks, placed above and below the consonant letters
and called massoretic points, indicated the vowels exactly. The pronunciations below
are modern Israeli pronunciations.

'unleavened bread'	מ צָ ה	[matsá]
'universe'	תֵ בֶ ל	[tévɛl]
'sprig'	נֵ צֶ ר	[nétsɛr]
'nephew'	אַ חְ יָ ן	['axyán]
'quarrel'	רִ י ב	[riv]

Answer either of these questions: Why were the massoretic points not placed between
the consonants? Why were the vowel signs not developed as early as the consonant signs?

_____

_____

_____

D. Some writers feel that the history of writing shows a movement from syllabic to alphabet
writing. How far had the form of Hebrew writing of the ninth century B.C. moved?

_____

_____

_____

EXERCISE 7: English Sounds and Spellings

The Consistency of English Spelling

English spelling appears chaotic and orderly by turns. For example, the phoneme /ɪ/ is spelled in a variety of ways: it occurs in the words *hit, sieve, England, women, busy, myth,* and *build.*[5] The spellings are *i, ie, e, o, u, y,* and *ui.* From the following list of words, compile the spellings of the vowels and consonants that follow the list.

hut	put	does	obey	easily	guard	ghost
veil	weight	along	dungeon	rate	wolf	rough
blood	porpoise	pain	villain	steak	give	none
would	gauge	play	book	physics	thin	trait

/ə/ _____

/ʌ/ _____

/ʊ/ _____

/e/ _____

/g/ _____

/f/ _____

/z/ _____

/s/ _____

Which are more consistent, vowels or consonants? _____

English Spelling Reform

Various systems of reformed spelling have been devised as solutions to the irregularities of English spelling. The British Simplified Spelling Society published its system in 1940, and Axel Wijk published his system in 1959. Below you will find a passage spelled according to each system. The British Society's is on the left, Wijk's is on the right.[6]

We instinktivly shrink from eny chaenj in whot iz familyar; and whot kan be mor familyar dhan dhe form ov wurdz dhat we have seen and riten mor tiemz dhan we kan posibly estimaet? We taek up a book printed in Amerika, and *honor* and *center* jar upon us every tiem we kum akros dhem; nae, eeven to see *forever* in plaes of *for ever*

We instinctivly shrink from eny chainge in whot iz familiar; and whot can be more familiar than the form ov wurds that we hav seen and written more times than we can posibly estimate? We take up a book printed in America, and *honor* and *center* jar upon us every time we cum across them; nay, even to see *forever* in place ov *for ever*

[5] Robert A. Hall, Jr., *Sound and Spelling in English* (New York: Chilton Books, 1961), p. 30.

[6] Axel Wijk, *Regularized English* (Stockholm: Almquist & Wiksell, 1959), pp. 324–25. Copyright Almquist & Wiksell, 1959. Reprinted with permission.

atrakts our atenshon in an unplezant wae. But dheez ar iesolaeted kaesez; think ov dhe meny wurdz dhat wood hav to be chaenjd if eny real impruuvment wer to rezult. . . . But dhaer iz soe much misapprehenshon on dhis point, and such straenj statements ar maed, dhat it bekumz necessary to deel widh dhis objekshon in sum deetael.

attracts our attention in an unplezant way. But theze ar isolated cases; think ov the meny wurds that wood hav to be chainged if eny real improovement wer to rezult. . . . But there iz so much misapprehension on this point, and such strainge statements ar made, that it becums necessary to deal widh this objection in sum detail.

A. How do these two systems treat the plural morpheme? In the spaces below, write in all the plural nouns of the passage as spelled by each system.

British Society	Wijk
wurdz	wurds
_____	_____
_____	_____
_____	_____

What is the principle that each system follows here?

British _____

Wijk _____

B. How does each system treat the shwa (/ə/)? To find out, list the first seven words from each passage that contain a shwa. Then try to account for the spellings of shwa. (There is room for disagreement over whether some of the words are pronounced with shwa.)

British Society	Wijk
_____	_____
_____	_____
_____	_____
_____	_____
_____	_____
_____	_____
_____	_____

Can you find any pattern in either of these systems?

C. As you have discovered, neither system uses the shwa itself, partly because the public might be alienated from spelling reform by a new symbol. Also, the use of the shwa obscures the relationships between some words. How many letters or letter groups do the two words in the box below have in common? (Remember that **ti** often stands for /š/.) _____ On the lines at the right, write the phonemic transcriptions for these words. How many phonemes do they have in common, position by position? _____ The ordinary spellings give more clues to their relationship than do the phonemic transcriptions.

a	b	o	l	i	sh			
a	b	o	l	i	ti	o	n	

_____

_____

Write out the phonemic transcriptions for the following pairs of words, and notice how the ordinary spelling gives clues to their relationships.

human _____   minister _____

humanity _____   ministerial _____

civil _____   ether _____

civility _____   ethereal _____

tutor _____   moral _____

tutorial _____   morality _____

injure _____   medicine _____

injurious _____   medicinal _____

Write the phonemic transcriptions of your pronunciation of these artificial words.

kembress (as a noun) _____

kembressional _____

condolve (verb) _____

condolution _____

hycrate (verb) _____

hycratory _____

The rules you followed in changing the pronunciation of the artificial words and the real words above are quite firmly in your mind, although they are complicated. Since we already know how to change /əbalɨš/ (in a midwestern pronunciation) to /æbəlɪšən/, we don't need the shwa or other new symbols to tell us how.

SCHOOLS AND THEORIES 15

EXERCISE 1: Identification of Schools of Grammar

The following passages, particularly the sections italicized for additional emphasis, are representative of schools and theories of linguistics treated by Bolinger in *Aspects of Language*. The nine approaches discussed are *traditional grammar, the Prague School, American structuralism, tagmemics, the Firthians, stratificational grammar, transformational-generative grammar, generative semantics,* and *case grammar*. Historical linguistics, discussed in Chapter 13, is also included here, since it represents a unique point of view. Each of the passages below has been selected to characterize the views of one particular school. In some cases the views of two schools seem very much alike; for example, the discussion of universals by traditional grammar and by transformational, or formal, linguistics. Many of the notions of the later schools had their roots in earlier centuries. One of the major axioms of descriptive linguistics, proposed in the early twentieth century—to describe language as it is rather than as it ought to be—is found in the works of a grammarian of the early nineteenth century. He writes:

> Language is conventional, and not only invented, but, in its progressive advancement, *varied* for purposes of practical convenience. Hence it assumes any and every form which those who make use of it choose to give it. We are, therefore, as *rational* and *practical* grammarians compelled to submit to the necessity of the case; to take the language as it *is*, and not as it *should be*, and bow to custom.[1]

By "custom," however, he means the custom of the best speakers and writers (see passage 1). The notion of universals, found in the first sentences of passage 1, is accepted by the transformational grammarians. Write the name of the school most closely related to each passage below. (Italics have been added; explanatory remarks are in brackets.)

---

[1] Samuel Kirkham, *English Grammar* (Rochester, N.Y.: William Alling, 1835), p. 18.

1. _____traditional grammar_____ "Grammar may be divided into two species, universal and particular. UNIVERSAL GRAMMAR explains the principles which are common to all languages. PARTICULAR GRAMMAR applies those general principles to a particular language, modifying them according to its genius, *and the established practice of the best speakers and writers by whom it is used.*"[2]

2. _____ There is no scientific use in mere description of a language; *history is the only object of linguistics.*[3]

3. _____ "Sound-laws have no exception" and *"No exception without a rule."*[4]

4. _____ *"Language is a system whose parts can and must all be considered in their synchronic solidarity.* Since changes never affect the system as a whole but rather one or another of its elements, they can be studied only outside the system. Each alteration doubtless has its countereffect on the system, but the initial fact affected only one point; there is no inner bond between the initial fact and the effect that it may subsequently produce on the whole system. The basic difference between successive terms and coexisting terms, between partial facts and facts that affect the system, precludes making both classes of fact the subject matter of a single science."[5]

5. _____ "While, according to the structure of our European languages, we always tend to look for the expression of singularity or plurality for the sake of clearness of expression, there are other languages that are entirely indifferent towards this distinction. A good example of this kind is the Kwakiutl [an American Indian language of the Pacific Northwest spoken by a people of the same name]. It is entirely immaterial to the Kwakiutl whether he says, *There is a house* or *There are houses.* The same form is used for expressing both ideas, and the idea of singularity and plurality must be understood either by the context or by the addition of a special adjective."[6]

6. _____ "The writer has attempted to satisfy six requirements which seem essential for a correct [phonological] system, but which no other system that he knows of completely fulfills. (1) Range and criteria must be accurately and unambiguously defined. (2) *There must be no mentalism.* (3) The terminology must involve no logical contradictions; terms defined as variables, class names, and quality

---

[2] *Ibid.,* p. 17.

[3] Bloomfield's paraphrase of Hermann Paul's *Prinzipien der Sprachgeschichte* in "On Recent Works in General Linguistics," *Modern Philology* (Chicago: The University of Chicago Press, 1927), p. 217.

[4] The first quote is attributed to August Leskien, 1876; the second, to Karl Verner in John T. Waterman's *Perspectives in Linguistics* (Chicago: The University of Chicago Press, 1963), p. 50.

[5] Ferdinand de Saussure, *Course in General Linguistics,* trans. Wade Baskin (New York: McGraw-Hill, 1959), p. 87.

[6] Franz Boas, *Introduction to the Handbook of American Indian Languages,* Smithsonian Institution, Bureau of American Ethnology Bulletin no. 40, part 1 (Washington, D.C.), p. 29.

names must be consistently used in those values. (4) No material should be excluded which might prove to be of grammatical importance, and none should be included which cannot be of grammatical importance. (5) *There must be no circularity; phonological analysis is assumed for grammatical analysis, and so must not assume any part of the latter. The line of demarcation between the two must be sharp.* (6) The way should be left open for the introduction of any criteria whatsoever on the grammatical level, barring mentalism."[7]

7. _____ "*The linguistic processes of the 'mind' as such are quite simply unobservable; and introspection about linguistic processes is notoriously a fire in a wooden stove.* Our only information about the 'mind' is derived from the behavior of the individual whom it inhabits. To interpret that behavior in terms of 'mind' is to commit the logical fallacy of 'explaining' a fact of unknown cause by giving that unknown cause a name, and then citing the name x as the cause of the fact. 'Mind' is indeed a summation of such x's, unknown causes of human behavior."[8]

8. _____ "It is not unreasonable to insist that any linguistic theory worthy of the name be expected to give enough insight into the nature of language to afford practical suggestions as to what we may find in the grammar of a previously unstudied language. *A codification of such suggestions yields discovery procedures.*"[9]

9. _____ "Trubetzkoy phonology tried to explain everything from articulatory acoustics and a minimum set of phonological laws taken as essentially valid for all languages alike, flatly contradicting the American (Boas) tradition that languages could differ from each other without limit and in unpredictable ways, and *offering too much of a phonological explanation where a sober taxonomy* [classification and labeling] *would serve as well.*"[10]

10. _____ "The well-founded pessimism which derives from the difficulties to be faced in studying languages not native to the linguist may, to an unknown extent, be mitigated by (even at present far from nonexistent) advantages to be derived from approaching 'exotic' languages with a highly specific, substantively rich theory of a language justified on the basis of the not insignificant range of distinct languages for which native linguists exist or can be expected to exist quite naturally. However, the possibilities so afforded will depend very much on overcoming the incredible harm done by that still dominant, extraordinarily exaggerated, habit of thought illustrated by the slogan 'describe each language in its own terms.' It will depend very much, that is, on the realization that *the description of every aspect of a particular*

[7] Charles F. Hockett, "A System of Descriptive Phonology," *Language* 18 (1942): 20–21.

[8] W. Freeman Twaddell, "On Defining the Phoneme," *Language Monographs* No. 16 (1935), as reprinted in Martin Joos, *Readings in Linguistics I* (Chicago: The University of Chicago Press, 1957), p. 57.

[9] Robert E. Longacre, *Grammar Discovery Procedures* (The Hague: Mouton, 1968), p. 13.

[10] Martin Joos, Epilogue to Bloch's "Phonemic Overlapping," in Martin Joos, *Readings in Linguistics I*, p. 96.

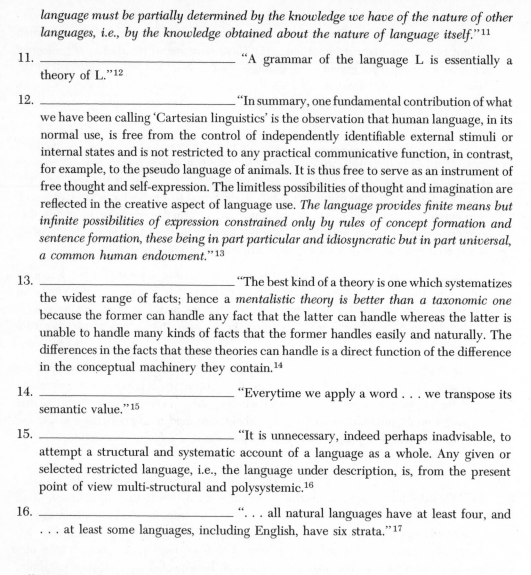

language must be partially determined by the knowledge we have of the nature of other languages, i.e., by the knowledge obtained about the nature of language itself."[11]

11. _____ "A grammar of the language L is essentially a theory of L."[12]

12. _____ "In summary, one fundamental contribution of what we have been calling 'Cartesian linguistics' is the observation that human language, in its normal use, is free from the control of independently identifiable external stimuli or internal states and is not restricted to any practical communicative function, in contrast, for example, to the pseudo language of animals. It is thus free to serve as an instrument of free thought and self-expression. The limitless possibilities of thought and imagination are reflected in the creative aspect of language use. *The language provides finite means but infinite possibilities of expression constrained only by rules of concept formation and sentence formation, these being in part particular and idiosyncratic but in part universal, a common human endowment."*[13]

13. _____ "The best kind of a theory is one which systematizes the widest range of facts; hence a *mentalistic theory is better than a taxonomic one* because the former can handle any fact that the latter can handle whereas the latter is unable to handle many kinds of facts that the former handles easily and naturally. The differences in the facts that these theories can handle is a direct function of the difference in the conceptual machinery they contain.[14]

14. _____ "Everytime we apply a word . . . we transpose its semantic value."[15]

15. _____ "It is unnecessary, indeed perhaps inadvisable, to attempt a structural and systematic account of a language as a whole. Any given or selected restricted language, i.e., the language under description, is, from the present point of view multi-structural and polysystemic.[16]

16. _____ ". . . all natural languages have at least four, and . . . at least some languages, including English, have six strata."[17]

[11] Footnote 6 in Paul Postal, "A Note on 'Understood Transitively,'" *International Journal of American Linguistics* 32, no. 1 (January 1966): 93.

[12] Noam Chomsky, *Syntactic Structures* (The Hague: Mouton, 1957), p. 49.

[13] Noam Chomsky, *Cartesian Linguistics* (New York: Harper & Row, 1966), p. 29.

[14] Jerrold J. Katz, "Mentalism in Linguistics," *Language* 40, no. 2 (1964): 127.

[15] Sergeij Karcevskij, as quoted in Joseph Vacheck, *A Prague School Reader in Linguistics* (Bloomington, Ind.: Indiana University Press, 1964), p. 85. Cf. Malinowski's "if a word is used in a different context, it cannot have the same meaning," in D. T. Langendoen *The London School of Linguistics: A Study of the Linguistic Theories of B. Malinowski and S. R. Firth*, Research Monograph No. 46 (Cambridge, Mass.: M.I.T. Press, 1968), p. 31.

[16] J. R. Firth, "Synopsis of Linguistic Theory," in *Studies in Linguistic Analysis*, a special publication of the Philological Society (Oxford, 1957), section XII.

[17] Sydney Lamb, *Outline of Stratificational Grammar* (Washington, D.C.: Georgetown University Press, 1966), p. 1.

17. _____ "The generation of a sentence does not start with a syntactic structure but with a structured meaning, called the remote structure, which all the rules together then convert to a surface structure."[18]

18. _____ "The sentence in its basic structure consists of a verb and one or more noun phrases, each associated with the verb in a particular case relationship."[19]

EXERCISE 2: Grammatical Versus the Functional Approach

Classify the following schools according to the approach with which they can be best identified. The *grammatical approach* relates to the sentence and its parts; the *functional approach* entails the sentence and the systematic functions of its parts.

School	Grammatical	Functional
1. case grammar		X
2. classical generative grammar	X	
3. generative semantics		
4. stratificational grammar		
5. structural grammar		
6. systemic grammar		
7. tagmemics		
8. traditional grammar		

EXERCISE 3: Reed-Kellogg Diagrams[20]

This exercise presents the Reed-Kellogg method of diagramming sentences. This traditional method has been popular in many high schools and grade schools since the late nineteenth century.

---

[18] Dwight Bolinger's characterization of one of the schools of grammar in *Aspects of Language,* 2nd ed. (New York: Harcourt Brace Jovanovich, 1975), p. 542.

[19] Charles J. Fillmore, "The Case for Case," in *Universals in Linguistic Theory,* ed. Emmon Bach and Robert T. Harms (New York: Holt, Rinehart and Winston, 1968), p. 21.

[20] Much of the information in this exercise is taken from H. A. Gleason, Jr., *Linguistics and English Grammar* (New York: Holt, Rinehart and Winston, 1965).

A. The first step is to find the noun of the subject and the verb of the predicate. In the sentences below, the nouns and verbs are underlined, and only the nouns and verbs have been diagrammed. The complete subjects of the sentences are in parentheses.

Sentence	Rudimentary Noun + Verb Diagram
(**Horses**) run.	Horses | run
(**He**) soon arrived.	He | arrived
(**The two men**) left for the garage.	men | left

The following sentences are divided into subject and predicate, with the subjects in parentheses. Underline the verb in each of the predicates. (In part B, you will diagram each sentence.)

1. (My car) always starts.

car \| starts

2. (The cycle that had the blowout) ran into a post.

3. (They) chose him the leader.

4. (The old vacuum sitting in the closet) worked most of the time.

B. The noun is the heart of the subject. Everything else in the subject modifies the noun. Study the examples above. There, the noun of each subject is underlined. Now underline the nouns in the subjects of sentences 2 through 4 above, and then draw the rudimentary *noun + verb* diagrams in the spaces provided.

C. The sentence type *subject + verb + object* is one of the most common in English. It is diagrammed this way:

Bakers | make | bread

The first vertical line, which crosses the base line, separates the noun of the subject from the verb of the predicate. The vertical line extending to the base line separates the object of the verb from the verb. In the examples below, the nouns of the subjects and the verbs of the predicates are underlined. The objects are in parentheses. The rudimentary diagrams follow.

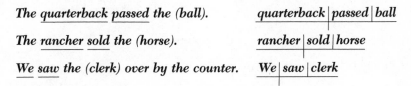

The quarterback passed the (ball).   *quarterback | passed | ball*

The rancher sold the (horse).   *rancher | sold | horse*

We saw the (clerk) over by the counter.   *We | saw | clerk*

Draw the rudimentary diagrams of the following sentences.

1. James led the gang.

James | led | gang

2. They elected him.

3. They elected the president.

4. John hated the long walk.

D. A prepositional phrase is diagrammed below the line in this way:

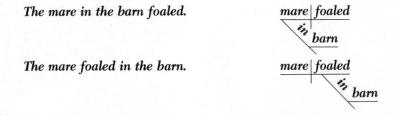

The mare in the barn foaled.

The mare foaled in the barn.

Another very common sentence type in English is *subject + verb + indirect object + direct object*. The Reed-Kellogg diagrams treat the indirect object like the prepositional phrase in such sentences as **He gave a bone to the dog.**

He gave a bone to the dog.   He | gave | bone
                                         to   *dog*

He gave the dog a bone.   He | gave | bone
                                          dog

Draw the rudimentary diagrams of these sentences.

1. He brought the horse to the minister.

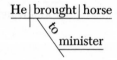

He | brought | horse
           to
           minister

2. He brought the horse to the water.

3. He offered her his hand.

4. He offered his hand to her.

E. The Reed-Kellogg system includes a number of different sentence types under the next feature. The feature is a line slanting to the left.

The horse seems tired.   horse | seems \ tired

(a) The sentence type represented above has three elements: subject, linking verb, and adjective. A linking verb is any verb except a form of *be* (***is, was,*** and so on) that can be substituted for ***seems*** in ***The horse seems tired.***

(b) Another sentence type is *subject + be + adjective.*

The horse is tired.   horse | is \ tired

Diagram these sentences and indicate the sentence type, *a* or *b*.

1. __*a*__ The doctor appeared overworked.

doctor | appeared \ overworked

2. _____ The wind grew sluggish.

3. _____ John was busy.

(c) A third sentence type diagrammed this way is *subject + be + noun,* in which the noun has the same referent as the subject.

My father is an engineer.   father | is \ engineer

(d) A fourth sentence type is *subject + linking verb + noun,* in which the noun has the same referent as the subject.

John became an architect.   ***John | became \ architect***

Diagram these sentences and indicate the sentence type, *c* or *d*.

4. __*c*__ John was president.

$$\underline{John \mid was \backslash president}$$

5. ____ John became president.

6. ____ He remained the deputy.

(e) Another pattern is *subject + **be** + adverb*. According to this system, a word that expresses place or time, such as ***there*** or ***then,*** and follows a form of ***be***, is an adverb.

The man is here.

Diagram the following sentences and indicate the sentence type—*a, b, c, d,* or *e.*

7. __*a*__ The horse in the barn appears underexercised.

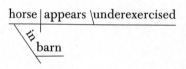

8. ____ John is outside.

9. ____ He remained the mayor in town.

10. _____ The ground under the hay is frozen.

11. _____ The grocery store is the forum of the town.

F. The next diagram feature is the line slanted to the right.

They named him president.   **They | named/president | him**

The teacher considered him stupid.   **Teacher | considered/stupid | him**

The two sentence types are *noun + verb + noun + noun,* in which the last two nouns have the same referent, and *noun + verb + noun + adjective,* in which the adjective modifies the second noun. The Reed-Kellogg system does not distinguish nouns from adjectives in these sentences. **President** and **stupid** in the sentences above are called *objective complements.* The word order is changed because the diagramming reflects the relationships between the words, not their order in the sentence. The relationship of **stupid** to **considered** is regarded as closer than the relationship of **stupid** to **him;** *to consider stupid* is thought of almost as a unit with **him** as object.

Diagram these sentences, and indicate whether the last word is a noun or an adjective.

1. _adj._ I thought Peter sick.

I | thought/sick | Peter

2. _____ They selected her queen.

3. _____ He called the child an idiot.

G. Modifiers are slung below the horizontal line on slant lines in the Reed-Kellogg system.

The three new coon hounds quickly found the scent.

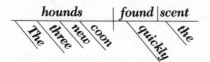

The plot was clear before the beginning of the first commercial.

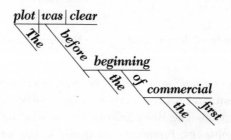

In this system of diagramming, no change is made in the diagram of the first sentence if *quickly* comes at the end of the sentence. Notice also that this diagram treats *coon* and *the* as modifiers of equal status. A word that is slung below a noun is called an *adjective,* and a word that is slung below a verb is called an *adverb.*

Diagram these sentences.

1. On Tuesday, the frustrated crowd named him their leader for the march.

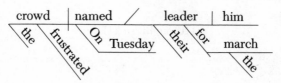

2. She rapidly taught him the Greek alphabet by constant repetition.

3. He arrived on the third flight.

4. The old boy never liked her kind of food.

EXERCISE 4: Schools of Grammar: Theory and Practice

In the following reading, Sven Jacobson compares four of the systems of grammatical analysis discussed by Bolinger. As you read, try to evaluate the advantages and disadvantages of each of the systems.

READING: The Problem of Describing Syntactic Complexity [21]

Sven Jacobson

One of the most complex of human activities is linguistic performance. All over the world scholars and scientists who have set themselves the task of describing language in its many different aspects are grappling with a number of intricate questions. One such problem is the relationship between function and form,° which is one of the major topics of syntax.

From my own schooldays I remember how in parsing exercises we were asked to analyse a sentence simultaneously from two different viewpoints: the part of speech (= the form

---

[21] Sven Jacobson, "The Problem of Describing Syntactic Complexity," *Studia Neophilologica* 40 (1968): 114–29. Reprinted by permission of Swets & Zeitlinger, who hold the right to reprint volumes 1–40 of *Studia Neophilologica*.

° By "form" I mean not only the occurrence of bound morphemes, such as plural endings, but also the presence of structure words, such as articles, and the order in which the various elements occur in the sentence.

class) was to be written under each word and the part of the sentence (= the function class) over each word or word-group. We were told always to keep the two types of analysis strictly apart and not to mix them. Such mixing is, however, not uncommon in some grammatical literature; one example is the well-known formula S V O (subject-verb-object).

Anyone who undertakes to analyse language in a really scientific way will soon find that the simple parsing technique that we were taught at school is not sufficient. For example, some words and word-groups can have several functions simultaneously, and elements that belong together functionally are often discontinuous in the sentence, so that one requires some special system of indicating their relationship. Also, in a discourse the various sentences can be described as links in a chain which are dependent on each other, so that full understanding of each separate sentence is usually achieved only by reference to what precedes or follows. A great deal of time and effort has been spent by linguists on the problem of how to achieve a grammatical description that accounts for these and other syntactic complexities, while at the same time satisfying the highest requirements as to brevity, accuracy and clarity. Some schools of linguists have tried to reach this goal by evolving systems in which ordinary explanations in words are supplemented with graphic or algebraic notation or even both these devices in combination. It has been objected that as a result their descriptions have often become totally inaccessible to the untutored public and thus hardly satisfy the demand for clarity. To this one might answer that clarity does not necessarily mean "simple and easy for the beginner." Moreover, one may wonder, as Sydney Lamb does,° how far, for instance, physics and chemistry or even a fine art like music would have advanced if scientists and composers had been dissuaded from using notational devices that require special study before they are understood.

In this article I propose to concentrate on one single example and demonstrate how it might be described syntactically by different linguistic schools. The example has been specially chosen because of its intricate syntactic relationships and runs as follows:

People moved to the cities. Especially was this the case in England.†

No doubt the attention of most readers will be focused on the adverb *especially*, which here fulfills a threefold function (cf. Jacobson 1964, p. 49):

(a) it is conjunctive, i.e. it links the two sentences together (the nature of the linking is described below under (c));

(b) it modifies the sentence it introduces; in fact its sentence modification is so strong that it is followed by the same kind of inverted word-order that we find in interrogative sentences;

(c) it directs our attention to the prepositional phrase *in England*, with which it may be said to form a split structure; this structure, in its turn, can be said to be a discontinuous modifier of the verb-phrase of the first sentence; if we put the three discontinuous constituents together, we get one long verb-phrase: *moved to the cities especially in England.*

° Lamb 1966, p. 8.

† The two sentences of this example may be assumed to form part of an account of the social upheaval caused in Europe by the Industrial Revolution. For two similar (but longer) examples excerpted from British books, see Jacobson 1964, pp. 47 and 49.

Undoubtedly it is of great interest to see how different grammatical systems might tackle the problem of describing these three functions of *especially* within the general framework of a syntactic description of the two-sentence example in which it occurs. For this purpose I shall choose the following four types of grammatical approach:

(*a*) Immediate-constituent (IC) analysis.
(*b*) Tagmemics.
(*c*) Transformational grammar.
(*d*) Stratificational grammar.

Immediate-Constituent Analysis

Leonard Bloomfield, in his epoch-making book *Language* (1933), introduced the notion of levels of structure and said that at each level there are as a rule two immediate constituents. During the 1940's immediate-constituent analysis was further developed, especially by Rulon Wells, C. C. Fries, and W. Nelson Francis.[*]

The binary cuts made at each level of structure have frequently been rendered graphically. One of the major problems encountered here has, however, been the denotation of discontinuous constituents. W. Nelson Francis' solution is to use "Chinese boxes," some of which are so shaped as to depict the nature of such constituents. Fig. 1 shows Francis' diagram of a sentence with IC's A and B, where A is split into two parts by B, as in, for instance, *do you swim* (see Francis 1958, p. 295).

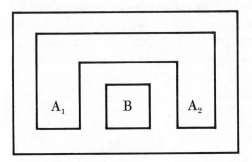

Figure 1   Discontinuous constituents.

In immediate-constituent analysis each pair of IC's is taken to form a structure, the type of which may be indicated by means of various symbols or other devices. In the system used by Francis (1958, pp. 294–96) an arrow denotes modification, a P predication (i.e. subject-predicate relationship), and a C complementation. Prepositions are attached in a small box directly to their objects. On the basis of Francis' system the example chosen for

[*] See Wells 1947, Fries 1952, and Francis 1958.

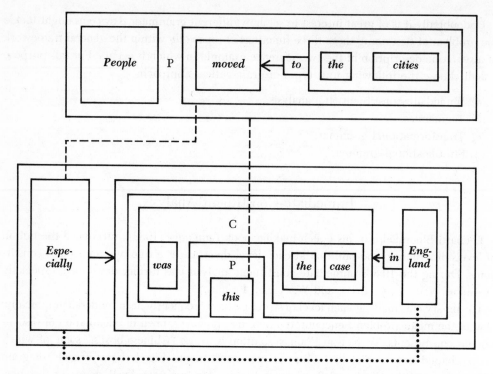

Figure 2 Immediate-constituent analysis of the two sentences.

this article may be rendered as in Fig. 2. In order to complete the description, I have added a dotted line to show the special referential, i.e. attention-directing, relationship between *especially* and *in England* (cf. Jacobson 1964, p. 42). Similarly, a broken line denotes the conjunctive function of *especially* by linking this adverb to the constituent *moved to the cities*. Another broken line indicates that the demonstrative pronoun *this* points back to the whole previous sentence.

Tagmemics

The linguistic approach that is termed tagmemics was originated by Kenneth L. Pike, who in 1954 began the publication of his three-volume work *Language in relation to a unified theory of the structure of human behavior*. As his basic term Pike first used the word grameme but later changed it to tagmeme. Recently he has published a comprehensive list of contributors to tagmemic theory (see Pike 1966). The best popularizers of this theory are probably Benjamin Elson and Velma Pickett. In their book *An Introduction to Morphology and Syntax*, p. 57, they define a tagmeme as "a grammatical unit which is the correlation of a grammatical function or slot with a class of mutually substitutable items occurring in that slot." H. A. Gleason, Jr., in *Linguistics and English Grammar*, p. 140, characterizes tagmemic analysis as "a slot-and-filler technique combined with certain characteristic views of the general nature of language systems." Tagmemicists do not use diagrams but have instead evolved a rather complex algebraic notational system. Thus the slot and the filler of a tagmeme are symbolized by letters and separated by a colon, and tagmemes which are obligatory in a construction are preceded by + and those which are optional by ±. Tagmemes and the constructions into which they enter may be identified and described at several different levels.

With the use of tagmemic technique the previous two-sentence example may be analysed as follows.

(a) *Discourse level.°* At this level each of the two sentences [plus the function it fills] constitutes one tagmeme denoted in the following way:

+Base:Ind Sent±Sequence:Seq Sent.

The first sentence (*People moved to the cities*) forms a base consisting of an independent sentence, to which the second sentence (*Especially was this the case in England*) is added to an optional sequence consisting of a sequence sentence.

(b) *Sentence level.* For the sake of brevity I shall concentrate on the second sentence, which may be analysed as follows:

±C:padv+Base:eCl.

The first tagmeme consists of a connector slot (C) filled by a particularizing adverb (padv). After thus accounting for *especially,* I have denoted the rest of the sentence as a base slot filled by an equational clause (eCl), i.e., one containing a copula followed by a nounal complement. At the sentence level a symbol denoting the type of intonation may be added. A functional feature that seems impossible to account for, at this or any other level, is the connective nature of *this.*

(c) *Clause level.* Here I again analyse the second sentence, though this time I regard *especially* not as a connector but as a manner tagmeme, whose slot (Ma) is filled by a manner adverb (madv):

±MA:madv+eP:cn+S:dpr+L:l.
└─────────── ± ───────┘

The second tagmeme consists of an equational predicate slot (eP) filled by a copula followed by a noun (cn), the third of a subject slot (S) filled by a demonstrative pronoun (dpr), and the fourth by a location slot (L) filled by a locative phrase (l). The line marked ± and tying the ± of the first tagmeme to the + of the fourth tagmeme means that both these tagmemes are optional, with the reservation that the first tagmeme does not occur without the fourth. This line thus serves the purpose of indicating that a special relationship exists between *especially* and *in England.* Alternatively, we may drop the first tagmeme and regard *especially . . . in England* as a discontinuous allotagma of the L:1 tagmeme (for further analysis, see (d)). The inverted word-order of the clause is not indicated in the

° Discourse is here used in the sense "connected speech or writing." Cf. Harris 1952, p. 18.

tagmemic analysis; it is simply regarded as an inverted allotagma of the eP:cn tagmeme. This word-order is here not emic, i.e. it is not distinctive in the way it is when it turns a declarative clause into an interrogative one.

(d) *Phrase level.* At this level I shall only analyse the discontinuous allotagma *especially . . . in England,* mentioned above:

±Ad:padv + R:prep + A:np.

The slot of the first tagmeme is an attention-director (Ad) filled by a particularizing adverb (padv), that of the second a relater (R) filled by a preposition (prep), and that of the third an axis (A) filled by a proper noun (np).

Transformational Grammar

The more accurate term for what is usually called "transformational grammar" is "transformational generative grammar." This grammatical approach came into prominence in 1957 when Noam Chomsky published his little book *Syntactic Structures.* Since then an enormous amount of work has been done not only in the form of applying transformational rules to more and more aspects of linguistics, such as semantics,[*] phonology,[†] and stylistics,[‡] but also in the form of popularizing the basic rules for use in schools.[§] Whereas immediate-constituent analysis and tagmemics mainly describe the *state* of linguistic forms and relations as they appear in the surface structure, i.e. the actual spoken or written language, transformational grammar principally describes the *transition* from deep structure to surface structure. The deep structure of a sentence is considered as being composed of the underlying abstract forms and relations which constitute its semantic basis. This dynamic technique has a strong explanatory power. For example, it accounts in a very clear way for ambiguities like *the shooting of the soldiers,* and explains the difference between such ostensibly similar constructions as *John is easy to please* and *John is eager to please.*

Unfortunately, as far as the theme of this article is concerned, the point of departure in transformational grammar has been the sentence, and very little research has so far been devoted to analysing relations at the discourse level. The following description of how the two interrelated sentences included in the example may be generated can therefore only be tentative.

For the purpose of a treatment of inter-sentence relations it seems suitable to recognize three types of sentences: independent sentences, embedded sentences (= subordinate clauses) and sequence sentences. Any discourse contains at least one independent sentence, which may be followed by an infinite number of sequence sentences. To the ordinary formula for sentence generation (S → NP + VP) should therefore be added an optional symbol Seq.

We now turn to the generation of the two sentences. This may be performed as follows:

[*] See, for instance, Katz and Fodor 1963 and Abraham and Kiefer 1966.
[†] See, for instance, Halle 1963.
[‡] See, for instance, Ohmann 1964.
[§] See, for instance, Roberts 1964 and Thomas 1966.

1. THE FIRST SENTENCE (S$_1$)

Phrase-structure rules

$S_1 \rightarrow NP + VP + Seq$
$NP \rightarrow Det + N + Pl$

$Det \rightarrow \begin{Bmatrix} \varnothing \\ the \end{Bmatrix}$

$Pl \rightarrow \begin{Bmatrix} \varnothing \\ \text{-es} \end{Bmatrix}$

$VP \rightarrow Aux + MV$
$Aux \rightarrow Past$
$MV \rightarrow V_i + Dir$
$Dir \rightarrow Prep + NP$
$Seq \rightarrow S_2$

Abbreviations

NP = noun phrase
VP = verb phrase
Det = determiner
Pl = plural
$\varnothing$ = zero
Aux = auxiliary
MV = main verb
V_i = intransitive verb
Dir = adverbial of direction
Seq = sequence sentence

Lexicon (in simplified form):

N: people, city
V_i: move
Prep: to

By successively applying the phrase-structure rules and then inserting words from the lexicon, we get the terminal string

People + *Past* + move + to + the + city + -es.

After applying first an obligatory transformation that shifts *Past* to the position after *move* and then morphophonemic (or, in the case of the written language, morphographemic) rules, we finally get as a result the surface structure *People moved to the cities*.

2. THE SECOND SENTENCE (S$_2$)

This sentence is based on the previous sentence and may be said to have the following semantic content: "That people moved to the cities was the case in a special degree (and manner) in England." We must therefore use rules that generate a deep structure containing this information.

Phrase-structure rules

$S_2 \rightarrow NP + VP$
$NP \rightarrow Det + N + Sg(S)°$

$Det \rightarrow \begin{Bmatrix} Art \\ Dem \end{Bmatrix}$

Abbreviations (except those given above)

Sg = singular
Art = article
Dem = demonstrative
Loc = locative

° Note that optional elements are placed within brackets and are not preceded by a plus sign.

$$\text{Art}\rightarrow\begin{Bmatrix}\text{a(n)}\\\text{the}\\\varnothing\end{Bmatrix}$$

Dem→this

Sg→∅

VP→Aux+MV+Loc

Aux→Past

MV→Be+Pred+Dg/Ma

Pred→NP

Dg/Ma→Prep+NP+Morph

Morph→-ly+Emph

Loc→Prep+NP

Pred = predicative

Dg/Ma = adverbial whose meaning is a mixture of degree and manner

Morph = special morpheme(s)

-ly = adverb morpheme

Emph = emphasis morpheme

PRO_{Ni} = a deletable indefinite noun that may be translated by "thing" or "circumstance." See Thomas 1966, p. 87. Ni stands for "noun inanimate."

Lexicon

N: PRO_{Ni}, case, degree/manner, England

Prep: in

In the derivation of the terminal string the optional symbol S listed in the rewriting of NP will be used twice, first to re-introduce S_1 and then to embed S_3, which will be a relative clause whose generation I will not deal with here. Suffice it to say that it gives this terminal string:

wh + degree/manner + *Past* + be + especial.

The terminal string of the whole of S_2, with S_1 and S_3 embedded, will be as follows:

This + PRO_{Ni} + People + *Past* + move + to + the + city + -es + *Past* + be + the + case + in + a + degree/manner + wh + degree/manner + *Past* + be + especial + -ly + Emph + in + England

This may be read in plain English as "This circumstance that people moved to the cities was the case in a degree (and manner) which was special in England."

Various transformations will now be applied to the terminal string. Among these may be mentioned the deletion of PRO_{Ni} and the repeated S_1, so that all that remains of the first NP is the word *this*. Moreover, the degree/manner adverbial is followed by the adverb morpheme *-ly*, which transforms it into *especially*, and also an emphasis morpheme, which shifts it to the front and inverts the order of *this* and *Past*+be.

Figs. 3–5 show phrase-markers that graphically render the deep structure of the example. Similar tree diagrams can be drawn for the surface structure. Fig. 6 shows that of the second sentence. Here, because of the changed word-order, the derivational paths from Dg/Ma and Aux+be to S_2 no longer pass VP, as they do in the deep structure (see Fig. 4). This may seem a perfunctory way of accounting for discontinuities, but transformationalists argue that it is at the deep structure diagrams that one must look to see where the various elements really belong.

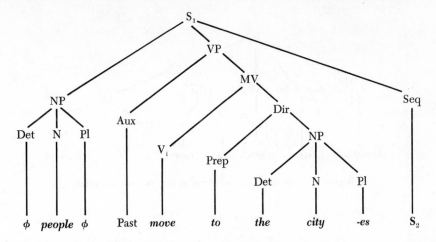

Figure 3 The deep structure of the first sentence.

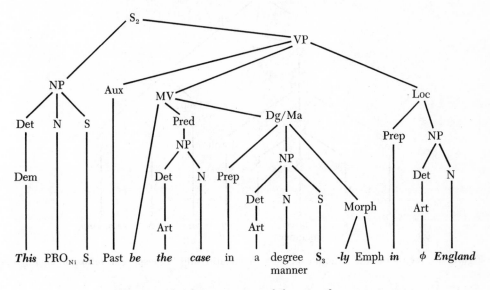

Figure 4 The deep structure of the second sentence.

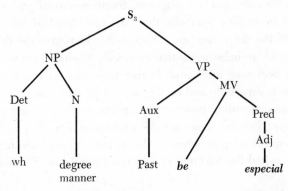

Figure 5 The deep structure from which the adjectival modifier *especial* is derived.

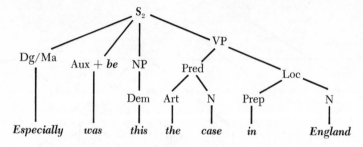

Figure 6 The surface structure of the second sentence.

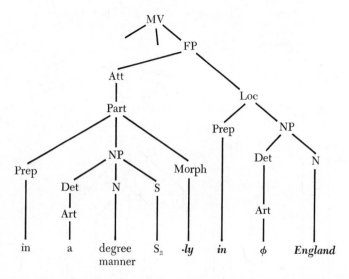

Figure 7 Deep structure diagram showing the relationship between *especially* and *in England.*

As appears from the rules and tree diagrams, transformational grammar does not express syntactic functions by explicit symbols; they are considered as inherent in the graphic subconfigurations of the deep structure.° Figs. 3–5, which give the deep structure of the example, fail, however, to indicate (*a*) that *especially* assumes a connective function when it is moved to the beginning of S₂ and (*b*) that there is a special functional relationship between the elements *especially* and *in England.* A possible solution might be to draw a special tree diagram comprising these two elements (see Fig. 7) and attach it to the MV node of the phrase-marker that shows the deep structure of S₁ (Fig. 3). This phrase-marker would then represent the deep structure of the surface string *moved to the cities especially in England.* I have called this addition to S₁ a function-phrase (FP) and suggest the intro-

° See Chomsky 1965, pp. 68–74.

duction of a rule that automatically deletes such a phrase in the transformational process, as the elements of its terminal string also occur elsewhere. It should be noted that in this function-phrase the node dominating what later becomes *especially* is not called Dg/Ma but Att (= attention-director), which is specified as Part (= particularizer). A special morphophonemic rule should be introduced that gives the element that is configuratively combined with an attention-director emphatic stress and intonation. If, as in the present case, this element occurs in a deletable function-phrase, then there should be a transformational rule to ensure that the emphatic stress and intonation are transferred to the same element in the undeleted counterpart.

The procedures of transformational grammar at first seem complicated, but they have the advantage of being algorithmic, i.e., they account for the generation of the surface structure in a mechanical way, so that a machine would be able to perform the operations necessary. And a machine does not mind performing a great number of operations whose products are simply deleted after they have served their purpose. To some extent such a process resembles the working of the human brain which, in a similar manner, performs a great number of tedious operations of which we, happily, are unaware, as our conscious minds simply concentrate on the result.

Stratificational Grammar

Stratificational grammar is one of the latest branches on our flourishing linguistic tree. Its main proponent is Sydney Lamb, who first published its basic tenets in an article entitled "MT (= machine translation) Research at the University of California, Berkeley" in 1961. This article was followed by his *Outline of Stratificational Grammar,* which was published in a multilithed edition in 1962 and in a revised printed edition in 1966. Although H. A. Gleason, Jr., devotes the whole of his book *Linguistics and English Grammar* to other types of grammatical approach, he says that his "own preference and conviction run to stratificational grammar" (p. vi).°

Stratificational grammar uses a graphic notation which resembles the charts drawn by engineers to represent interconnections at, for instance, an automatic telephone exchange. The main emphasis of this grammar is on the relationships between linguistic elements. These relationships can be analysed within several different strata, and it is not necessary for the linguist to complete his analysis within one stratum before going on to the next.

The graphic notation may be accompanied by an algebraic notation, but this is considered subsidiary and is only used to describe the linguistic graphs. A graph is made up of lines branching off at nodes which have the property of showing direction. The nodes are always turned in the branching direction, which may be upwards, i.e. towards meaning, or downwards, i.e. towards expression. If two or more branching lines touch each other when they converge at a node, they are unordered; if, on the other hand, there is some space between them, they operate from left to right.

° For further works on stratificational grammar, see the bibliography in Lamb 1966 and footnote 64 in Hockett 1966.

The two concepts of meaning and expression correspond to the concepts of deep structure and surface structure in transformational grammar. Thus impulses are to be'thought of as moving downwards in the production process and upwards in the decoding process. Fig. 8 is an attempt to give a graphic analysis of the example at the level of the lexemic, i.e. syntactic, stratum. The graph is somewhat simplified; though, for example, intonation and juncture play a lexemic as well as a phonemic role, the lines and nodes pertaining to these concepts have been omitted. Quite consistent is, however, the exclusion of such derivations as *especially* < *especial* + *ly* and *moved* < *move* + *past*, as these belong to the morphemic stratum.

A look at the graph shows the following noteworthy features:

(*a*) If we read the terminal lexemes, i.e. the words, from left to right and add the marks of punctuation that correspond to intonation and juncture, we get the unchanged version of the example: *People moved to the cities. Especially was this the case in England.*

(*b*) At the Pred node of S_1 three ordered lines branch off. The third leads to *especially* and further to *in England*, which shows that there is a relationship between these elements, so that we can read *People moved to the cities especially in England.*

(*c*) The meaning of the lexeme *this* is explained by a line leading from the Subj node of S_2 to the node S_1, i.e. the subject *this* refers back to the whole previous sentence.

(*d*) The emphasis lexeme has first shifted *especially* to the front, then reversed the order of *the case* and *was*, and lastly placed *this* between these two elements.

Like transformational grammar, stratificational grammar has proved a valuable tool for mechanical linguistic operations, especially machine translation. Typically, Sydney Lamb's first article on stratificational grammar (see above) was concerned with machine translation

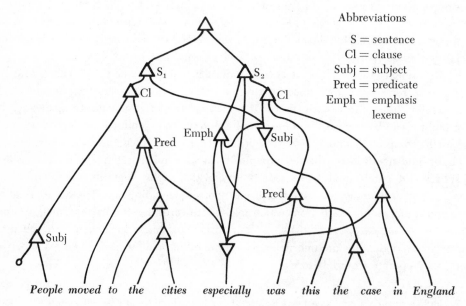

Figure 8 The two sentences analysed at the level of the lexemic stratum.

and his latest bears the title "Stratificational linguistics as a basis for machine translation" (see Lamb 1968?).

Conclusion

It is difficult to judge which of the four linguistic systems dealt with in this article offers the best description of the type of syntactic complexity that the particular example presents, for all of them have both advantages and disadvantages. Naturally these systems have been invented to cater for a very wide range of linguistic problems, and we should not be too surprised if they do not give ready-made answers to all questions concerning some specific points of grammar. As this article shows, I have consequently had to suggest several additions and amendments to the presentations I have found in the handbooks. Nor should we be surprised if, along with more or less satisfactory answers to the particular questions asked, we are also supplied with a great deal of additional information. After all, the aim of the article was to obtain these answers within the general framework of a syntactic description.

Personally I tend to favour the graphic presentation offered by stratificational grammar, as it seems to satisfy to a somewhat greater extent than the others the requirements mentioned earlier, namely, those of brevity, accuracy, and clarity. It is too early to judge, however, whether stratificational methods will also prove superior as regards the description of other types of syntactic complexity than those dealt with in this article.

References

Abraham, Samuel, and Kiefer, Ferenc, 1966. *A Theory of Structural Semantics*. The Hague: Mouton.

Bloomfield, Leonard, 1933. *Language*. New York: Henry Holt.

Chomsky, Noam, 1957. *Syntactic Structures*. The Hague: Mouton.

—— 1965. *Aspects of the Theory of Syntax*. Cambridge, Mass.: M.I.T. Press. Elson, Benjamin, and Pickett, Velma, 1965. *An Introduction to Morphology and Syntax*. Santa Ana, Calif.: Summer Institute of Linguistics.

Francis, W. Nelson, 1958. *The Structure of American English*. New York: The Ronald Press.

Fries, Charles C., 1952. *The Structure of English*. New York: Harcourt Brace Jovanovich.

Gleason, H. A., Jr., 1965. *Linguistics and English Grammar*. New York: Holt, Rinehart and Winston.

Halle, Morris, 1962. "Phonology in Generative Grammar," *Word*, 18, pp. 54–72.

Harris, Zellig S., 1952. "Discourse Analysis." *Language*, 28, pp. 18–23.

Hockett, Charles F., 1966. "Language, Mathematics, and Linguistics." In Thomas A. Sebeok (ed.), *Current Trends in Linguistics* (The Hague: Mouton), pp. 155–304.

Jacobson, Sven, 1964. *Adverbial Positions in English*. Stockholm: AB Studentbok.

Katz, Jerrold J., and Fodor, Jerry, 1963. "The Structure of a Semantic Theory." *Language*, 39, pp. 170–210.

Lamb, Sydney, 1961. "MT Research at the University of California, Berkeley." In H. P. Edmundson (ed.), *Proceedings of the National Symposium on Machine Translation*. Englewood Cliffs, N.J.: Prentice-Hall.

—— 1966. *Outline of Stratificational Grammar*. Washington, D.C.: Georgetown University Press.

—— 1968? "Stratificational linguistics as a basis for machine translation." In Bulcsu Laszlo (ed.), *Approaches to Language Data Processing*. The Hague: Mouton.

Ohmann, Richard, 1964. "Generative Grammars and the Concept of Literary Style." *Word*, 20, pp. 423–29.

Pike, Kenneth L., 1954–60. *Language in relation to a unified theory of human behavior,* Vols. I–III. Glendale, Calif.: Summer Institute of Linguistics.

———— 1966. "A Guide to Publications Related to Tagmemic Theory." In Thomas A. Sebeok, *Current Trends in Linguistics* (The Hague: Mouton), pp. 365–94.

Roberts, Paul, 1964. *English Syntax.* New York: Harcourt Brace Jovanovich.

Thomas, Owen, 1966. *Transformational Grammar and the Teacher of English.* New York: Holt, Rinehart and Winston.

Wells, Rulon S., 1947. "Immediate Constituents." *Language,* 23, pp. 81–117.

The Criteria for Evaluating Analyses

What is the function of a grammar? _____

_____

_____

_____

_____

_____

Hjelmslev's criteria are internal consistency, exhaustiveness, and simplicity. As you read through the article, what criteria occurred to you? _____

_____

_____

_____

Which description appeals to you most? Why? _____

_____

_____

_____

Which description is least appealing? Why? _____

_____

_____

_____

LANGUAGE AND THE PUBLIC INTEREST 16

EXERCISE 1: *Webster's Third New International Dictionary:* On Pronunciation

Webster's Third New International Dictionary of 1961 is based scrupulously on the actual practice of English speakers and on the statements of the grammarians who suggest how men ought to speak. The dictionary records both. If someone wanted to find out how a word, say ***wharf,*** is pronounced by cultured people across the country, he or she would do well to look in this dictionary. It lists eight pronunciations, in abbreviated form. Write them out in full here. _____

_____

_____

What does the dictionary say about the status of these pronunciations? Are any of them necessarily forbidden to an educated person? Would any necessarily cause an adverse reaction in an educated audience in his or her own part of the country? The dictionary gives such information. Study the section on pronunciation in the "Explanatory Notes," which starts on page 16a. Does the lack of a usage label or mark perhaps signify that a pronunciation

is heard in all parts of the country? _____ What exactly does the fact that a pronunciation is unmarked signify?

_____

_____

What are the acceptable pronunciations of the following words? Underline the pronunciation that you use.

foreign _____

barn _____

with _____

aunt _____

fog _____

new _____

_____

The pronunciation of words is necessarily affected by the sounds in surrounding words. *Webster's Third* gives these variations in pronunciations for some words. Supply the variations for these two words and the environments that cause the variation.

creel _____

root _____

The dictionary sometimes marks a pronunciation as coming from a particular region. Write down the regional pronunciation for the following words and name the regions. (The small number at the beginning of the word will help lead you to the right entry.)

greasy _____

_____

[1] creek _____

_____

[1] Negro _____

_____

[1] the _____

_____

[1] -ing (verbal suffix) _____

_____

Some of the words have pronunciations that are labeled "substandard" or "chiefly substand-ard." Look in the "Explanatory Notes" for the label "substandard" and summarize what is meant by the term. _____

_____

_____

Look up the following words and write down the substandard pronunciations and their full labels.

because _____

ask _____

athlete _____

didn't _____

[1] extra _____

The editors had difficult decisions to make in applying the labels "substandard" and "chiefly substandard." The first two of the three words discussed below have pronunciations marked "chiefly substandard" or "chiefly in substandard speech," and the third is bluntly marked "substandard." There are not many words with this blunt label in the dictionary. In the light of the information given below about these words, discuss on what basis these different labels were applied in *Webster's Third.*

_____

_____

_____

_____

wash \\'wo(ə)rsh, 'wärsh\\ *Webster's Third* labels these "chiefly substandard." Hans Kurath and Raven I. McDavid, Jr., basing their statement on the evidence gathered for the *Linguistic Atlas of the United States and Canada,* say that "In Pennsylvania west of the Susquehanna River and in West Virginia, an /r/ rather generally makes its appearance between the low back vowel and the /š/ of *wash* and *Washington.* This usage survives also in the Valley of Virginia and the Pennsylvania settlements farther south. In other areas that preserve postvocalic /r/, this intrusive /r/ is rare."[1]

borrow \\'bärē, 'bäri\\ *Webster's Third* labels this "chiefly in substandard speech." Kurath and McDavid write, "The variant ending in /i/ is characteristic of Southern and South Midland folk speech; it occurs here also, with varying frequency, in the speech of the middle class, but is rare in cultivated speech. Outside the South and the South Midland only scattered instances of /i/ have been observed, except in southeastern Maine and adjoining parts of New Hamsphire."[2] The incidence of /i/ in cultivated speech is about 4 percent.

Once, twice \\'wənzt, -n(s)t\\, \\'twīst\\ *Webster's Third* spells these *oncet* and *twicet,* and labels these "substandard." Kurath and McDavid write, "An added /t/ occurs in *once* and *twice* throughout the Midland and the South, excepting only the Piedmont of Virginia. It is more frequent in *once* than in *twice.* Though most common in folk speech, it is widely used by middle-class speakers, especially in the South Midland."[3]

[1] Hans Kurath and Raven I. McDavid, Jr., *The Pronunciation of English in the Atlantic States* (Ann Arbor, Mich.: University of Michigan Press, 1961), pp. 169–70. The status labels of *once, twice, borrow,* and *wash* were first studied by Jean Malmstrom, "Webster's Third on Nonstandard Usage," *Publication of the American Dialect Society* 41 (April 1964): 1–6.

[2] *Ibid.,* p. 173.

[3] *Ibid.,* p. 179.

It is a curious fact that some words have common pronunciations that many people dislike. These pronunciations are marked with ÷, which is called an *obelus*. Summarize what this symbol means.

_____

_____

Write down first what your own pronunciations of the following words are and then the pronunciations that the dictionary has marked with the obelus as disapproved of by many people.

eczema _____

baptist _____

February _____

licorice _____

rodeo _____

pumpkin _____

Is there a pronunciation of *licorice* acceptable everywhere? _____

Can a pronunciation marked with an obelus still be an accepted pronunciation? _____

EXERCISE 2: *Webster's Third New International Dictionary:* On Word Usage

Look up the phrase **greasy grind.** How does the dictionary label it? _____

Summarize the definition of this label that is given in the "Explanatory Notes." _____

_____

_____

Can a word that has the label "slang" ever be appropriately used in contexts that are not marked by extreme informality? _____ Give the meanings of the words and phrases below that are labeled "slang."

mary _____

up for grabs _____

cornball _____

Look up the word [5]*like* as used in **he talked stuttering-like.** How is this word labeled?

_____ What does this label mean? (Check the "Explanatory Notes.")

What are the differences between the meanings of this label and "slang"? _____

_____

Look up the following words and give the meanings that are labeled "substandard" and the exact wording of the label.

learn (meaning 'teach') _____

wore out _____

²suspicion _____

Some of the words in the dictionary are proper only to certain areas of the country or to certain countries. Look up the words below and give the restricted meaning and the region to which it is restricted.

mary _____

lay by _____

leave out _____

leave over _____

mutton corn _____

screw _____

The information in the dictionary that is at once the most plentiful and the most difficult to use as a source of information about usage is the citation. This is the quotation, often ascribed to a particular person or publication, that illustrates the word in use. Consider the word ¹*eve.* One citation is clearly poetical: <from morn to noon he fell, from noon to dewy *eve*—John Milton>. No label is needed to show that the word is part of the language of poetry. Look up the word *morn* and write the names and occupations of the people quoted. (You may not be able to find the occupations of all of them.) In what contexts would

you expect to find it used? _____

_____

_____

_____

_____

Look up the citations for the following words and describe the kinds of books or contexts in which they would appear to be especially appropriate.

pearly (meanings 4, 5, and 6) _____

pearl (meaning 'teeth') _____

lay off (as in **lay off me**—note the style of the citation) _____

³even (meaning 1b) _____

sputnik _____

husband (meaning 'hoarder') _____

mark (meaning 'one to be swindled') _____

neck (meaning 'fondle and kiss') _____

EXERCISE 3: *Webster's Third New International Dictionary: On Inflections*

The dictionary gives information about the appropriateness of various inflected forms. Write down the labels for the following italicized words in the uses illustrated.

brung (preterite) _____

have *wore* _____

you *was* (plural) _____

you *is* (plural) _____

ain't (meaning 'have not') _____

John and *her* are here _____

between you and *he* _____

Often the labels are not definite; usage is somewhat divided. Summarize the information contained in the entries for the following italicized words.

He talked to my sister and *I.* _____

_____

Our people and *us* are here. _____

_____

The dictionary often makes distinctions between speech and writing in its discussions of usage, especially usage of inflections. Your summaries of some of the usage information just above should carefully discriminate between what is proper to speech and what is proper to writing. Write summaries of what *Webster's Third* has to say about the following forms in both speech and writing. Note also the differences between the facts of actual usage and the positions taken by some grammarians.

ain't (meaning 1c) _____

_____

me (as in *it's me*) _____

_____

me (as in *me and John went yesterday*) _____

_____

us (as in *it was us*) _____

_____

which (as in *it was raining there yesterday, which kept us from going*) _____

_____

_____

whom (as in *the man whom you took to dinner*) _____

_____

EXERCISE 4: The Desk Dictionary

There is much more in a good desk dictionary than is apparent in casual, everyday use. You have already been introduced to its etymological information in Chapter 7. This exercise is designed to introduce you to some of the principles and practices of your own dictionary. If the desk dictionary you use does not have the information requested, indicate this in the space provided for the answer.

A. The Main Entry

    1. What is the name of your dictionary? _____

       Does your dictionary list not just words but also phrases as main entries? _____

       If so, give one. _____

       Does it include phrases within the main entries? _____

       If so, give an example. _____

2. Where does your dictionary list names of places? _____

3. Where does it put abbreviations and their meanings? _____

_____

4. Where are the biographical names in your dictionary? _____

5. Does your dictionary have separate main entries for *junior* used as noun and as adjective? _____

   If not, how are these two words separated? _____

6. Does your dictionary give any principles of order that determine whether the noun or the adjective form of *junior* should come first? (Look in the front matter, the introductory material, of the dictionary.) In some dictionaries the older forms come

   first. _____

   _____

7. How does your dictionary indicate word division for purposes of hyphenation?

   _____

8. Where are variant spellings of the word *pajamas* listed? Does *pyjamas* have its own

   main entry? _____

9. What are the variants of *dexterous?* _____

   Of *caddy?* _____

   Which of the two spellings of each word is preferred by the dictionary? _____

   _____ State the principle you used to

   decide which spelling, if either, is preferred. _____

   _____

10. Write the American spelling of the following words.

    gaol _____   cheque _____

    kerb _____   colour _____

    tyre _____   behaviour _____

    cyder _____

11. Does your dictionary set apart words and phrases it considers foreign? _____

    How? _____

    _____

B. Pronunciation
  1. Copy the vowel and diphthong symbols that your dictionary uses for English sounds. For each sound you use in your own speech, write two words in which the sound is used. Do not use the same examples as the dictionary.

  _____

  _____

  _____

  _____

  _____

  _____

  _____

  _____

  _____

  _____

  _____

  _____

  _____

  _____

  _____

  _____

  _____

  _____

  _____

  _____

  2. How does your dictionary mark the varying degrees of stress within a word? Give
     one example. _____

3. Earlier in this chapter you investigated the pronunciations of **wharf** and what *Webster's Third New International Dictionary* says about the status of these pronunciations. Compare your desk dictionary with *Webster's Third*. Give the variant pronunciations listed in your dictionary for the word **wharf**, and indicate which one is yours by underlining it. Spell out each pronunciation completely; do not use abbreviations.

_____

_____

What does your dictionary say about the status of these pronunciations? Are they all used by educated speakers? _____

_____

What determines which pronunciation comes first? _____

_____

_____

Does your dictionary state that the first pronunciation is preferred? _____

If so, on what page is this stated? _____

4. What labels does your dictionary use to indicate that the acceptability of a pronunciation is restricted in some way? (Include regional as well as usage labels.)

_____

5. If your dictionary does not list a particular pronunciation of a word, does this mean that pronunciation is in some way proscribed or necessarily characteristic only of uneducated speakers? (Look in the front matter for this information.) _____

_____

_____

C. Parts of Speech

What are the functional labels or parts of speech given in the dictionary for the following italicized words in the given contexts?

1. Do you *like* working there? _____

2. *Like* father, *like* son. _____

3. He bought a suit of *like* cut. _____

4. Is the iron hot enough to melt *solder?* _____

5. Please *solder* this joint. _____

D. Inflected Forms
   Write all the forms the dictionary gives for the following. Indicate the usage level of each form.

   1. plural of *brother-in-law* _____
   2. plural of *cupful* _____
   3. plural of *index* _____
   4. plural of *datum* _____
   5. plural of *alumnus* _____
   6. preterite of *dive* _____
   7. past participle of *dive* _____
   8. past participle of *drink* _____
   9. preterite of *work* _____

   Write down the usage levels of the following words in the situations illustrated.

   10. He talked to my sister and *I.* _____
   11. Our people and *us* are here. _____
   12. me (as in *it's me*) _____
   13. me (as in *me and John went yesterday*) _____
   14. us (as in *it was us*) _____

   Compare the usage prescriptions or descriptions with the descriptions of *Webster's Third,* which you studied in Exercise 3.

E. Capitalization
   Underline the letters that should be capitalized.
   1. schick test   6. verner's law
   2. ouija board   7. irish setter
   3. caustic soda   8. marcel wave
   4. garand rifle   9. peking man
   5. artesian well   10. crepe de chine

F. Definitions
   1. Read the explanatory notes of your dictionary to see which meaning of a word is

      listed first. Is the oldest meaning given first, the most common, or what? _____

      _____

      Is the order of the meanings always the same? _____

2. The word *float* can mean one thing to a zoologist and another to the pilot of a seaplane. Sometimes these specialized meanings are marked by special labels, such as *Aeron.* or *Zool.* Give a specialized meaning of each of the following words.

set _____

rest _____

fundamental _____

highball _____

free _____

3. Compose six short sentences, using six of the different meanings of **needle**. A reader should be able to guess your meaning from the sentence.

_____

_____

_____

_____

_____

_____

4. Often, instead of giving a full definition of a word, a dictionary will give a synonym. Or, in addition to a definition, the dictionary will refer the reader to another word or words, where more information is given. Look through your dictionary and write two words for which synonyms, rather than definitions, are given. Write the synonyms also.

    dispend   *Obs. to pay out, expend, spend*

_____   _____

_____   _____

Give two words for which meanings are supplemented by cross-references to other words. List the words that supplement the definition.

    hobble   *fetter, hamper, impede*

_____   _____

_____   _____

5. Dictionaries, especially those of limited size, cannot include all the meanings of complex words. Write in brief form the definitions given in your desk dictionary for the following words, and then sketch the various ways in which the definitions are

limited or inaccurate. In thinking about **breakfast,** for example, you might wish to deal with that breakfast which some restaurants claim to serve twenty-four hours a day.

breakfast _____

_____

lunch _____

_____

dinner _____

_____

supper _____

_____

G. Miscellaneous Sections

Most dictionaries give a variety of information in other parts of the book besides the main vocabulary. Different dictionaries give different information. Does your dictionary discuss punctuation? _____ Manuscript preparation? _____ Does it give proofreading symbols? _____ A history of the English language? _____ An essay on dialect and usage? _____ Detailed information on pronunciation? _____ A section on English given names? _____ Italicization? _____ Capitalization? _____ Rimes? _____ Does it have an index? _____

H. Sources of Information

The dictionary maker does not compose his own definitions arbitrarily but bases his definitions and usage statements on how words are actually used and sometimes on how some grammarians say they ought to be used. Read the preface to your dictionary, and anything else of relevance, to find what the sources of information were for your dictionary. Be as detailed as possible.

_____

_____

_____

_____

_____

_____

_____

EXERCISE 5: From Colloquial to Formal

The following strictures are paraphrased from a widely used handbook for writers. Each is sensible at one level, but limits the capabilities of the language at another. After each stricture, indicate the ways in which it is limiting.

1. *Calculate, guess,* and *reckon* should not be used for *think* or *expect* in formal prose.

   _____

   _____

   _____

2. *Contact* should not be used with the meaning 'open communication with'. _____

   _____

   _____

3. *Put in* should not be used for *spend* in formal prose. *He put in a hard day at the laboratory* is not formal. _____

   _____

   _____

4. *Size up* is colloquial for the formal *judge* or *estimate.* _____

   _____

   _____

EXERCISE 6: Doctrines of Usage

Seventeenth- and Eighteenth-Century England

Browsing through grammars of English from the last three centuries turns up interesting ideas about "good English" and the task of the grammarian. This passage is from the dedicatory poem in *The English Grammar* by Joseph Aickin (London, 1693) and is addressed to Aickin.

> Great *Chaucer* did at first the Tongue refine
> But you from all its dregs have clear'd the wine.
> *Wallis,* and *Cooper* did with *Wharton* try,
> And by degrees the Tongue did Rectifie.
> But still there wanted a more perfect Rule,
> An *English Grammar* for the English School.

The dedication gives to the grammarian the task of perfecting the language by giving it rules, something the four named poets could not do completely. The following passage from Aickin's *Grammar* opens his preface.

> The Daily obstructions and difficulties, that occur in teaching and Learning our Mother Tongue, proceed from the want of an English Grammar, by Law establish'd, the Standard of education, as in other Tongues; For no Tongue can be acquired without Grammatical rules; since then all other Tongues, and Languages are taught by Grammar, why ought not the English Tongue to be taught so too. Imitation will never do it, under twenty years; I have known some Foreigners who have been longer in learning to speak English and yet are far from it: the not learning by Grammar, is the true cause. Hence it cometh, that Children go ten or eleven years or more to School, and yet do not attain the Perfection of the English Tongue: Nay some scarce learn to read and write well in that time: but are forced at length to go to Latin Schools to attain its perfection: and sooner become masters of the Latine, than their own Tongue. The want of such a Grammar, which ought to be the standard of the English Tongue, is the cause of all this. . . .

Aickin assumes that everyone should learn English like a foreign language from a grammar book, even native speakers. What does Aickin consider the task of the grammarian?

_____

_____

_____

Like Aickin, Bishop Robert Lowth, publishing about seventy years later, distrusted the normal English of his time. The passage below is from the preface of his *A Short Introduction to English Grammar* (London, 1762).

> The English Language hath been much cultivated during the last two hundred years. It hath been considerably polished and refined; it hath been greatly enlarged in extent and compass; its force and energy, its variety, richness, and elegance, have been tried with good success, in verse and in prose, upon all subjects, and in every kind of stile: but whatever other improvements it may have received, it hath made no advances in Grammatical accuracy.
>
> It is now about fifty years since Doctor *Swift* made a public remonstrance, addressed to the Earl of Oxford, then Lord Treasurer, of the imperfect State of our Language; alledging in particular, that in many instances it "offended against every part of Grammar." *Swift* must be allowed to have been a good judge of this matter. He was himself very attentive to this part, both in his own writings, and in his remarks upon those of his friends: he is one of our very best prose writers. Indeed the justness of this complaint, as far as I can find, hath never been questioned; and yet no effectual method hath hitherto been taken to redress the grievance of which he complains.
>
> But let us consider how, and in what extent, we are to understand this charge brought against the *English* Language. Does it mean, that the *English* Language as it is spoken by the politest part of the nation, and as it stands in the writings of our most approved authors, oftentimes offends against every part of Grammar? Thus far, I am afraid, the charge is true.

Can you conjecture what Bishop Lowth means by *Grammar* in the next-to-last sentence?

_____

_____

_____

Later in the preface he laments the trust people have in the way they speak.

> It is not owing then to any peculiar irregularity or difficulty of our Language, that the general practice both of speaking and writing it is chargeable with inaccuracy. It is not the Language, but the practice, that is in fault. The truth is, Grammar is very much neglected among us: and it is not the difficulty of the Language, but on the contrary the simplicity and facility of it, that occasions this neglect. Were the Language less easy and simple, we should find ourselves under a necessity of studying it with more care and attention. But as it is, we take for granted, that we have a competent knowledge and skill, and are able to acquit ourselves properly, in our own native tongue: a faculty solely acquired by use, conducted by habit, and tried by the ear, carries us on without reflection; we meet with no rubs or difficulties in our way, or we do not perceive them; we find ourselves able to go on without rules, and we do not so much as suspect that we stand in need of them.

By asserting the simplicity of English, Bishop Lowth is saying that it has fewer inflections than Latin. He is apparently under the impression that children learning a highly inflected language from their parents, such as Russian children, have great difficulty with the task. Bishop Lowth wrote that "It is not the Language, but the practice, that is in fault." What source of information about the English *language* can you imagine that would give data

significantly at odds with the actual *practice* of English speakers? _____

_____

_____

Bishop Lowth himself limits his sources of information. He would not, of course, study the common speech. On the other hand, he writes:

> Our best Authors for want of some rudiments of this kind have sometimes fallen into mistakes, and been guilty of palpable errors in point of Grammar. The examples there given [in Notes which give common errors of usage by these best authors] are such as occurred in reading, without any very curious or methodical examination: and they might easily have been much increased in number by any one, who had leisure or phlegm enough to have gone through a regular course of reading with this particular view.

He rejects both the common speech and the writings of the best authors. What is the source

of his data? _____

_____

Nineteenth-Century America

Samuel Kirkham in *English Grammar in Familiar Lectures* (Rochester, N.Y., 1823) followed Bishop Lowth and the traditions of the eighteenth-century English grammarians. Let us start with several of his key definitions. "English Grammar is the art of speaking and writing the English language with propriety." The standard is "the established practice of the best speakers and writers by whom it is used."

> By the phrase, *established practice*, is implied reputable, national, and present usage. A usage becomes *good* and *legal*, when it has been long and generally adopted. *The best speakers and writers*, or such as may be considered good authority in the use of language, are those who are deservedly in high estimation; speakers, distinguished for their elocution and other literary attainments, and writers, eminent for correct taste, solid matter, and refined manner. (1835, 41st edition, pp. 17–18)

How do you think Kirkham would distinguish those writers deservedly in high estimation from those undeservedly in high estimation? What objective method of choosing would he have? _____

_____

_____

The eighteenth-century English pronouncements on usage were generally *ipse dixit* in base, even though the grammarians said they only followed good usage. Kirkham does the same: in a note later in his text (p. 35) he betrays his attitude toward the "best writers."

> To demonstrate the utility, and enforce the necessity, of exercising the learner in correcting *false Syntax*, I need no other argument than the interesting and undeniable fact, that Mr. Murray's labours, in this department, have effected a complete revolution in the English language, in point of verbal accuracy. Who does not know, that the best writers of this day, are not guilty of *one* grammatical inaccuracy, where those authors who wrote before Mr. Murray flourished, are guilty of *five?* And what has produced this important change for the better? Ask the hundreds of thousands who have studied "Mr. Murray's exercises in *False Syntax*."

Kirkham refers to the "best writers" both here and in his definitions reprinted above. Does he actually use their practice as his standard? _____ On what standard did Mr. Murray base his principles? _____ Could he have based them on the standard of the best writers of his day? Why? _____

_____

_____

We have seen what Kirkham's attitude toward the best speakers and writers was; let us look at his attitude toward the English language. He expresses it in an apology for his book near the end of his preface.

> That the work is defective, the author is fully sensible: and he is free to acknowledge, that its defects arise, in part, from his own want of judgment and skill. But there is another and a more serious cause of them, namely the anomalies and imperfections with which the language abounds. This latter circumstance is also the cause of the existence of so widely different opinions on many important points; and, moreover, the reason that the grammatical principles of our language can never be indisputably settled. But principles ought not to be rejected because they admit of exceptions. He who is thoroughly acquainted with the genius and structure of our language, can duly appreciate the truth of these remarks.

The word *genius* here is of uncertain meaning, but the attitude toward English is clear. What is the task of the grammarian, according to Kirkham?

Kirkham expresses the old idea that language improves with age.

> In the early and rude state of society, mankind are quite limited in their knowledge, and having but few ideas to communicate, a small number of words answers their purpose in the transmission of thought. This leads them to express their ideas in short, detached sentences, requiring few or none of those *connectives*, or words of transition, which are afterwards introduced into language by refinement, and which contribute so largely to its perspicuity and elegance. The argument appears to be conclusive, then, that every language must necessarily have more parts of speech in its refined, than in its barbarous state. (p. 28)

Where else in these readings has the idea of the progress of English been expressed?

One of the most interesting passages in Kirkham's little book is the exhortation "to the young learner," much of which is reprinted here.

> You are about to enter upon one of the most useful, and, when rightly pursued, one of the most interesting studies in the whole circle of science. If, however, you, like many a misguided youth, are under the impression that the study of grammar is dry and irksome, and a matter of little consequence, I trust I shall succeed in removing from your mind, all such false notions and ungrounded prejudices; for I will endeavour to convince you, before I close these lectures, that this is not only a pleasing study, but one of real and substantial utility; a study that directly tends to adorn and dignify human nature, and meliorate the condition of man. Grammar is a leading branch of that learning which alone is capable of unfolding and maturing the mental

powers, and of elevating man to his proper rank in the scale of intellectual existence;—of that learning which lifts the soul from earth, and enables it to hold converse with a thousand worlds.

The similarity to a passage from the 1693 *English Grammar* of Joseph Aickin is striking:

Learning is an inestimable Jewel, exceeding the worth of all the Riches of the Earth; for it makes men fit for any Employment either in Church or State. It restores that Knowledge of good, which *Adam* lost by his fall, and thereby entailed Ignorance upon his Posterity. It distinguisheth Man from Beasts, and all Terrestrial Creatures. It teacheth us the Knowledge of God and the true way to Heaven.

Kirkham resumes:

In pursuing any and every other path of science, you will discover the truth of these remarks, and feel its force; for you will find, that, as grammar opens the door to every department of learning, a knowledge of it is indispensable: and should you not aspire at a distinction in the republick of letters, this knowledge cannot fail of being serviceable to you, even if you are destined to pass through the humblest walks of life. I think it is clear, that, in one point of view, grammatical knowledge possesses a decided advantage over every other branch of learning. Penmanship, arithmetick, geography, astronomy, botany, chymistry, and so on, are highly useful in their respective places; but not one of them is so universally applicable to practical purposes, as this. In every situation, under all circumstances, on all occasions;—when you speak, read, write, or think, a knowledge of grammar is of essential utility.

Note the appeal to usefulness; this is a distinctively American passage. Kirkham continues:

You are aware, my young friend, that you live in an age of light and knowledge;—an age in which science and the arts are marching onward with gigantick strides. You live, too, in a land of liberty;—a land on which the smiles of Heaven beam with uncommon refulgence. The trump of the warriour and the clangour of arms no longer echo on our mountains, or in our valleys; "the garments died in blood have passed away;" the mighty struggle for independence is over; and you live to enjoy the rich boon of freedom and prosperity which was purchased with the blood of our fathers. These considerations forbid that you should ever be so unmindful of your duty to your country, to your Creator, to yourself, and to succeeding generations, as to be content to grovel in ignorance. Remember that "knowledge is power;" that an enlightened and virtuous people can never be enslaved; and that, on the intelligence of our youth, rest the future liberty, the prosperity, the happiness, the grandeur, and the glory of our beloved country. Go on, then, with a laudable ambition, and an unyielding perseverance, in the path which leads to honour and renown. Press forward. Go, and gather laurels on the hill of science; linger among her unfading beauties; "drink deep" of her crystal fountain; and then join in "the march of fame." Become learned and virtuous, and you will be great. Love God and serve him, and you will be happy.

Place in parentheses the phrases of the above passages by Kirkham that relate grammar to patriotism. Place in brackets the phrases that relate grammar to other virtues. Underline phrases that relate reputation, power, or money to grammar.

STYLE 17

EXERCISE 1: Purpose and Style

In each of the following pairs of sentences, choose the example that best carries out the intent of the writer, and give a reason for your selection.

1. a. Yóu discárd that!
   b. Yóu thrów thát awáy!

   b   Since the intent is to be assertive, the choice of the two-part verb is a good one, because it allows for more accents in the expression. (Final demonstratives are normally unaccented.)

2. a. Get ríd of that old junk!
   b. Throw that old junk awáy!

   _____

   _____

   _____

   _____

3. a. They were reluctant to bring the matter up.
   b. They were reluctant to bring up the matter.

   _____

   _____

   _____

   _____

4. a. They plan to discard the others, but they intend to keep this one.
   b. They plan to discard the others, but this one they intend to keep.

_____

_____

_____

5. a. Marci was pleased about becoming a mother.
   b. Marci was happy as a lark about becoming a mother.

_____

_____

_____

EXERCISE 2: Avoiding Distractions

The following sentences are somewhat troublesome. They generally reflect a writer's first attempt at expressing an idea. Some are ambiguous, some are imprecise, others do not take advantage of prosody to direct the reader. Rewrite each sentence; in the case of ambiguous sentences, only one of the senses needs to be preserved.

1. The great American wit Will Rogers has made a healthy comeback.
   Revision: *There is a great deal of interest nowadays in the great American wit Will Rogers.*

2. Jimmy R. likes our new $599 system almost as much as his dog.
   Revision: _____

   _____

3. John: See, I can kick my head. I bet you can't.
   Stan: Yes, I can. (He kicks John's head.)
   John: Did I say something wrong?

   Revision of John's initial remark: _____

   _____

4. The revolutionaries believed that people not governments should have the power.
   Revision: _____

   _____

   _____

5. He bothers me so that I want to kill him.

Revision: _____

_____

6. After that we were no longer worried.

Revision: _____

_____

7. Now that you two are out of the race, my job of appointing the next director is easier.

Revision: _____

_____

8. If the Middle Eastern countries do not make peace, they will bring on a serious catastrophe upon the world.

Revision: _____

_____

_____

9. Help stamp out and eliminate redundancies.

Revision: _____

10. Such a form of action would have been inoperable at that point in time.

Revision: _____

_____

_____

A LETTER TO THE EDITOR

You will have to put more in black and white on paper about the dogs. I hate them. If they want pets, let them take care of them. I see by the St. Paul paper, they are putting out poison. Who wants their Blvd. all crapped and shrubbery ruined. When they have a leash, it's so long, they take them to the bushes. Have you ever watched it? The dog catchers cannot pick them up any more as Mayor Cohen stopped tranquillizers. How can they catch them? Not these mean police dogs, the people feel safe about it. Cats are getting just as numerous. The thrifties in newspapers is forever having ads to give away the culprits. The whole world is in an uproar. You better mention in your paper about all the Halloween vandalism. That day should not be allowed any more. Happened to read your paper. I hope you stress it.

—A concerned reader

What is the basic stylistic problem of the writer of the preceding letter to the editor?

_____

_____

EXERCISE 3: Syntax and New Information

A statement can be the response to any of several questions. For example, *I've got to write a 2000-word theme* can be an answer to
1. What's the trouble?
2. What do you have to do?
3. What do you have to write?
If you wanted to answer each of the questions above as briefly as possible, using the basic sentence *I've got to write a 2000-word theme,* how would you respond to

1. _____ *got to write a 2000-word theme* _____

2. _____

3. _____

What is the difference in questions 1, 2, and 3 that allows for different short responses to

the three questions? _____

_____

_____

EXERCISE 4: Punctuation

The importance of intonation in communication is seldom recognized until one begins to express oneself in writing, and even then it is not entirely appreciated. Punctuate the following seemingly bizarre, self-contained utterances in such a way that they would be understood on first reading.

1. Time flies you can't they fly too fast

2. Mary where John had had had had had had had had had been correct Mary would have been wrong

3. Other than that one thought he was not there

4. Where do we go from here asked Jefferson to Washington

5. This is not all it is cracked up to be sure

EXERCISE 5: Normative Grammar—Nineteenth Century

In Samuel Kirkham's *English Grammar,* published in 1835, the following sentences are given as examples of "false syntax." The words that Kirkham considers wrong or misplaced are italicized. Some of the same examples still appear in handbooks of English. What are your *personal* reactions to these sentences? Place **A, B,** or **C** beside each sentence to denote *acceptable, questionable,* or *not acceptable* respectively. Compare your results with those of your classmates.

1. ____ Great pains *has* been taken to reconcile the parties.

2. ____ The sincere *is* always esteemed.

3. ____ The variety of the productions of genius, like that of the operations of nature, *are* without limit.

4. ____ Time and tide *waits* for no man.

5. ____ Patience and diligence, like faith, *removes* mountains.

6. ____ Man's happiness or misery *are,* in a great measure, put into his own hands.

7. ____ The prince, as well as the people, *were* blameworthy.

8. ____ The nation was once powerful; but now *they are* feeble.

9. ____ The multitude eagerly *pursues* pleasure as *its* chief good.

10. ____ Much depends on this *rule* being observed.

11. ____ *Who* did you talk with?

12. ____ *Who* did you give the book to?

13. ____ He is a man *who* I greatly respect.

14. ____ Which of those two cords is the *longest?*

15. ____ I was at a loss to determine which was the *wiser* of the three.

16. ____ Be composed, it is *me.*

17. ____ The French language is *spoke* in every state in Europe.

18. ____ These things should be *never* separated.

19. ____ I shall work today, unless it *rains.*

20. ____ They were all well but *him.*

EXERCISE 6: Normative Grammar—Twentieth Century

The following article by George W. Feinstein, "Letter from a Triple-threat Grammarian," is representative of pointers taught in rhetoric nowadays. Compare Feinstein's concerns with Kirkham's. To what degree is each bound by tradition, and to what degree does clarity dictate such rules?

_____

_____

_____

_____

_____

Dear sir; you never past me in grammer because you was prejudice but I got this here athaletic scholarship any way. Well, the other day I finely get to writing the rule's down so as I can always study it if they ever slip my mind.

1. Each pronoun agrees with their antecedent.
2. Just between you and I, case is important.
3. Verbs has to agree with their subjects.
4. Watch out for irregular verbs which has crope into our language.
5. Don't use no double negatives.
6. A writer mustn't shift your point of view.
7. When dangling, don't use participles.
8. Join clauses good, like a conjunction should.
9. Don't write a run-on sentence you got to punctuate it.
10. About sentence fragments.
11. In letters themes reports articles and stuff like that we use commas to keep a string of items apart.
12. Don't use commas, which aren't necessary.
13. Its important to use apostrophe's right.
14. Don't abbrev.
15. Check to see if you any words out.
16. In my opinion I think that an author when he is writing shouldn't get into the habit of making use of too many unnecessary words that he does not really need in order to put his message across.
17. In the case of a business letter, check it in terms of jargon.
18. About repetition, the repetition of a word might be real effective repetition—take, for instance, Abraham Lincoln.
19. As far as incomplete constructions, they are wrong.
20. Last but not least, lay off clichés.[1]

---

[1] George W. Feinstein, "Letter from a Triple-threat Grammarian," *College English* 21, no. 7 (April 1960), p. 408. Reprinted with the permission of the National Council of Teachers of English and George W. Feinstein.

EXERCISE 7: Bureaucratic Style

Bureaucrats who administer federal funding programs have the task of writing regulations that will guarantee that the intent of the legislators is carried out. The regulations must go into great detail; if they do not, unqualified applicants might claim subjectivity on the part of the administrators. The unusual complexity of the regulations challenges good writers; unfortunately, a bureaucrat is usually no better a writer than anyone else. In this exercise, your task is to improve portions of a passage that is both bureaucratic and accurate. As you read through the passage, consider what effect sentence length, embedding, and jargon have on comprehensibility.

> With respect to the issue of funding programs in a local prime sponsor[2] area which are unique to that area, the Council decided that the legislative provisions of section 106[3] allow such funding to (1) enhance the coordination and delivery of employment and training services of State or local governmental agencies, and for (2) carrying out special model training and employment programs and related services, including programs for offenders and others with special employment barriers. In the instances where statewide significance is not evident and yet 4% funding[4] is legislatively permissible, the Council has asked that the respective prime sponsor(s) assume a portion of the funding responsibilities for the program or project. Additionally, the prime sponsor(s) will be asked to supply programmatic justification for the non-inclusion of the program or project in question under Title I plans. It is the Council's desire that no program or project be funded in a prime sponsor area without the concurrence of the local prime sponsor(s).[5]

Rewrite the following wordy phrases. Be careful not to lose any of the original meaning.

with respect to the issue of _____

where statewide significance is not yet evident _____

_____

to supply programmatic justification for the non-inclusion of the program or project

_____

Substitute a word or a phrase for the following jargon elements.

prime sponsor _____

special employment barriers _____

additionally _____

[2] A prime sponsor is a unit of government with 100,000 or more inhabitants that administers manpower programs.
[3] Of the applicable federal law.
[4] Four percent funding is the name for the type of funding under discussion.
[5] *Report on the Governor's Special Grants: 4%. Comprehensive Employment and Training Act.* U.S. Department of Labor, Manpower Administration, Governor's Office of Manpower and Human Development, State of Illinois (Springfield, Ill.: 1975), p. 3.

Rewrite the third sentence of the passage in normal English. _____

_____

_____

_____

_____

_____

EXERCISE 8: A Rhetorical Jigsaw Puzzle

Each numbered sentence or group of sentences below is a separate unit of an imaginary article on photography. When they are put together in the correct order, the units make up a general treatment of a subject. Label each one according to the type of rhetorical device it represents (introduction, statement of point, restatement, signpost transition, comparison, summary statement, example, and punch line), and then order the parts so that they form the best possible article.

1. And finally, there are the telephoto lenses. _____ *signpost transition* _____

2. But what the wide-angle gains in some ways, it loses in others. It "stretches" lines and curves them. When you get to the widest angles of all—the "fisheye" lenses—distortion is so extreme that what you see just barely resembles the real world. _____

_____

3. You can take just about any aspect of vision and compare it with what one of these lenses records. The results are bound to be different. _____

_____

4. And the next time someone tells you that the camera doesn't lie, just reply that if that is the case, then it must be the eye that doesn't tell the truth. _____

_____

5. But how about the wide-angle lens? _____

6. Have you ever tried comparing what you see with what you get? Normal, my eye.

_____

7. A telephoto shot of a highway, for example, gives the impression that all the cars are stacked up on top of one another. _____

8. There isn't really any way to get around it. All you can do is select the most suitable

kind of distortion and try to use it to your advantage. _____

_____

9. So you can see that "normal" is at best a very relative term. _____

_____

10. "The camera doesn't lie." That's a line everyone has heard at least a thousand times, and it sounds reasonable enough. But any photographer knows that the reverse is true.

_____

11. First of all, take the so-called "normal" lens. _____

12. So the wide-angle lens isn't very truthful either. _____

_____

13. The eye takes in a much wider angle; everything it directs itself to is automatically in focus. Under normal circumstances it works in conjunction with another eye to create a stereoscopic image, and it is constructed in a different way, giving a somewhat different perspective. _____

14. The fact is that the camera can't tell the truth no matter how hard it tries. _____

_____

15. Again, you might think that these lenses are essentially true to life, even though they make things that are far away seem closer, something the eye doesn't do. _____

_____

16. Let's just consider the case of lenses and what they do to the images they record.

_____

17. You might think that a wide-angle lens is more normal than the "normal" lens. After all, it has a greater range of vision, more like the eye, and it keeps things in focus over a much deeper field than the "normal" lens. _____

_____

18. But they also compress the image, making things look much closer to each other.

_____

The correct order is _____, _____, _____, _____, _____, _____, _____,

_____, _____, _____, _____, _____, _____, _____, _____,
                                                                             (A)   (B)   (C)

_____, _____.
(D)   (E)

On what bases did you order the sentences marked A–E?

A. _____

B. _____

C. _____

D. _____

E. _____

READING: The Principles of Newspeak[6]

George Orwell

As you read this fictional description of the development of a language that makes certain modes of thought impossible, destroys precision, reduces the range of and distorts the expression of feeling, consider whether any such transition is taking place in present-day English. For example, does the use of the acronym *NATO* in place of *North Atlantic Treaty Organization* serve to obscure the apparent contradiction that two member nations, Turkey and Greece, are not North Atlantic nations? What effects does the unification of opposites have when it occurs in such expressions as *Teller, father of the H-bomb?* (The father, a giver and supporter of life, generates the H-bomb for the annihilation of life.) What other ominous signs of Newspeak do you find in our daily use of language? As you read the article, make any comments you have in the space provided below.

_____

_____

_____

_____

_____

_____

_____

_____

_____

_____

[6]George Orwell, *1984* (New York: Harcourt Brace Jovanovich, 1949), pp. 303–14. Copyright 1949 by Harcourt Brace Jovanovich, Inc. Reprinted by permission of Brandt & Brandt, Mrs. Sonia Brownell Orwell, and Secker & Warburg.

Newspeak was the official language of Oceania and had been devised to meet the ideological needs of Ingsoc, or English Socialism. In the year 1984 there was not as yet anyone who used Newspeak as his sole means of communication, either in speech or writing. The leading articles in the *Times* were written in it, but this was a tour de force which could only be carried out by a specialist. It was expected that Newspeak would have finally superseded Oldspeak (or Standard English, as we should call it) by about the year 2050. Meanwhile it gained ground steadily, all Party members tending to use Newspeak words and grammatical constructions more and more in their everyday speech. The version in use in 1984, and embodied in the Ninth and Tenth Editions of the Newspeak dictionary, was a provisional one, and contained many superfluous words and archaic formations which were due to be suppressed later. It is with the final, perfected version, as embodied in the Eleventh Edition of the dictionary, that we are concerned here.

The purpose of Newspeak was not only to provide a medium of expression for the world-view and mental habits proper to the devotees of Ingsoc, but to make all other modes of thought impossible. It was intended that when Newspeak had been adopted once and for all and Oldspeak forgotten, a heretical thought—that is, a thought diverging from the principles of Ingsoc—should be literally unthinkable, at least so far as thought is dependent on words. Its vocabulary was so constructed as to give exact and often very subtle expression to every meaning that a Party member could properly wish to express, while excluding all other meanings and also the possibility of arriving at them by indirect methods. This was done partly by the invention of new words, but chiefly by eliminating undesirable words and by stripping such words as remained of unorthodox meanings, and so far as possible of all secondary meanings whatever. To give a single example. The word *free* still existed in Newspeak, but it could only be used in such statements as "This dog is free from lice" or "This field is free from weeds." It could not be used in its old sense of "politically free" or "intellectually free," since political and intellectual freedom no longer existed even as concepts, and were therefore of necessity nameless. Quite apart from the suppression of definitely heretical words, reduction of vocabulary was regarded as an end in itself, and no word that could be dispensed with was allowed to survive. Newspeak was designed not to extend but to *diminish* the range of thought, and this purpose was indirectly assisted by cutting the choice of words down to a minimum.

Newspeak was founded on the English language as we now know it, though many Newspeak sentences, even when not containing newly created words, would be barely intelligible to an English-speaker of our own day. Newspeak words were divided into three distinct classes, known as the A vocabulary, the B vocabulary (also called compound words), and the C vocabulary. It will be simpler to discuss each class separately, but the grammatical peculiarities of the language can be dealt with in the section devoted to the A vocabulary, since the same rules held good for all three categories.

The A vocabulary. The A vocabulary consisted of the words needed for the business of everyday life—for such things as eating, drinking, working, putting on one's clothes, going up and down stairs, riding in vehicles, gardening, cooking, and the like. It was composed almost entirely of words that we already possess—words like *hit, run, dog, tree, sugar, house, field*—but in comparison with the present-day English vocabulary, their number was extremely small, while their meanings were far more rigidly defined. All ambiguities and shades of meaning had been purged out of them. So far as it could be achieved, a Newspeak word of this class was simply a staccato sound expressing *one* clearly understood concept. It would have been quite impossible to use the A vocabulary for literary purposes or for political or philosophical discussion. It was intended only to express simple, purposive thoughts, usually involving concrete objects or physical actions.

The grammar of Newspeak had two outstanding peculiarities. The first of these was an almost complete interchangeability between different parts of speech. Any word in the language (in principle this applied even to very abstract words such as *if* or *when*) could be used either as verb, noun, adjective, or adverb. Between the verb and the noun form, when they were of the same root, there was never any variation, this rule of itself involving the destruction of many archaic forms. The word *thought,* for example, did not exist in Newspeak. Its place was taken by *think,* which did duty for both noun and verb. No etymological principle was followed here; in some cases it was the original noun that was chosen for retention, in other cases the verb. Even where a noun and verb of kindred meaning were not etymologically connected, one or other of them was frequently suppressed. There was, for example, no such word as *cut,* its meaning being sufficiently covered by the noun-verb *knife.* Adjectives were formed by adding the suffix *-ful* to the noun-verb, and adverbs by adding *-wise.* Thus, for example, *speedful* meant "rapid" and *speedwise* meant "quickly." Certain of our present-day adjectives, such as *good, strong, big, black, soft,* were retained, but their total number was very small. There was little need for them, since almost any adjectival meaning could be arrived at by adding *-ful* to a noun-verb. None of the now-existing adverbs was retained, except for a very few already ending in *-wise;* the *-wise* termination was invariable. The word *well,* for example, was replaced by *goodwise.*

In addition, any word—this again applied in principle to every word in the language—could be negatived by adding the affix *un-*, or could be strengthened by the affix *plus-*, or, for still greater emphasis, *doubleplus-.* Thus, for example, *uncold* meant "warm," while *pluscold* and *doublepluscold* meant, respectively, "very cold" and "superlatively cold." It was also possible, as in present-day English, to modify the meaning of almost any word by prepositional affixes such as *ante-, post-, up-, down-*, etc. By such methods it was found possible to bring about an enormous diminution of vocabulary. Given, for instance, the word *good*, there was no need for such a word as *bad*, since the required meaning was equally well—indeed, better—expressed by *ungood*. All that was necessary, in any case where two words formed a natural pair of opposites, was to decide which of them to suppress. *Dark*, for example, could be replaced by *unlight*, or *light* by *undark*, according to preference.

The second distinguishing mark of Newspeak grammar was its regularity. Subject to a few exceptions which are mentioned below, all inflections followed the same rules. Thus, in all verbs the preterite and the past participle were the same and ended in *-ed*. The preterite of *steal* was *stealed*, the preterite of *think* was *thinked*, and so on throughout the language, all such forms as *swam, gave, brought, spoke, taken*, etc., being abolished. All plurals were made by adding *-s* or *-es* as the case might be. The plurals of *man, ox, life* were *mans, oxes, lifes*. Comparison of adjectives was invariably made by adding *-er, -est* (*good, gooder, goodest*), irregular forms and the *more, most* formation being suppressed.

The only classes of words that were still allowed to inflect irregularly were the pronouns, the relatives, the demonstrative adjectives, and the auxiliary verbs. All of these followed their ancient usage, except that *whom* had been scrapped as unnecessary, and the *shall, should* tenses had been dropped, all their uses being covered by *will* and *would*. There were also certain irregularities in word-formation arising out of the need for rapid and easy speech. A word which was difficult to utter, or was liable to be incorrectly heard, was held to be ipso facto a bad word; occasionally therefore, for the sake of euphony, extra letters were inserted into a word or an archaic formation was retained. But this need made itself felt chiefly in connection with the B vocabulary. *Why* so great an importance was attached to ease of pronunciation will be made clear later in this essay.

The B vocabulary. The B vocabulary consisted of words which had been deliberately constructed for political purposes: words, that is to say, which not only had in every case a political implication, but were intended to impose a desirable mental attitude upon the person using them. Without a full understanding of the principles of Ingsoc it was difficult to use these words correctly. In some cases they could be translated into Oldspeak, or even into words taken from the A vocabulary, but this usually demanded a long paraphrase and always involved the loss of certain overtones. The B words were a sort of verbal shorthand, often packing whole ranges of ideas into a few syllables, and at the same time more accurate and forcible than ordinary language.

The B words were in all cases compound words.° They consisted of two or more words, or portions of words, welded together in an easily pronounceable form. The resulting amalgam was always a noun-verb, and inflected according to the ordinary rules. To take a single example: the word *goodthink*, meaning, very roughly, "orthodoxy," or, if one chose

---

° Compound words, such as *speakwrite*, were of course to be found in the A vocabulary, but these were merely convenient abbreviations and had no special ideological color.

to regard it as a verb, "to think in an orthodox manner." This inflected as follows: noun-verb, *goodthink;* past tense and past participle, *goodthinked;* present participle, *goodthinking;* adjective, *goodthinkful;* adverb, *goodthinkwise;* verbal noun, *goodthinker.*

The B words were not constructed on any etymological plan. The words of which they were made up could be any parts of speech, and could be placed in any order and mutilated in any way which made them easy to pronounce while indicating their derivation. In the word *crimethink* (thoughtcrime), for instance, the *think* came second, whereas in *thinkpol* (Thought Police) it came first, and in the latter word *police* had lost its second syllable. Because of the greater difficulty in securing euphony, irregular formations were commoner in the B vocabulary than in the A vocabulary. For example, the adjectival forms of *Minitrue, Minipax,* and *Miniluv* were, respectively *Minitruthful, Minipeaceful,* and *Minilovely,* simply because *-trueful, -paxful,* and *-loveful* were slightly awkward to pronounce. In principle, however, all B words could inflect, and all inflected in exactly the same way.

Some of the B words had highly subtilized meanings, barely intelligible to anyone who had not mastered the language as a whole. Consider, for example, such a typical sentence from a *Times* leading article as *Oldthinkers unbellyfeel Ingsoc.* The shortest rendering that one could make of this in Oldspeak would be: "Those whose ideas were formed before the Revolution cannot have a full emotional understanding of the principles of English Socialism." But this is not an adequate translation. To begin with, in order to grasp the full meaning of the Newspeak sentence quoted above, one would have to have a clear idea of what is meant by *Ingsoc.* And, in addition, only a person thoroughly grounded in Ingsoc could appreciate the full force of the word *bellyfeel,* which implied a blind, enthusiastic acceptance difficult to imagine today; or of the word *oldthink,* which was inextricably mixed up with the idea of wickedness and decadence. But the special function of certain Newspeak words, of which *oldthink* was one, was not so much to express meanings as to destroy them. These words, necessarily few in number, had had their meanings extended until they contained within themselves whole batteries of words which, as they were sufficiently covered by a single comprehensive term, could now be scrapped and forgotten. The greatest difficulty facing the compilers of the Newspeak dictionary was not to invent new words, but, having invented them, to make sure what they meant: to make sure, that is to say, what ranges of words they canceled by their existence.

As we have already seen in the case of the word *free,* words which had once borne a heretical meaning were sometimes retained for the sake of convenience, but only with the undesirable meanings purged out of them. Countless other words such as *honor, justice, morality, internationalism, democracy, science,* and *religion* had simply ceased to exist. A few blanket words covered them, and, in covering them, abolished them. All words grouping themselves round the concepts of liberty and equality, for instance, were contained in the single word *crimethink,* while all words grouping themselves round the concepts of objectivity and rationalism were contained in the single word *oldthink.* Greater precision would have been dangerous. What was required in a Party member was an outlook similar to that of the ancient Hebrew who knew, without knowing much else, that all nations other than his own worshiped "false gods." He did not need to know that these gods were called Baal, Osiris, Moloch, Ashtaroth, and the like; probably the less he knew about them the better for his orthodoxy. He knew Jehovah and the commandments of Jehovah; he knew, therefore, that all gods with other names or other attributes were false gods. In somewhat the same way, the Party member knew what constituted right conduct, and in exceedingly vague, generalized terms he knew what kinds of departure from it were possible. His sexual life, for example, was entirely regulated by the two Newspeak words *sexcrime* (sexual immorality) and *goodsex* (chastity). *Sexcrime* covered all sexual misdeeds whatever. It covered fornication, adultery, homosexuality, and other perversions, and, in addition, normal intercourse practiced for its own sake. There was no need to enumerate them separately, since they were all equally culpable, and, in principle, all punishable by death. In the C vocabulary, which consisted of scientific and technical words, it might be necessary to give specialized names to certain sexual aberrations, but the ordinary citizen had no need of them. He knew what was meant by *goodsex*—that is to say, normal intercourse between man and wife, for the sole purpose of begetting children, and without physical pleasure on the part of the woman; all else was *sexcrime*. In Newspeak it was seldom possible to follow a heretical thought further than the perception that it *was* heretical; beyond that point the necessary words were nonexistent.

No word in the B vocabulary was ideologically neutral. A great many were euphemisms. Such words, for instance, as *joycamp* (forced-labor camp) or *Minipax* (Ministry of Peace, i.e., Ministry of War) meant almost the exact opposite of what they appeared to mean. Some words, on the other hand, displayed a frank and contemptuous understanding of the real nature of Oceanic society. An example was *prolefeed*, meaning the rubbishy entertainment and spurious news which the Party handed out to the masses. Other words, again, were ambivalent, having the connotation "good" when applied to the Party and "bad" when applied to its enemies. But in addition there were great numbers of words which at first sight appeared to be mere abbreviations and which derived their ideological color not from their meaning but from their structure.

So far as it could be contrived, everything that had or might have political significance of any kind was fitted into the B vocabulary. The name of every organization, or body of people, or doctrine, or country, or institution, or public building was invariably cut down into the familiar shape; that is, a single easily pronounced word with the smallest number of syllables that would preserve the original derivation. In the Ministry of Truth, for example, the Records Department, in which Winston Smith worked, was called *Recdep*, the Fiction Department was called *Ficdep*, the Teleprograms Department was called *Teledep*, and so on. This was not done solely with the object of saving time. Even in the early decades of the twentieth century, telescoped words and phrases had been one of the characteristic features of political language; and it had been noticed that the tendency to use abbreviations of this kind was most marked in totalitarian countries and totalitarian organizations. Examples were such words as *Nazi, Gestapo, Comintern, Inprecorr, Agitprop*. In the beginning the practice had been adopted as it were instinctively, but in Newspeak it was used with a conscious purpose. It was perceived that in thus abbreviating a name one narrowed and subtly altered its meaning, by cutting out most of the associations that would otherwise cling to it. The words *Communist International*, for instance, call up a composite picture of universal human brotherhood, red flags, barricades, Karl Marx, and the Paris Commune.

The word Comintern, on the other hand, suggests merely a tightly knit organization and a well-defined body of doctrine. It refers to something almost as easily recognized, and as limited in purpose, as a chair or a table. *Comintern* is a word that can be uttered almost without taking thought, whereas *Communist International* is a phrase over which one is obliged to linger at least momentarily. In the same way, the associations called up by a word like *Minitrue* are fewer and more controllable than those called up by *Ministry of Truth*. This accounted not only for the habit of abbreviating whenever possible, but also for the almost exaggerated care that was taken to make every word easily pronounceable.

In Newspeak, euphony outweighed every consideration other than exactitude of meaning. Regularity of grammar was always sacrificed to it when it seemed necessary. And rightly so, since what was required, above all for political purposes, were short clipped words of unmistakable meaning which could be uttered rapidly and which roused the minimum of echoes in the speaker's mind. The words of the B vocabulary even gained in force from the fact that nearly all of them were very much alike. Almost invariably these words—*goodthink, Minipax, prolefeed, sexcrime, joycamp, Ingsoc, bellyfeel, thinkpol,* and countless others—were words of two or three syllables, with the stress distributed equally between the first syllable and the last. The use of them encouraged a gabbling style of speech, at once staccato and monotonous. And this was exactly what was aimed at. The intention was to make speech, and especially speech on any subject not ideologically neutral, as nearly as possible independent of consciousness. For the purposes of everyday life it was no doubt necessary, or sometimes necessary, to reflect before speaking, but a Party member called upon to make a political or ethical judgment should be able to spray forth the correct opinions as automatically as a machine gun spraying forth bullets. His training fitted him to do this, the language gave him an almost foolproof instrument, and the texture of the words, with their harsh sound and a certain willful ugliness which was in accord with the spirit of Ingsoc, assisted the process still further.

So did the fact of having very few words to choose from. Relative to our own, the Newspeak vocabulary was tiny, and new ways of reducing it were constantly being devised. Newspeak, indeed, differed from almost all other languages in that its vocabulary grew smaller instead of larger every year. Each reduction was a gain, since the smaller the area of choice, the smaller the temptation to take thought. Ultimately it was hoped to make articulate speech issue from the larynx without involving the higher brain centers at all. This aim was frankly admitted in the Newspeak word *duckspeak*, meaning "to quack like a duck." Like various other words in the B vocabulary, *duckspeak* was ambivalent in meaning. Provided that the opinions which were quacked out were orthodox ones, it implied nothing but praise, and when the *Times* referred to one of the orators of the Party as a *doubleplusgood duckspeaker* it was paying a warm and valued compliment.

The C vocabulary. The C vocabulary was supplementary to the others and consisted entirely of scientific and technical terms. These resembled the scientific terms in use today, and were constructed from the same roots, but the usual care was taken to define them rigidly and strip them of undesirable meanings. They followed the same grammatical rules as the words in the other two vocabularies. Very few of the C words had any currency either in everyday speech or in political speech. Any scientific worker or technician could find all the words he needed in the list devoted to his own speciality, but he seldom had more than a smattering of the words occurring in the other lists. Only a very few words were common to all lists, and there was no vocabulary expressing the function of Science as a habit of mind, or a method of thought, irrespective of its particular branches. There was, indeed, no word for "Science," any meaning that it could possibly bear being already sufficiently covered by the word *Ingsoc.*

From the foregoing account it will be seen that in Newspeak the expression of unorthodox opinions, above a very low level, was well-nigh impossible. It was of course possible to utter heresies of a very crude kind, a species of blasphemy. It would have been possible, for example, to say *Big Brother is ungood.* But this statement, which to an orthodox ear merely conveyed a self-evident absurdity, could not have been sustained by reasoned argument, because the necessary words were not available. Ideas inimical to Ingsoc could only be entertained in a vague wordless form, and could only be named in very broad terms which lumped together and condemned whole groups of heresies without defining them in doing so. One could, in fact, only use Newspeak for unorthodox purposes by illegitimately translating some of the words back into Oldspeak. For example, *All mans are equal* was a possible Newspeak sentence, but only in the same sense in which *All men are redhaired* is a possible Oldspeak sentence. It did nót contain a grammatical error, but it expressed a palpable untruth, i.e., that all men are of equal size, weight, or strength. The concept of political equality no longer existed, and this secondary meaning had accordingly been purged out of the word *equal.* In 1984, when Oldspeak was still the normal means of communication, the danger theoretically existed that in using Newspeak words one might remember their original meanings. In practice it was not difficult for any person well grounded in *doublethink* to avoid doing this, but within a couple of generations even the possibility of such a lapse would have vanished. A person growing up with Newspeak as his sole language would no more know that *equal* had once had the secondary meaning of "politically equal," or that *free* had once meant "intellectually free," than, for instance, a person who had never heard of chess would be aware of the secondary meanings attaching to *queen* and *rook.* There would be many crimes and errors which it would be beyond his power to commit, simply because they were nameless and therefore unimaginable. And it was to be foreseen that with the passage of time the distinguishing characteristics of New-speak would become more and more pronounced—its words growing fewer and fewer, their meanings more and more rigid, and the chance of putting them to improper uses always diminishing.

When Oldspeak had been once and for all superseded, the last link with the past would have been severed. History had already been rewritten, but fragments of the literature of the past survived here and there, imperfectly censored, and so long as one retained one's knowledge of Oldspeak it was possible to read them. In the future such fragments, even if they chanced to survive, would be unintelligible and untranslatable. It was impossible to translate any passage of Oldspeak into Newspeak unless it either referred to some technical process or some very simple everyday action, or was already orthodox (*goodthinkful* would be the Newspeak expression) in tendency. In practice this meant that no book written before approximately 1960 could be translated as a whole. Prerevolutionary literature could only be subjected to ideological translation—that is, alteration in sense as well as language. Take for example the well-known passage from the Declaration of Independence:

We hold these truths to be self-evident, that all men are created equal, that they are endowed by their Creator with certain inalienable rights, that among these are life, liberty and the pursuit of happiness. That to secure these rights, Governments are instituted among men, deriving their powers from the consent of the governed. That whenever any form of Government becomes destructive of those ends, it is the right of the People to alter or abolish it, and to institute new Government . . .

It would have been quite impossible to render this into Newspeak while keeping to the sense of the original. The nearest one could come to doing so would be to swallow the whole passage up in the single word *crimethink*. A full translation could only be an ideological translation, whereby Jefferson's words would be changed into a panegyric on absolute government.

A good deal of the literature of the past was, indeed, already being transformed in this way. Considerations of prestige made it desirable to preserve the memory of certain historical figures, while at the same time bringing their achievements into line with the philosophy of Ingsoc. Various writers, such as Shakespeare, Milton, Swift, Byron, Dickens, and some others were therefore in process of translation; when the task had been completed, their original writings, with all else that survived of the literature of the past, would be destroyed. These translations were a slow and difficult business, and it was not expected that they would be finished before the first or second decade of the twenty-first century. There were also large quantities of merely utilitarian literature—indispensable technical manuals and the like—that had to be treated in the same way. It was chiefly in order to allow time for the preliminary work of translation that the final adoption of Newspeak had been fixed for so late a date as 2050.

D
E 9
F 0
G 1
H 2
I 3
J 4